CHARLOTTE BRONTË: TRUCULENT SPIRIT

CHARLOTTE BRONTË: TRUCULENT SPIRIT

by

Valerie Grosvenor Myer

VISION
and
BARNES & NOBLE

Vision Press Limited
Fulham Wharf
Townmead Road
London SW6 2SB

and

Barnes & Noble Books
81 Adams Drive
Totowa, NJ 07512

ISBN (UK) 0 85478 306 7
ISBN (US) 0 389 20763 2

Library of Congress Cataloging-in-Publication Data

Myer, Valerie Grosvenor.
  Charlotte Bronte: truculent spirit.

  (Critical studies series)
  1. Brontë, Charlotte, 1816–1855—Criticism and
interpretation. I. Title. II. Series.
PR4169.M94 1987   823'.8   87-15499
ISBN 0-389-20763-2

**In memory of
my grandfather, Henry Jones,
who collected good books**

First published in the U.S.A. 1987

Printed and bound in Great Britain by
L.R. Printing Services Ltd.,
Crawley, W. Sussex.
Phototypeset by Galleon Photosetting,
Ipswich, Suffolk.
MCMLXXXVII

Contents

Acknowledgements

The trip to northern libraries was made possible by a generous grant from the Welsford Research Fund by Newnham College, Cambridge. I must thank, for exceptional patience and generosity, Dr. Juliet R. V. Barker, curator-librarian at the Brontë Parsonage Museum, Haworth, and her assistant, Sally Johnson; C. D. W. Sheppard, Vanessa Hinton and Jo Charlesworth at the Brotherton Collection, Leeds University; Glenise Matheson and Anne Young at the John Rylands Library, Manchester University; Christine Lingard, Language and Literature Department, Central Library, Manchester; and Odette Rogers, Fitzwilliam Museum, Cambridge. For general support and advice I must thank Professor Philip Collins, Nora Crook, Michael Edwards, Judith Fisher, Sylvia Greybourne, Jeannette Honan, Professor Park Honan, Professor Ian Jack, Tony Jasper, Dr. Pamela Kenny, Alison McRobb, Ken May, Professor Arthur Pollard, Dr. Roy Porter, Dr. Mark Seaward, Dr. Sally Shuttleworth, Margaret Smith and Professor Christopher Stead. Finally I must thank my husband, Michael Grosvenor Myer, for his research and editorial skills.

References: the best available editions of Charlotte Brontë's novels are the Clarendon *Jane Eyre*, *Shirley* and *Villette*. At the time of writing, *The Professor* is forthcoming. However, the three-volume arrangement is confusing for readers who have access only to cheaper editions, so references are by chapter only, numbered consecutively. Biographical information, easily available in standard sources, is not referenced. Letters are referenced by recipient and (sometimes conjectural) date. Critical commentary, however, is fully referenced. Abbreviations used are as follows: *B.S.T.*, *Brontë Society Transactions* (I am grateful for permission to quote); *N.C.F.*, *Nineteenth Century*

Fiction; *N.Q.*, *Notes and Queries*; *P.M.L.A.*, *Publications of the Modern Language Association.*

Notes on English usage: the town of Keighley is pronounced 'Keethley', though the pronunciation 'Keely' is also in use; in the nineteenth century 'Keetly' was recorded. Lord David Cecil is correctly referred to by his full title or, for brevity, 'Lord David'; 'Lord Cecil' is a solecism, as is 'the Rev. Brontë, the Rev. Brocklehurst, etc.'; we write 'The Rev. Patrick Brontë' or 'The Rev. Mr. Brontë'.

Introduction

The reader will find references to critics of various persuasions throughout this book. I have not spelt out anywhere my own critical position which I would describe as eclectic humanism. While not going so far as Adorno and his followers, who deny intentionality of signification, I cannot escape the Freudian influence which directs us to look for unconscious meanings. While I hold no brief for Marxism, I must agree with Terry Eagleton that 'we are all Marxists now' (*Myths of Power: A Marxist Study of the Brontës*, Introduction), if only insofar as we look now not to 'psychology' in reading novels, but to money and class as psycho-dynamic determinants. With the extreme relativism which will have no truck with interpretation or with value-judgements, I have little sympathy; while such approaches can be liberating in small doses in that they question ossified hierarchies of value, they ultimately lead nowhere. Because I have no quarrel with 'bourgeois ideology', I affirm the value of art, as traditionally conceived.

Cambridge, 1987   V.G.M.

1

'Three Weird Sisters' and Socks for Mr. Nicholls

—The Brontë girls . . . couldn't slip down to the pub. So they had to take up writing. (Elizabeth Taylor, *At Mrs. Lippincote's*)

'Three weird sisters, Charlotte and Emily and Anne', went the refrain of a comic song in the Cambridge University Footlights revue of 1953. The university audience could be relied upon to appreciate this witty conflation of *Macbeth* and one of Britain's best-known true stories. The yoking of the two heterogeneous ideas is accomplished by the pun on 'weird'. The lyricist, Colin Pearson, touched a resonant string: like Shakespeare's three witches, the Brontë girls are associated with storm and violence, lightning flashes, heath and moorland. Like the witches, the sisters were secretly and mysteriously inventive, creators of magic. Robert Bernard Martin has described *Jane Eyre* as 'a witch's broth of ingredients'.[1] *Jane Eyre* is full of allusions to *Macbeth* and, like Shakespeare's play, is structured on contrasts between light and darkness, with running patterns of imagery. The novel includes, like *Macbeth*, prophecy, portents and magic. Like the black and midnight hags, the Brontës were female, though their professional self-presentation was, like that of the witches, sexually ambiguous. Fearing they would be judged not as writers but as women, the sisters appropriated masculine pseudonyms (though as Robert Keefe points out, Charlotte was calling herself 'Charles Thunder' and 'Charles Townsend' before there was any need to anticipate a sexually biased audience[2]).

Biased, however, that audience was. Writing to her publisher's

11

reader, W. S. Williams, on 16 August 1849, Charlotte noted wryly that the literary critic of the *Economist* 'praised [*Jane Eyre*] if written by a man, and pronounced it "odious" if the work of a woman'. The sisters were praised for the 'masculine power' of their writing, but condemned as unwomanly and improper. Reviewing *Shirley* for the *Edinburgh Review*, G. H. Lewes reverted to *Jane Eyre*:

> . . . A more masculine book, in the sense of vigour, was never written. Indeed, that vigour often amounts to coarseness,—and that is certainly the very antipode to 'ladylike'. The same over-masculine vigour is even more prominent in *Shirley*. . . .[3]

Charlotte's reply was a bitter epigram (undated): 'I can be on my guard against my enemies, but God deliver me from my friends!' The attack rankled. She wrote to Lewes again on 19 January 1850:

> My dear Sir,—I will tell you why I was so hurt by that review . . . because after I had said earnestly that I wished critics would judge me as an *author*, not as a woman, you so roughly—I even thought so cruelly—handled the question of sex.

More than half a century later, G. K. Chesterton told the Brontë Society that Lewes 'represented the worst elements in mid-Victorian England' and regretted that Charlotte listened to his advice to avoid melodrama.[4] Charlotte proceeded to write *Shirley*, imagining that sober realism was what the public wanted (see Chapter 13). Mrs. Gaskell's biography was written in part to defend Charlotte against the charge of 'coarseness'[5] (see my Chapter 3) and to show how 'noble' was Charlotte's character. The word 'noble' runs through nineteenth-century appreciations of Charlotte, especially in early numbers of the *Brontë Society Transactions*. Like Mrs. Gaskell, early speakers were anxious to guard Charlotte's moral reputation, to defend the 'nobility' of her character, the 'purity' of her mind, and to stress her lifetime of 'duty and self-sacrifice'. That the woman whose works breathed 'hunger, rebellion and rage', in Matthew Arnold's famous words about *Villette*, should have sacrificed her independence to the 'selfish old man', in the words of Charlotte's friend Mary Taylor, filled them not with the 'gloomy anger' which burdened Mary (letter to Ellen Nussey, Wellington, 19 April 1856), but with relief that Charlotte was a tamed creature, a true angel-in-the-house at heart. T. Wemyss-Reid, addressing the Brontë Society at Halifax, 15 January 1898, for example, praised her 'noble' life of 'self-sacrificing devotion to duty'.[6] He also recalled the days when mention of the sisters had 'aroused conflicting emotions', because the picture of Yorkshire people had been considered unflattering, but that was over now. Other contributors to the *Transactions* conclude that Charlotte was a good girl after all; she was a Yorkshire lass they could be proud of. They repeatedly thank the Brontë girls for glorifying Yorkshire, putting it on the map and forcing the rest of the world to notice it. The Brontë Society's attitude early on was possessive, based on local patriotism, a defence against limiting judgements such as those of Leslie Stephen[7] and Mrs. Humphry Ward.[8]

For Thackeray, Charlotte had been 'an austere Little Joan of Arc'; for other Victorians, she became a secular Miss Valiant-for-Truth, a diminutive Miss Greatheart-in-the-body-of-a-weak-and-feeble-woman, a heroic example of courage, self-help and victory over circumstance. Charlotte was frequently compared to Shakespeare and praised for her 'passion' and her 'poetry'. It was a commonplace of Brontë Society commentary at the turn of the century that the Brontë sisters, or at any rate Charlotte and Emily, had introduced the intensity, lyricism and imagery of Romantic poetry into the novel, though the references remained uncharted, the pattern of the imagery was for a long while unexamined, and, as M. H. Scargill pointed out in 1950, 'passion' was undefined.[9] The word seems to have been a single blanket term for various violent emotions (see my Chapter 3). Edmund Gosse, addressing the Brontë Society in 1904, deplored the 'whitewashing' of Charlotte, and praised 'a certain admirable ferocity' in her.[10] Appreciations, especially of Charlotte, in the extended metaphorical style current throughout the nineteenth century and after, tended to reflect her own vocabulary and imagery, and, like much of her own most effective writing, to be expressed in terms of physical sensation. The words 'acrid' and 'pungent' were used to describe her unique 'flavour'. Both these words are taken from *Jane Eyre* itself: Rochester smiles an 'acrid' smile in the presence of Bertha (Ch. 26), and, as Margaret Smith observes in her important essay, 'The manuscripts of Charlotte Brontë's novels', Rochester's 'sarcasm' was first described by Charlotte as 'sharp' and later altered to 'pungent'.[11] As for the image of 'fire' which burns in Jane herself and is as pervasive an image in the novel as that of blood in *Macbeth*, people repeatedly take it over to describe their own responses. Prince Mirsky, in 1923, writes of the 'red-hot fire of emotion which seems to burn in its flames all the numerous inconsistencies and absurdities in . . . *Jane Eyre*'.[12] Lord David Cecil writes of Charlotte's 'central white-hot fire'[13] and her 'volcanic imagination', which 'throws a lurid glare'.[14]

By 1900, it had become customary to apologize for writing 'yet another Brontë book',[15] and in 1903 Leonard W. Lillingstone wrote in the *Connoisseur*, 'We have heard so much of the Brontës that their books have an interest quite other than the literary one',[16] a comment frequently made. Henry James's complaint is well known:

> . . . the fashion has been, in looking at the Brontës, so to confound the cause with the result that we cease to know . . . what we are talking about. They represent the ecstasies, the high-water mark of sentimental judgement.[17]

There has long been controversy as to the 'relevance' or otherwise of biographical material to literary criticism, a conflict never satisfactorily resolved. The Brontë picture is complicated by Charlotte being the subject of a famous biography, Mrs. Gaskell's *Life*, itself a work of literature. We are left with the problem of how to evaluate a biography by a novelist with an eye for a good story but an anxious concern, as a friend, for her subject's reputation. How do we evaluate it, either intrinsically, or in relation to its usefulness to us, students of Charlotte's mature work? As Annette Tromly writes, 'Shortly after her death, Brontë—the writer of fiction—was herself fictionalized by a novelist who had been asked to become a biographer'.[18] 'Mrs. Gaskell was the first and greatest of the Brontë legend-mongers', said Dr. Donald Hopewell, a president of the Brontë Society.[19] 'If a single issue has bedevilled Brontë studies, it has been the extent to which we can read the novels from the evidence of the life . . . and . . . discern an autobiographical voice in the fiction', writes Tromly.[20]

'The Brontë story' is part of British mythology. The works, or at any rate *Jane Eyre* and *Wuthering Heights*, are part of a living cultural tradition in a way matched by few of our great authors, in that the names of their characters are known to the uneducated and the outline of the stories remembered. On any Bank Holiday, 2,000 visitors are likely to pour through the small house with its Museum extension. The original Museum was opened in 1895, housed in the Penny Bank, and in 1915 a total of 54,000 had attended. In 1927, Sir James Roberts, a local man, bought the parsonage for the then considerable sum of £3,000 and presented it to the village. In 1946, a record year, the Museum had 37,903 visitors. In 1970, there were 100,000, and since then the number has doubled. Haworth, once so isolated, now has a large coach park and is crowded with trippers almost every day of the year; the cobbled street has its Brontë hairdressing salon and its Brontë tearooms. Emily would have hated it. Suffering and consumptive, the sisters have become secular saints, their remote, wind-lashed home a place of pilgrimage. The Brontë girls exist for us, like film stars and royalty, as icons: they are emblems of loneliness, anguished love, despair and courage; of indomitable minds in frail, short-lived bodies; of frustrations compensated by intellectual and creative power. Emily and Anne fit the stereotype of the artist who dies young in poverty, after unrewarded struggle; Charlotte and Anne are the most famous governesses in history, sacrificial victims to the harsh Victorian social and economic system, over which Charlotte, at least, finally triumphed to assert herself as a brilliantly successful writer. Her first published novel, *Jane Eyre* (1847) was met with a degree of notice few have achieved before or since; it managed to be at once a *succès d'estime* and *succès de scandale*. Many of the 200,000 visitors who flock every year to Haworth imagine that 'Jane Eyre' lived there. There is no longer any excuse for such ignorance. Upstairs at the Museum there is a visual aid giving the facts and dates of the Brontë story.

The Brontës and their stories, real and imaginary, form a romantic nexus which has filtered through, in some form, to the consciousness of people who do not read nineteenth-century novels. The family and their works had become legend long before the invention of film and television. Charlotte alone lived to become a celebrity, though fame arrived too late for her to enjoy it, in her moorland parish, sisters gone, and with an ailing father to take care of. The story ends with the tragi-comedy of her marriage to her father's curate, who had served seven years for his Rachel, and her death before she had been married a year.

How much evidence from the life do we take into account? How relevant is it that recorded in the *Brontë Society Transactions* we read a report by Mr. Jonas Bradley, of the *Yorkshire Observer* (19 June 1916), about the Brontë centenary, telling us that 'Mrs. Tempest, who had the proud privilege of knitting a pair of socks for the Rev. A. B. Nicholls . . . was present'?[21] A remote and even comic connection, we may think, but the omitted phrase was 'under Charlotte's supervision and instruction'. Mrs. Tempest was taught sewing and knitting by Charlotte in the Sunday school. Charlotte's fine motor control, despite her bad eyesight, her delicate skills with pen and needle, the results of which have come down to us, come into focus. Is the sofa Emily died on thereby different from all other sofas? Does it matter that, according to Geoffrey Fox Bradby, there are some half-dozen combs with burned teeth, all alleged to be the one the dying Emily dropped on to the hearth?[22] The reasonable reader will probably feel that the works hold priority of interest, yet many admit to that fascination with extraneous matters which at its highest is scholarship and at its lowest the worship of relics. Is it sentimentality to be moved by the sight of the hair of the famous dead, especially when woven into mourning rings? To note with a pang that Charlotte's letter to Miss Wooler about her anxieties for Anne, written just before setting off to Scarborough, on 16 May 1849, is written on black-edged paper, because she was in mourning for Emily?

To Margaret Wooler.

Haworth, May 16th, '49.

My dear Miss Wooler,—I will lose no time in thanking you for your letter and kind offer of assistance. We have, however, already engaged lodgings. I am not myself acquainted with Scarbro' but Anne knows it well—having been there three or four times—she had a particular preference for the situation of some lodgings (No. 2 Cliff). We wrote and, finding them disengaged, took them at 30s. per week. Your information is notwithstanding valuable—should we find this place in any respect ineligible—it is a satisfaction to be provided with directions for future use.

Next Wednesday is the day fixed for our departure; Ellen Nussey accompanies us at her own kind and friendly wish. I would not refuse her society but I dared not urge her to go, for I have little hope that the excursion will be one of pleasure or benefit to those engaged in it. Anne is extremely weak. She herself, has a fixed impression that the sea-air will give her a chance of regaining strength—that chance therefore we must have.

Having resolved to try the experiment—misgivings are useless—and yet—when I look at her—misgivings will rise. She is more emaciated than Emily was at the very last—her breath scarcely serves her to mount the stairs however slowly. . . .

This item, letter 442 in the Shakespeare Head Brontë, is printed with a page footnote saying that opposite the reference to Ellen, 'Miss Wooler has added a pencil note: "Anne had implored E. to accompany her but I did not know it." ' There is a mystery about this footnote. The original is in the Fitzwilliam Museum, Cambridge, No. 7 in the sequence of letters to Miss Wooler. As I read it, the pencilled note says not 'I' but 'C'. The curves are not conspicuous, but the slanting vertical stroke has 'hooks' at top and bottom on the right-hand side. Professor Clifford Allbutt, Miss Wooler's nephew, who presented the letters to the Museum, says in a scribbled note above it that the handwriting is his aunt's. Professor Mildred Christian, according to an anonymous hand-written annotation on the typed Fitzwilliam letter-list, believes that the hand is Ellen Nussey's, but the Museum has no confirming letter from Professor Christian.

Mrs. Gaskell (*Life*, Ch. 17), writes that Ellen proposed that Anne should go and visit her family. Charlotte wrote on 24 March to Ellen (letter quoted in Mrs. Gaskell):

> I have read your kind note to Anne, and she wishes me to thank you sincerely for your friendly proposal. She feels, of course, that it would not do to take advantage of it, by quartering an invalid upon the inhabitants of ——; but she intimates there is another way in which you might serve her, perhaps with some benefit to yourself as well as her.

Charlotte then goes on to say that if Anne does go to the seaside, 'could you be her companion? . . . you would be put to no expense. This, dear E., is Anne's proposal; I make it to comply with her wish.' Charlotte then goes on to warn Ellen that Anne might die when alone with Ellen, which 'would be terrible'.

Charlotte suggests putting off the excursion till June and pleads, 'Write such an answer to this note as I can show Anne.'

It is clear from this letter that Charlotte did know Anne had asked Ellen to accompany her; indeed the request was made through Charlotte, so Charlotte in fact lied to Miss Wooler that Ellen was coming 'at her own kind and friendly wish'. If Ellen wrote the note, why should she write what was not true, that 'C' (meaning, presumably, Charlotte) did not know about Anne's request? Or did Miss Wooler write that note; and did she write 'I' or 'C'?

Mrs. Gaskell quotes the letter from Anne, dated 5 April 1849 (now in the Parsonage Museum at Haworth, BS5), meeting the objections of Ellen's 'friends' to Ellen's

> taking the responsibility of accompanying me under present circumstances. But I do not think there would be any great responsibility. . . . It would be as a companion not as a nurse that I should wish for your company. . . . I have no horror of death; if I thought it inevitable, I think I could quietly resign myself to the prospect, in the hope that you, dear Miss Nussey, would give as much of your company as you possibly could to Charlotte and be a sister to her in my stead. . . . I long to do some good in the world before I leave it. . . .

The account of Anne's death in Mrs. Gaskell's *Life* is Ellen's (the manuscript is now at Haworth). Mrs. Gaskell wrote to Miss Wooler, acknowledging the packet of letters, on 12 November [?1855]. This letter (also in the Fitzwilliam Museum, with Miss Wooler's copy of the *Life*, inscribed by the author) says:

> I like them better than any other series of hers that I have seen; (a few to 'Emily' those to Miss Nussey, and some to Mr. Smith;) I am sure you will allow me to apply to you with any questions that may suggest themselves to me in the course of my work. . . . I hope you and your hostess continue as well satisfied with each other as you spoke of being when I had the pleasure of seeing you at Brookroyd. . . . (Letter 272, *Letters of Mrs. Gaskell*, ed. Chapple and Pollard).

Mrs. Gaskell had been introduced to Miss Wooler by Ellen the previous October. In a letter tentatively dated 20 December 1855 (Letter 275a), Mrs. Gaskell writes to Ellen,

I *do* want you to come . . . it would not be right to conceal from you the actual state of nothingness in which the Memoir is at present. About your account of Anne Brontë's death we will talk when I see you, it seems to me very desirable to have it from an eye-witness. . . .

Ellen visited Mrs. Gaskell at her home, Plymouth Grove, Manchester, in early January 1857, and stayed several days, looking over the *Life*, according to Winifred Gérin's *Elizabeth Gaskell* (Ch. 15).[23] Mr. Brontë had embargoed Ellen's inspection, and Ellen tended to be jealous of those close to Charlotte. In later life Ellen became possessive and acrimonious on the subject of her celebrated friend, as the extant correspondence shows. She must have felt herself pushed out by Mr. Brontë, and her account of Anne's death is an apparently self-effacing exercise in self-dramatization. Ellen tells the story of arriving at Leeds station at the appointed time, not knowing Anne was worse and could not keep the appointment. Ellen tells us 'it struck her as strange at the time—and it almost seems ominous to her fancy now' that she saw two separate coffins placed on hearses. Next day she arrived 'just in time to carry the feeble, fainting invalid into the chaise which stood at the gate to take them down to Keighley' (*Life*, Ch. 17).

Being in at Anne Brontë's death was possibly the greatest event of Ellen's life, and Ellen made the most of her reflected glory. Ellen is of interest to posterity only as Charlotte's friend and she both enjoyed and resented this. Staying with Mrs. Gaskell while Miss Wooler's letters were in Mrs. Gaskell's possession, could Ellen have pencilled a note on the letter in question, drawing Mrs. Gaskell's attention to her own importance as a friend so dear that Anne, unbeknown to Charlotte, had particularly requested her presence? She must have known that Mrs. Gaskell knew Charlotte knew, so why should the well-bred Ellen have scrawled on a letter belonging to somebody else? Perhaps as a former pupil, awarded a copy of Mrs. Chapone's *Letters on the Improvement of the Mind* as a prize for 'good and ladylike conduct' when at Roe Head, inscribed by Miss Wooler, Ellen hoped to be forgiven. If Professor Christian is right in her attribution, Ellen was perhaps giving Mrs. Gaskell a hint. Mrs. Gaskell, however, did not take it, and did not use the letter in the *Life*. Possibly such speculation is unnecessary;

while I believe the scribbled note to be in Ellen's handwriting, it may have been added later. When Clement Shorter was editing *The Brontës Life and Letters* (published 1908), Ellen scrawled helpfully on letters and on envelopes.

A further complication is that Shorter, for reasons best known to himself, transcribes the letter falsely as saying '(by Anne's expressed wish)', though the original letter is perfectly clear. This editorial meddling is inexcusable. The printed texts are unreliable; the originals of many letters surviving in printed versions are lost. Clement Shorter discovered A. B. Nicholls in Ireland in the 1890s and persuaded Nicholls to overcome his lifelong hatred of publicity to the extent of handing over Charlotte's papers, wrapped in brown paper, from the back of a cupboard. Shorter told Nicholls and Ellen that he intended to produce a definitive biography and edition of the Brontë works and paid money. Nicholls and Ellen were left with the impression that these payments were in respect of loan rights only. Shorter was financed by T. J. Wise, who claimed to be setting up a Charlotte Brontë museum in Kensington, where everything would be preserved in one place. However, Shorter made his transcriptions, frequently publishing limited editions in partnership with Wise. Wise then took over the manuscripts, split them up (sometimes separating letters into their component sheets) and sold them. Ellen was appalled to find some of her letters passing into the hands of collectors. The originals on which the printed texts are based are scattered. Signatures have been chopped off by autograph hunters. Ellen and others have scrawled on letters and envelopes. J. Horsfall Turner (editor of Patrick Brontë's works) stamped his holdings with his name. And, as will be clear from the foregoing discussion, letters have been printed in censored, inaccurate or incomplete versions. Fortunately, at the time of going to press, a definitive edition of the letters is planned, though some problems may be insoluble.

Joan Stevens's essay, 'Woozles in Brontëland',[24] shows how errors get repeated. The only surviving letter from Charlotte to Mary Taylor is now in the John Rylands library, University of Manchester. It says quite clearly that there was a *thunderstorm* on the July day Charlotte and Anne set off to London to confront their publisher. (Mary, who destroyed the rest of Charlotte's letters, kept this one because of its historic importance.) Printed versions of the letter give 'snowstorm'. The girls were not 'shown up', but went into a back room, to meet George Smith. Stevens shows how few Brontë 'scholars' pass the test: most of them have accepted the July snowstorm as freak Yorkshire weather. Stray letters keep turning up, and are printed in the *Brontë Society Transactions*. Charlotte's habit of using dashes instead of full stops, sometimes instead of commas, colons or semi-colons, makes her holograph letters lively reading. In print (with honourable exceptions) punctuation is regularized. She wrote fast and fluently, with few erasures. Charlotte's epistolary hand is clear and legible, despite an idiosyncratic 'x' that looks like 'f' or long 's'. The letters are freer than the exquisite formal penmanship of the *Devoirs* and the *Jane Eyre* manuscript, and unlike the hasty, cramped scrawl of the Roe Head Journal. Unlike the miniscule 'print' of the juvenilia, they are written to be read.

Relic-hunting started early. The book-collector Sidney Bidell, in a letter to Ellen Nussey now in the Parsonage Museum at Haworth (unfortunately dated simply 2 May), wrote:

I attended a sale of autograph letters yesterday, among them was one from Charlotte Brontë to Mrs. Gaskell dated 26 September 1850. With the letter went a portrait of herself and her father, view of Haworth Parsonage and small tray made from oak out of Haworth Church. To my astonishment, the whole fetched £6.5s., of course the letter was the great thing.

A gentleman sitting next to me who had been a collector and seller all his life (now about 70 years) was equally astonished with myself at the sudden rise in value of Charlotte Brontë's autograph letters.

A letter of Robert Burns dated 15th January 1795 fetched only £13, and a Lord Byron £6.

In haste . . .

Ellen Nussey died in 1897, aged 80. Her funeral was attended by several members of the Brontë Society, then nearly four years old.

Professor Mildred Christian has produced a list of Brontë manuscripts in the United States. Christine Alexander's bibliography of Charlotte's manuscripts shows some as 'untraceable'. Frances Beer has edited a recent Penguin edition of the juvenilia of Jane Austen and Charlotte Brontë. Beer says in her Introduction, 'I am convinced that Brontë's juvenilia have been

chronically undervalued because they have been so terribly difficult to read.' Beer has used the Shakespeare Head and Gérin as
her copy-texts, and, in her anxiety to make Charlotte readable,
has fallen over backwards by cutting out 'distracting verbosity',
modernizing punctuation, capitalization and hyphenation, has
introduced paragraphing and replaced Charlotte's dashes by
'the commas, semicolons, and periods that their usage seemed
intended to designate'. Such an edition is presumably intended
for the university student of English, but the Penguin editorial
policy of modernizing texts limits their value. Great literature is
frequently reprinted for unsuspecting students with up-to-date
introductions and texts which perpetuate old errors, or are so
ruthlessly modernized as to mislead. While the flood of Brontë
commentary pours on unabated, much of it is not soundly
based.

T. Wemyss-Reid, in the address cited above, tells us that the
'good people of the Browning Society . . . carried away by their
passion for research', appealed to Browning 'to know whether a
certain passage in one of his poems had a particular meaning
not apparent on the surface'. Browning replied that he did not
know, adding, 'but if you ask the Browning Society I have no
doubt they will be able to tell you.' Reid adds complacently,
'We have not yet begun to analyse every passage in *Jane Eyre* or
Wuthering Heights in order to discover some occult meaning.
. . . happily the exquisite simplicity and clearness of the
language in which both Charlotte and Emily conveyed their
thoughts . . . will leave but little room for the labours of
investigators of the type of the Browning Society. . . .'

We have now. The investigators have moved in. The novels
have been trawled for arcane and even unintentional messages,
as we shall see. Recent criticism has alerted us to the prob-
lematics of narrative, persona and point of view. Charlotte's
works offer a rich mine to the delver, as they are rhetorical,
metaphorical, structured on antitheses, and deal with emotional, spiritual and socio-economic conflict. Charlotte's novels
have been 'deconstructed',[25] so that we find her more, not
less, interesting than we did. 'Psycho-biographical' criticism,
generally on Freudian lines, is currently out of vogue, but it has
produced some fresh and challenging interpretations, which are
not easily dismissed, though some are solemnly absurd. Feminists

have discerned suppressed anger in Charlotte's work, though John Maynard and others have pointed out that Charlotte's anger was articulate. Helene Moglen sees Charlotte as a masochist, while Margot Peters believes she, in effect, committed suicide. How far are these questions extra-literary? My own view is that it is impossible to distinguish the woman who suffers from the artist who creates, to separate Charlotte the novelist, letter-writer and editor of her sisters' work from Charlotte the bereaved, Charlotte the unrequited lover, Charlotte consumed with ambition, because these emotional experiences fuelled and shaped her fictions. Her personality and talent, like other people's, were moulded both by her environment and her resistance to the pressures of her peculiar life.

As for M. Heger, the leap in maturity in the writing of both Emily and Charlotte after Brussels can only be due to him. We do not know for certain when Emily's poems were written, but when Charlotte and Emily went to Brussels, it seems they had written mainly adolescent fantasies of sex and violence. Heger fired them with his own enthusiasm for the latest European literature. Mrs. Humphry Ward was the first to point out that, in addition to their Celtic heritage, the girls learned from European culture: brilliant and hungry, they eagerly seized on the books Heger gave and lent them. The influences on Emily were German, whereas Charlotte soaked up Lamartine[26] and Bernardin de Saint-Pierre.[27] Heger imposed standards of style and structure (*'Etudiez donc la forme'*[28]), pushed them to extend themselves. Like Mr. Brontë, Heger considered Emily cleverer than Charlotte, which possibly put Charlotte on her mettle. With Heger, the girls worked at degree level, forced to think in French for themselves. A student at a collegiate university with a tutorial system would be lucky today to find the close individual attention, the quality of stimulus, Heger offered to Charlotte and Emily. The certificate of proficiency he presented to Charlotte was not a mere 'fancy diploma' as John Maynard thinks.[29] French-speaking people judge foreigners by their ability to speak good French, and do not easily give away documents certifying they can do it. The diploma represented real achievement on Charlotte's part, and was a genuine qualification for teaching, in an age when such validation for clever women had not been organized. Rude things have been

23

said about Charlotte's French, but her French biographer, Ernest Dimnet, considered her written French better than Heger's.[30] That she lacked the stamina and the temperament for successful teaching over a long period was not Heger's fault. His comments on Charlotte's work are in themselves an essay on the nature of genius and the necessity for discipline. He uses a series of metaphors: a weight is more easily lifted with the help of a lever; nature makes the painter, but he needs to study colour and perspective; it is not the jeweller who makes the diamond, but without him it remains a pebble. The doctrine is that of Gauthier's *Emaux et Camées*. Heger concludes, '*Poëte ou non, étudiez donc la forme. Poëte vous serez plus puissant et vos oeuvres vivront. . . .*' Here Charlotte's master is giving her an inspiring message: she will be a *powerful* poet if she listens to him, and her works *will live*. The '*vous*' is arguably impersonal, but Charlotte took it personally and engraved the message on her heart. That the '*pauvre coeur blessé*', the '*pauvre coeur malade*' was ravished away was not perhaps the teacher's intention, though he probably manipulated Charlotte's crush on him to make her work harder. Emily, who did not 'draw well' with him at all, according to Charlotte's letter to Ellen Nussey (Brussels, May 1842), worked for work's sake, undistracted by emotional involvement. Charlotte strove to please her exacting taskmaster. The long-term result was *Villette*.

This study is selective. *Jane Eyre* will dominate, as so much has been written on it; about *The Professor* there is little said or to say. I shall have almost nothing to say about Charlotte's poems, agreeing with Tom Winnifrith that Charlotte was probably the worst poet in the family after her father.[31] My excursions into Angria will be minimal. I am tempted to agree with Charles Burkhart that 'Angria is a bore'.[32] Unlike some commentators, I lay no claim to intimacy with Charlotte: her work and her personality are puzzlingly antinomian (in the philosophical, not the religious, sense). She courted fame and shunned publicity; she was fascinated by, yet feared, violence. Her novels breathe revolt and an aspiration towards dominance, while her life shows a pattern of submission, so that her friend Sir James Kay-Shuttleworth could describe her, after her death, as a 'Christian heroine who could bear her cross with the firmness of a martyr saint'. She was a shy, prim spinster who shocked her contemporaries by writing about 'passion'. She was proud and touchy, because of poverty and an equivocal social status. She was conscious of a powerful intelligence, which she made others aware of. Nervous herself, she made other people uncomfortable because she was often tongue-tied; her silence and searching glance made others suspect she was watching and judging them. She had the prejudices, political and religious, inherited from her Ulster Protestant father. As a versifier she was mediocre, yet her prose is wonderfully poetic, showing the digested influence of Byron and Milton, both of whom she often quotes directly. She was a wonderful letter writer: her letters are full of personality and eloquence, and prose-poetry. She wrote movingly of her dead sisters, in a letter to James Taylor, 22 May 1850:

> For my part, I am free to walk over the moors; but when I go out there alone, everything reminds me of the times when others were with me, and then the moors seem a wilderness, featureless, solitary, saddening. My sister Emily had a particular love for them, and there is not a knoll of heather, not a branch of fern, not a young bilberry leaf, not a fluttering lark or linnet, but reminds me of her. The distant prospects were Anne's delight, and when I look round she is in the blue tints, the pale mists, the waves and shadows of the horizon.

The woman who could write that commands our attention and our respect. But A. O. J. Cockshut writes, 'Was our distaste for Charlotte Brontë due to a base feeling of superiority, to shame perhaps at having enjoyed her books when we were fourteen?'[33] Charlotte is often spoken of disparagingly as a 'woman's writer', a purveyor of schoolgirl dreams. Patricia Meyer Spacks tells us that her husband learned early that Charlotte was 'escape reading for girls'.[34] Kate Millett writes,

> Literary criticism of the Brontës has been a long game of masculine prejudice wherein the player either proves they can't write and are hopeless primitives, whereupon the critic sets himself up like a schoolmaster to edit their stuff and point out where they went wrong, or converts them into case-histories from the wilds, occasionally prefacing his moves with a few pseudo-sympathetic remarks about the windy house on the moors, or old maidhood, following with an attack on every truth the novels contain, · waged by anxious pedants who fear

Charlotte might 'castrate' them or Emily 'unman' them with her passion.[35]

Carolyn Heilbrun writes: 'The work of most male critics on the Brontës . . . will probably with time seem simply an aberration of the critics' cultural bias.'[36]

Female critics have recently made it their business to ask in what ways Charlotte speaks for us as women, though there is still disagreement about what she says and what she means. We are in the process of rediscovering Charlotte.

The Brontës have always attracted commentators on the lunatic fringe; Maud Margesson wrote a book called *The Brontës and their Stars* in 1928, explaining their talents by charting the positions of the planets. John Malham-Dembleby, in 1911, despite some intelligent remarks on nomenclature and sources, was convinced that Charlotte wrote all the Brontë works and that, craftily swopping sexes as well as other determining characteristics, she put the Haworth family, including Tabby, with of course M. Heger, into everything she wrote. More respectable critics have been impelled to ferret out mysteries, clues, secrets, to offer exclusive revelations. Such claims are mostly spurious; one might ask why critics find the stance of inspired seer-prophet so satisfying, each with his monopoly of insight; and why other people want to weave a circle round them thrice and believe them.

I have no axe to grind, although I hope to offer some thoughts on Victorian religion to those who ignore it. I look briefly over the last half-century of criticism and interpretation of Charlotte's three major novels, with a few excursions into her life, to draw conclusions of my own. Not all the questions I raise have answers. Those working on Charlotte's reputation in the nineteenth century will find little in this book, but my bibliography may be helpful. I call Miss Brontë Charlotte not because I claim familiarity but to distinguish her from her sisters. Acquaintance with the story of Charlotte's life is assumed.

NOTES

1. Robert Bernard Martin, *The Accents of Persuasion*, p. 58.
2. Robert Keefe, *Charlotte Brontë's World of Death*, p. 31.
3. G. H. Lewes, *Edinburgh Review*, 91 (January 1850), 153–57 (repr. in *The Brontës: The Critical Heritage*, ed. Miriam Allott, p. 163).
4. G. K. Chesterton, 'Charlotte Brontë and the Realists', *B.S.T.*, 4 (1907), 6. See also Franklin Gary, 'Charlotte Brontë and George Henry Lewes', *P.M.L.A.*, 51 (1936), 518–42, and K. Tillotson, 'Back to the Beginning of the Century', *B.S.T.*, 19 (1986), 14.
5. See Mrs. Gaskell's *Life of Charlotte Brontë*, Ch. 26.
6. T. Wemyss-Reid, *B.S.T.*, 2 (1899), 'The Brontës', 10.
7. See *The Critical Heritage*, pp. 413–23.
8. Introductions to the Haworth edition, extracts repr. in *The Critical Heritage*, p. 448 ff.
9. M. H. Scargill, 'All Passion Spent', *University of Toronto Quarterly*, 19 (January 1950), 120.
10. Edmund Gosse, *B.S.T.*, 2 (1904), 'The Challenge of the Brontës', 199.
11. Margaret Smith, 'The Manuscripts of Charlotte Brontë's Novels', *B.S.T.*, 18 (1983), 195.
12. Prince S. Mirsky, 'Through Foreign Eyes', *B.S.T.*, 6, 1923, 147.
13. Lord David Cecil, *Early Victorian Novelists*, p. 103.
14. Ibid., p. 114.
15. Early Brontë commentary is repetitive and turgid.
16. Leonard W. Lillingstone, 'The Brontës and their Books', *Connoisseur*, 5, No. 17 (January 1903), typescript in Brotherton Collection, Leeds, no pagination.
17. Henry James, 'The Lesson of Balzac', in *The Future of the Novel: Essays on the Art of Fiction*, ed. Leon Edel (New York: Vintage Books, 1956), p. 101.
18. Annette Tromly, *The Cover of the Mask*, p. 11.
19. Cited Anne Passell, *Charlotte and Emily Brontë: A Bibliography* (New York and London: Garland, 1979), p. 86.
20. Tromly, *The Cover of the Mask*, p. 10.
21. *B.S.T.*, 5 (1917), 182.
22. Geoffrey Fox Bradby, *The Brontës and Other Essays*, p. 37.
23. Winifred Gérin, *Elizabeth Gaskell* (Oxford: Oxford University Press, 1976), p. 174. And see Mrs. Gaskell, *Letters*, ed. Chapple and Pollard, to W. S. Williams (or perhaps George Smith, see Chapple and Pollard, p. 438n.), tentatively dated 19 January 1857: 'Miss Nussey was here last week reading the MS.'
24. Joan Stevens, 'Woozles in Brontëland', *Studies in Bibliography*, 24 (1971), 100.
25. For a definition of this and other terms from literary theory in relation to Charlotte Brontë, see Jeanette King's excellent Open University Guide, *Jane Eyre*.
26. For discussion of these influences, see E. M. Duthie, *The Foreign Vision of Charlotte Brontë*, and Lawrence Jay Dessner, 'Charlotte Brontë's Le Nid', *B.S.T.*, 16 (1973), 213–18.

27. See Duthie, *The Foreign Vision*, Ch. 6, and John Ware, 'Bernardin de Saint-Pierre and Charlotte Brontë', *Modern Language Notes*, 40 (1925), 381–82.
28. Heger's handwritten 'Observations' on Charlotte's essay '*La chute des feuilles*', repr. *B.S.T.*, 6 (1924), 244-47.
29. John Maynard, *Charlotte Brontë and Sexuality*, p. 22.
30. Ernest Dimnet, *Les Soeurs Brontë*, cited by Ernest Rhys, *B.S.T.*, 6 (1922), 91. Later carelessly translated by Louise Morgan Sill (London: Cape, 1927), so that Emily's famous 'That's right!' to the statement that religion was a matter between the individual and God is rendered as 'Well said!', without reference to the original. We read, too, of 'the stationer in the village of Greenwood', when clearly John Greenwood, the stationer of Haworth, is meant.
31. Tom Winnifrith, *The Poems of Charlotte Brontë* (Oxford: Basil Blackwell, for the Shakespeare Head Press, 1984), xii.
32. Charles Burkhart, *Charlotte Brontë: A Psychosexual Study of her Novels*, p. 33.
33. A. O. J. Cockshut, review of Robert Bernard Martin's *The Accents of Persuasion* and Inga-Stina Ewbank's *Their Proper Sphere, Essays in Criticism*, 17 (January 1967), 107.
34. Patricia Meyer Spacks, *The Female Imagination*, p. 228.
35. Kate Millett, *Sexual Politics* (paperback edn.), p. 147.
36. Carolyn Heilbrun, *Towards Androgyny*, p. 152.

2

Mr. Rockingham and Monsieur Beck

... her books cover nothing of the religious, the intellectual, and the purely animal sides of life. . . .—Lord David Cecil, 1934

Lord David Cecil's condemnation of Charlotte reigned for a quarter of a century, and lingered on until about 1970. In *Early Victorian Novelists* (1934) he wrote that Charlotte had 'no gift of form, no restraint, little power of observation, no power of analysis . . . her novels . . . are badly constructed, . . . improbable, . . . often ridiculous.'[1] 'Even at her best, she is not among the greatest drawers of character. . . .'[2] He mentions frequently her 'lack of restraint'.

Lord David's admiration was reserved for Emily. He made an apology to Charlotte in 1973, addressing the Brontë Society, deciding that

> *Jane Eyre* and *Villette* are only incoherent if they are judged by a conventional standard of a well-knit plot in which each incident follows logically on that which preceded it . . . what I had not grasped was that both books had more fundamental coherence, the coherence of a continuous theme.[3]

That Charlotte, whose descriptions of houses, rooms, weather and sensations have burned themselves into a million memories, should be accused of lacking 'observation' is astonishing. Even Malham-Dembleby was more acute: 'A recognizable idiosyncrasy of Charlotte Brontë's genius is the vivid minuteness with which she paints and records apparently unimportant details and happenings in her early childhood.'[4] As to her powers of creating character, her obituary in the *Leeds Mercury*, March 1855, said

> Mrs. Nicol [*sic*], formerly Miss Brontë, who under the *nom de plume* of Currer Bell, established a lasting reputation by the publication of 'Jane Eyre', 'Shirley' and 'Villette', all especially distinguished for great power of conception and vigorous portrayal of character, died on Saturday last. . . .

The local newspaper shows here a juster appreciation of Charlotte's true quality than does the Oxford don. As to Charlotte's powers of 'character-drawing', this was what the nineteenth century, obsessed with motivation and psychology, valued her for, and she earned the praise of Swinburne for it. Leslie Stephen put down Swinburne's gush,[5] and in his Introduction to the Works of Samuel Richardson digresses to have a go at Charlotte:

> Miss Brontë . . . showed extraordinary power in 'Jane Eyre'; but Jane Eyre's lovers, Rockingham [*sic*] and St. John, are painted from the outside; they are, perhaps, what some women think men ought to be, but not what any man of power at all comparable to Miss Brontë's could ever have imagined. Her most successful men—such as M. Paul in 'Villette'—are those who have the strongest feminine element in their composition. On the other hand, the heroines of male writers are for the most part unnaturally strained or quite colourless. . . . Milton could draw a majestic Satan, but his Eve is no better than a good managing housekeeper who knows her place.[6]

So anxious is Stephen to dismiss Rochester that he gets his name wrong. The remarks on Milton, however, show that he has digested Shirley Keeldar's comments on Milton (*Shirley*, Ch. 18):

> Milton was great; but was he good? His brain was right; how was his heart? He saw Heaven: he looked down on Hell. He saw Satan, and Sin his daughter, and Death their horrible offspring. Angels serried before him their battalions: the long lines of adamantine shields flashed back on his blind eyeballs the unutterable splendor of heaven. Devils gathered their legions in his sight: their dim, discrowned, and tarnished armies passed rank and file before him. Milton tried to see the first woman; but . . . it was his cook that he saw. . . .

Stephen, while dismissing Charlotte Brontë intellectually, has clearly been influenced emotionally by this magnificent passage, which exemplifies Charlotte's qualities at their best. In it she demonstrates her ability to respond to Milton's great poetry and to reflect its influence in new-minted poetic prose of her own, in order to make a serious intellectual-literary-moral-feminist point. (Like Lord David, Stephen shows the influence of Charlotte's potent imagery in his dismissal of her artistry.)

F. R. Leavis's suggestion that 'there is only one Brontë'[7] is well known. 'The genius, of course, was Emily.' Charlotte

> has a permanent interest of a minor kind. She had a remarkable talent that enabled her to do something firsthand and new in the rendering of personal experience, above all in *Villette*.

The Brontës are dismissed in a half-page 'note'.

Leavis's famous description of 'that astonishing work, *Wuthering Heights*' as 'a kind of sport' is not original. It comes from Professor George Saintsbury's address to the Brontë Society at Huddersfield on 14 January 1899. Professor Saintsbury said that Anne's work was 'the feeblest of the three'.... 'But *Wuthering Heights* and the four novels of Charlotte, though their total extent is not very great, give us practically all we want.' Emily Brontë was 'a poet rather than a novelist'; *Wuthering Heights* is

> too close upon the confines of the fairy tale, and there are many other technical drawbacks. If *Wuthering Heights* had stood alone it would have continued to be more or less alone—a kind of 'sport' as botanists say....[8]

Dr. Leavis has here characteristically reversed what he felt to be received opinion (that Charlotte was a greater novelist than her sister), while purloining (probably not with conscious recollection) Saintsbury's striking expression. The opinion that Emily was greater than Charlotte was in fact well established by the 1940s.[9]

Walter Allen takes over Lord David's judgement uncritically: 'As an artist, Charlotte Brontë had no taste, no restraint and no sense of the ridiculous.'[10] Jane Eyre 'has wit, but neither humour nor self-criticism'.[11] He allows *Jane Eyre* to be 'the first romantic novel in English', and writes sensitively about the theme of loneliness, noting that all Charlotte's heroines are 'in revolt against their circumstances, and they are in revolt as women'.[12] Allen is more perceptive than Lord David; he recognizes Charlotte as a forerunner of Lawrence, and notes that 'the passionate response is not to sex alone, but to all experience, to the whole living world'.[13]

Derek Traversi's account of 'The Brontë Sisters and *Wuthering Heights*' is a shamefully slipshod piece of work. The *Pelican Guide* is, unfortunately, still taken by students as authoritative. Traversi treats Charlotte with contempt, having made up his mind in advance that she cannot write. Her images are self-evidently 'embarrassing and absurd'.[14] Traversi continues:

> The blind Rochester is presented as a 'sightless Samson', a 'caged eagle whose gold-ringed eyes cruelty has extinguished'; and Jane, when she ventures at an earlier stage to meet her 'master's and lover's eye', receives a smile 'such as a sultan might, in a blissful and fond moment, bestow on a slave his gold and gems had enriched'. Similarly, the idealisation of M. Beck in *Villette* rises to heights of unreality. . . .

M. Beck? Madame Beck is a widow. Her cousin is Paul Emmanuel. In their haste to distance Charlotte's intensity these men invent imaginary characters. That Charlotte's reference to a sultan is part of a complex pattern of imagery involving sexual power-politics has escaped him. The master-slave-pupil nexus has been ably dealt with by feminist writers.

The first rehabilitation of Charlotte as artist came from M. H. Scargill in 1950. He rehearses dismissive judgements by Gerald Bullett and E. A. Baker,[15] and suggests that *Jane Eyre* is great because 'it speaks for all humanity' as a 'record of the eternal conflict between flesh and spirit . . . solved satisfactorily when all passion is spent'.[16] He argues that we make no demands of probability on the poet, but ask the novelist for a reproduction of life. *Jane Eyre* is a new type of novel:

> . . . the mad woman of the Gothic novel has been put to allegorical use. *Jane Eyre* contains the elements of fiction used as a poet employs language and imagery—to impose belief, even though it be by irrational means.[17]

'Was there ever a more powerful symbol of the ascetic than St. John Rivers?' asks Scargill.[18]

He concludes,

> If *Jane Eyre* is to be blamed because it doesn't do what *Tom Jones* and *Vanity Fair* do, then literary criticism is at fault . . . let us now admit that in *Jane Eyre* fiction has become poetry, and let us enlarge our idea of fiction accordingly.[19]

While *Tom Jones* and *Vanity Fair* seem to me to be different kinds of novel, and the poetic resonances of *Vanity Fair* are not to be under-estimated, it will become clear that my view of *Jane Eyre* is similar to Scargill's.

Critical opinion does not come from nowhere; like literature itself, it is rooted in traditions and influences, social and historical. It was Q. D. Leavis who next established, in a sustained way, the claims of *Jane Eyre* to be considered great, in her Penguin edition of 1966. The text reproduces misprints (the chestnut tree at Thornfield 'gasped ghastly' instead of 'gaped'; the condor in the Andes is 'wildest winged' instead of 'widest winged'), and instead of annotation at the end, Mrs. Leavis argues interpretative points. However, Scargill's and Shapiro's defences in 1950 and 1968 would seem to evince the diffused influence of L. C. Knights's essay, 'How Many Children had Lady Macbeth?' This essay was the single most important contribution to twentieth-century Shakespeare criticism, totally rechannelling the current. It argued against mining Shakespeare's plays for psychology and motive, and for looking at them as 'dramatic poems'. Knights's ultimate influence was to be reflected back into the study of novels for their poetic imagery. For a time Knights was a member of the *Scrutiny* group, which met at the house of the Leavises to produce the journal. Scargill's reading of *Jane Eyre* shows a digested influence of Knights's ideas. Mrs. Leavis's introduction to *Jane Eyre* is her freshest and most original work, staking out fresh ground. Writing as one who had the privilege of her individual supervision during my final year as an undergraduate at Cambridge, I must make my position clear. Her knowledge of Victorian social and religious history was unmatched, a wonderful resource for her pupils. Her critical opinions were arbitrary and rigid, often taken over as axioms from other people. She could see no merit, for example, in *Vanity Fair* or in *Jude the Obscure*. But, championing Charlotte, she wrote at her best. Mrs. Leavis knows the difference between Evangelicalism and Calvinism,

unlike Moglen[20] and Showalter,[21] though I cannot agree with
Mrs. Leavis that 'all the representatives or mouthpieces of
religion . . . are either "placed" or destroyed by ironic analysis'.[22]
Mrs. Leavis's analysis is broad and general. She is the first to
note that *Jane Eyre* and *Wuthering Heights* are 'strikingly controlled and schematic'.[23] Charlotte's prose is 'a mosaic, notice-
ably Regency in its combination of eighteenth-century exact-
ness and the new journalistic idiom . . . the magical quality of
her writing . . . the thrilling suggestiveness she conveys through
the simplest words'.[24] While this is true, much of Charlotte's
characteristic effect is achieved, as is Shakespeare's, by a blend
of simple native idiom with neologisms and exotic imports. Mrs.
Leavis accuses Charlotte of journalistic 'vulgarism' in using
'optics' for eyes, but there are precedents: in Quarles's *Emblems*,
we read, 'Look off, let not thy optics be/ Abus'd. . . .'[25] Leaving
Lowood, says Mrs. Leavis, Jane is 'like Christian in Doubting
Castle'.[26] The larger parallels with *The Pilgrim's Progress*, that
pattern-book for so many apparently secular novels, are not
pursued. At Moor House, the 'broken Reeds are replaced by
Rivers of life. . . . St. John represents the eighteenth-century
"Reason" founded on an education in the classics.'[27] Mrs.
Leavis finds in *Jane Eyre* an integrated story of personal growth
and fulfilment, in which the 'embittered little charity child finds
the way to come to terms with life and society'.[28]

Inga-Stina Ewbank's *Their Proper Sphere* (1967) said that
Charlotte's 'artistic principles brought her into conflict with the
principles of conventional femininity and involved her, willy
nilly, in a feminist rebellion'.[29] W. A. Craik, in the *Sphere History
of Literature in the English Language*, Vol. 6, writes of *Jane Eyre* as
'a fully achieved masterpiece' and *Shirley* as a 'misconceived
variant'. Craik insists, against F. R. Leavis, that Charlotte must
be 'judged by the highest standards'.[30]

In 1968, several voices were raised. Craik published *The
Brontë Novels*, which argued, in opposition to Lord David Cecil,
that far from all being Charlotte Brontë, her protagonists were
all distanced. Craik also pleaded for recognition of Charlotte as
artist, independently of her life. Dale Kramer published a
paper, 'Thematic Structure in *Jane Eyre*',[31] and Arnold Shapiro
published one called 'In Defense of *Jane Eyre*'.[32] Shapiro writes
to disagree with Richard Chase's 'The Brontës: or Myth

Domesticated'[33] and G. Armour Craig's 'The Unpoetic Compromise: On the Relation Between Private Vision and Social Order in Nineteenth-century English Fiction'.[34] Shapiro argues that in accusing Jane of 'cowardice' in leaving Rochester, Chase pays 'no attention to the terrible torment Jane undergoes . . . and the guilt and anguish she feels when she does leave'. Shapiro defends Jane's rejection of St. John as a refusal 'to turn away from humanity . . . to an other-worldly life-denying selfish existence nominally carried out in the name of God'.[35] Shapiro sees that Jane turns away from Helen Burns's other-worldliness. He recognizes that Rochester, promising to make the bejewelled Jane into an acknowledged beauty, 'has a false view of what she is'.[36] He quotes with approval R. B. Heilman's comment that Jane reacts to temptation not with the 'fear and revulsion of the popular heroines, but by a responsiveness which she barely masters'.[37] Shapiro observes that St. John's attempt to change Jane into what she is not parallels Rochester's. Jane does not receive 'supernatural aid' until she is ready and willing to respond to it.[38] Shapiro rejects Armour Craig's hostile reading that Jane triumphs over everybody and commits 'the most dreadful violence' in reducing the world to her own vision.[39] For Shapiro, *Jane Eyre* is 'concerned with the real problems of a real world',[40] and in support of his reading he cites Raymond Williams on novels of the 1840s about orphans, exposed children, governesses, 'expressing, even through the conventional forms, a radical human dissent'.[41]

Earl A. Knies's careful study, *The Art of Charlotte Brontë* (1969) was less influential, at least in Britain, than it deserved to be. In 1973 Nina Auerbach could still write that Charlotte Brontë was 'out of critical fashion'.[42]

Since the mid-'70s, there has been an explosion of feminist writing about Charlotte, focusing mainly on *Jane Eyre*. It may be worth pointing out that the generation of critics exemplified by Mrs. Leavis looked for harmony and resolution in works of art; when they found this 'unity' they honoured it with the metaphoric appellation of 'organic'. More recent criticism, influenced directly or indirectly by European Marxism, prefers to look at tensions, contradictions and evasions, in order to reveal socio-economic or unconscious meanings, and to scrutinize every narrative for indeterminacy.

Charlotte Brontë: Truculent Spirit

NOTES

1. Lord David Cecil, *Early Victorian Novelists* (paperback edn.), p. 113.
2. Ibid., p. 97.
3. *B.S.T.*, 16 (1973), 169.
4. John Malham-Dembleby, *The Key to the Brontë Works* (London and Felling-on-Tyne: Walter Scott Publishing Co. Ltd., 1911), p. 6.
5. Leslie Stephen, repr. *The Critical Heritage*, p. 413.
6. Leslie Stephen, Introduction to the works of Samuel Richardson (Henry Sotheran & Co., 1883), p. xxvii.
7. F. R. Leavis, *The Great Tradition* (London: Chatto and Windus, 1950), p. 27.
8. George Saintsbury, *B.S.T.*, 2 (April 1899), 26.
9. See Earl A. Knies, *The Art of Charlotte Brontë*, pp. 3–7.
10. Walter Allen, *The English Novel*, p. 193.
11. Ibid., p. 189.
12. Ibid., p. 192.
13. Ibid., p. 193.
14. Derek Traversi, 'The Brontë Sisters and *Wuthering Heights*', *Pelican Guide to English Literature*, Vol. 6, 258.
15. Gerald Bullett, *George Eliot* (London, 1947), and E. A. Baker, *The History of the Novel* (London, 1937), VIII, 36, cited Scargill, 120n.
16. Scargill, p. 121.
17. Ibid., p. 122.
18. Ibid., p. 123.
19. Ibid., p. 123.
20. Helene Moglen, *The Self Conceived*, p. 24.
21. Elaine Showalter, *A Literature of their Own*, p. 118.
22. Q. D. Leavis, Introduction to Penguin *Jane Eyre*, p. 18.
23. Ibid., p. 11.
24. Ibid., p. 26.
25. Quarles, *Emblems* 2:6.
26. Q. D. Leavis, *Jane Eyre* Introduction, p. 16.
27. Ibid., p. 24.
28. Ibid., p. 12.
29. Inga-Stina Ewbank, *Their Proper Sphere*, p. 161.
30. W. A. Craik, *Sphere History of Literature in the English Language*, Vol. 6, 146.
31. Dale Kramer, 'Thematic Structure in *Jane Eyre*', *Papers on Language and Literature*, 4 (Summer 1968), 288–98.
32. Arnold Shapiro, 'In Defense of Jane Eyre', *Studies in English Literature 1500–1900*, 8 (1968), 681–98.
33. Richard Chase, 'The Brontës: or Myth Domesticated', in *Forms of Modern Fiction*, ed. William Van O'Connor (Minneapolis: University of Minnesota Press, 1948).
34. G. Armour Craig, 'The Unpoetic Compromise: On the Relation Between Private Vision and Social Order in Nineteenth-century English Fiction', in *English Institute Essays*, 1955 (New York: Columbia University Press, 1956), 26–50.

35. Shapiro, p. 683.
36. Ibid., p. 689.
37. Robert Heilman, 'Charlotte Brontë's "New" Gothic', in *From Jane Austen to Joseph Conrad*, ed. Robert C. Rathburn and Martin Steinmann, Jr. (Minneapolis: University of Minnesota Press, 1958), pp. 118–32.
38. Shapiro, p. 695n.
39. Ibid., p. 697.
40. Ibid., p. 698.
41. Raymond Williams, *The Long Revolution*, p. 68.
42. Nina Auerbach, 'Charlotte Brontë: The Two Countries', *University of Toronto Quarterly*, 42:2 (Summer 1973), 328.

3

'How very corse!'

The true poet, quiet externally though he may be, has often a truculent spirit. . . . (*Shirley*, Ch. 4)

'There is a coarseness of tone throughout the writing of all these Bells', said the reviewer of Anne Brontë's *The Tenant of Wildfell Hall, Spectator*, 18 July 1848. The accusation of 'coarseness' was widespread, and it hurt. What did it mean? *Wildfell Hall* was intended as a sober tract, a warning against drink. It was read as sensation literature. As W. A. Craik points out, 'All three sisters unhesitatingly depicted drunkenness and degradation.'[1] Charlotte considered *Wildfell Hall* 'a mistake'[2] and refused to republish it after Emily and Anne were dead. 'Coarseness' was a broad term, covering unpleasant subjects, crude language and violence. The topic is raised by Charles Burkhart,[3] briefly discussed by Miriam Allott,[4] and handled in detail by Tom Winnifrith.[5] See also Edith M. Weir,[6] Eanne Oram and John Mitchell.[7]

'Coarseness' was also a term applied by sophisticated London readers to descriptions of provincial speech and lower-class manners. Sara Coleridge complained in a letter to Ellis Yarnall of Philadelphia in 1850 that though *Jane Eyre* and *Shirley* were 'full of genius', with 'spirit . . . glow and fire, a masculine energy of satire and picturesque description, which have delighted me', they also abounded in 'a certain hardness of feeling and plebean [*sic*] coarseness of taste'.[8] Sara, who was extremely intelligent, preferred the novels of Mrs. Marsh. London society people thought Charlotte was 'accustomed only to the narrow literalness of her own circle', so could not 'fall in with the easy badinage of . . . well-bred people'.[9] This citified narrowness is

mocked by Charlotte herself, in a speech put into the mouth of
Joe Scott (*Shirley*, Ch. 5), defiantly speaking in the dialect of his
region and class.

> We allus speak our minds i' this country, and them young
> parsons and grand folk fro' London is shocked at wer '*incivility*',
> and we like weel enow to gi'e 'em summat to be shocked at,
> 'cause it's sport to us to watch 'em turn up the whites o' their een,
> and spreed out their bits o' hands, like as they're flayed wi'
> boggards, and then to hear 'em say, nipping off their words short,
> like—'Dear! dear! Whet seveges! How very corse!'

'Flayed wi' boggards' needs translating: it means 'frightened by
ghosts', according to the editors of the Clarendon edition. The
refined daughters of the parsonage were bilingual, thanks to
Tabby, and Charlotte has here brilliantly projected herself as a
provincial workman, defending himself against such criticisms
as were made by her father's curates, depicted in their smug
typicality in *Shirley*. Her view of London society was less than
enchanted. Writing to Miss Wooler on 14 February 1850,
Charlotte noted:

> London people strike a provincial as being very much taken up
> with little matters about which no one out of particular town
> circles cares much ... I think I should scarcely like to live in
> London. ... (No. 8, Fitzwilliam Museum).

She preferred looking at Turner's water-colours to being
lionized. In the same letter she reports

> When I was in London a woman whose celebrity is not wider
> than her moral standard is elevated—and in each point she has
> no living superior—said to me, '*I have ever observed that it is to the
> coarse-minded alone—"Jane Eyre" is coarse*'. This ['obser' crossed
> out] remark tallied with what I had myself noticed; I felt its
> truth. ... Certain of the clergy have thought proper to be bitter
> against the work—some of them good men in their way—but
> men in whom the animal obviously predominates over the
> intellectual. I smile inwardly when I hear of their disapprobation.

Charlotte here seems to be saying that clergymen who object to
Jane Eyre must have dirty minds. Who the lady was who told
Charlotte what she wanted to hear we do not know. Clergymen
objected to the satirical portrayal of Brocklehurst; and the
picture of Lowood, immediately recognized as the Clergy

Daughters' School, Cowan Bridge, could be criticized on two counts: as an attack on religion, and as an example of insubordination. The criticisms of Elizabeth Rigby[10] and of the *Christian Remembrancer*[11] are too well known to repeat at length and are easily accessible in *Jane Eyre and Villette* (Macmillan Casebook, ed. Miriam Allott). However, some may have wondered what Rigby meant by writing that if *Jane Eyre* was written by a woman, it must be 'one who has . . . long forfeited the society of her own sex'. A cruel insult was cloaked as artistic judgement; ostracism was the punishment for the 'fallen woman', the unchaste. Rumour had it that the author of *Jane Eyre* was the cast-off mistress of Thackeray, the original of Becky Sharp taking revenge (that Thackeray, unknown to Charlotte, had a mad wife caused embarrassment all round when she dedicated the third edition to him). The accusation of immorality was grotesquely inapplicable to the virgins of Haworth, but nevertheless wounding. In the *Christian Remembrancer*, along with 'masculine power, breadth and shrewdness, combined with masculine hardness, coarseness and freedom of expression', Charlotte is accused of using slang. Mrs. Gaskell found in the manuscript of *The Professor*, rejected during Charlotte's lifetime, 'more coarseness,—& profanity . . . than in any of her other works'.[12] Charlotte's widower, the Rev. A. B. Nicholls, edited the manuscript after Charlotte's death. 'God damn your insolence' has been softened to 'Confound your insolence'. Margaret Smith thinks that Charlotte, sensitive to the accusation of bad language, apparently 'cleaned up' the manuscripts of *Shirley* and *Villette*.[13]

Winifred Gérin's biography of Charlotte tells us that Charlotte's godmother, Mrs. Atkinson, rejected Charlotte for having written an 'unwomanly' book.[14] Miss Wooler hastened to forgive. Charlotte wrote diplomatically (letter quoted above):

> You may and do object to certain phrases, exclamations &c., phrases and ['objections' crossed out] exclamations, however, which, viewing them from an artistic point of view, my judgement ratifies as consistent and characteristic—but I have not hitherto fancied you have withdrawn from me your esteem.

This sentence is uncharacteristically clumsy and even hesitant, which suggests some tension. Edwin Percy Whipple, writing

about *Jane Eyre*, *Wuthering Heights* and *The Tenant of Wildfell Hall*
in the *North American Review*, October 1848, said:

> When the admirable Mr. Rochester appears, and the profanity,
> brutality, and slang of the misanthropic profligate give their
> torpedo shocks to the nervous system . . . we are gallant enough
> to detect the hand of a gentleman in the composition. There are
> also scenes of passion, so hot, so emphatic, and condensed in
> expression, and so sternly masculine in feeling, that we are
> almost sure we observe the mind of the author of *Wuthering
> Heights* at work in the text.[15]

Charlotte's response was wry humour. She wrote to W. S.
Williams on 31 July 1848:

> What a bad set the Bells must be! What appalling books they
> write! Today, as Emily seemed a little better, I thought the
> 'Review' would amuse her, so I read it aloud to her and Anne. As
> I sat between them at our quiet but now somewhat melancholy
> fireside, I studied the two ferocious authors. Ellis, the 'man of
> uncommon talents, but dogged, brutal and morose', sat . . .
> looking, alas! piteously pale and wasted; it is not his wont to
> laugh, but he smiled half-amused and half in anger as he
> listened. Acton was sewing, no emotion ever stirs him to
> loquacity, so he only smiled too, dropping at the same time a
> single word of calm amazement to hear his character so darkly
> portrayed. I wonder what the reviewer would have thought of his
> own sagacity could he have beheld the pair as I did. . . . How I
> laugh in my sleeve when I read the solemn assertions that *Jane
> Eyre* was written in partnership, and that it 'bears the marks of
> more than one mind and more than one sex.'

Charlotte wrote to Williams on 21 September 1849:

> Margaret Hall called *Jane Eyre* a 'wicked book', on the authority
> of the *Quarterly*; an expression which, coming from her, I will here
> confess, struck somewhat deep. It opened my eyes to the harm
> the *Quarterly* had done. Margaret would not have called it
> 'wicked' if she had not been told so.

The real trouble was that Charlotte's book was erotic. As
Elizabeth Hardwick notes, readers were aware of an under-
current of sexual fantasy.[16] G. H. Lewes offended Charlotte by
announcing publicly, 'We have both written naughty books.'[17]
George Steiner writes, '*Jane Eyre* aroused hostility by its assumption of sexual readiness . . .—in a "decent" woman.'[18] It was

Lewes who observed that Jane Eyre is 'a creature of flesh and
blood, with very fleshly infirmities. . . .'[19] It is not easy to know
what Lewes means by 'infirmities'. This is vague and unsatis-
factory: Jane, unlike Lucy Snowe, is healthy. It is not clear
whether he means her disgust at the smell of burnt porridge or
her feelings about Rochester. His review of *Villette* clarifies,
however, the question of 'coarseness':

> . . . her Rochesters and Jane Eyre . . . are men and women of
> deep feeling, clear intellects, vehement tempers, bad manners,
> ungraceful, yet loveable persons. Their address is brusque,
> unpleasant, yet individual, direct, free from shams and conven-
> tions of all kinds. They outrage 'good taste', yet they fascinate
> . . . Janet captured all our hearts; not because she was lovely,
> lady-like, good, but because she was direct, clear, upright,
> capable of deep affections, and of bravely enduring great
> affliction.[20]

In other words, though *Jane Eyre* has 'too much melodrama
and improbability',[21] it scores because it is not like standard
fiction, but like real life. Too much 'realism', though, was a
challenge to notions of 'good taste'.

The presence of flesh and blood, of sense organs all over the
body surface sending messages along the nerves, is potent in
Charlotte's writing. People describe their first reading of *Jane
Eyre* in terms of physical excitement, echoing Charlotte's own
articulated response to life; they write of 'thrills', 'throbs',
'red-hot' and even 'white-hot' sensations. Charlotte, whose own
trembling seems to have been visible, transferred to readers her
own consciousness of the powerful heartbeat in her tiny frame,
the palpitations of her small extremities, her sensitivity to the
motion of blood flowing warm through her veins from 'the
sentient target of death', or 'running ice' (letter to Ellen Nussey,
9 April 1851, about her refusal of James Taylor—a real-life
parallel to Jane's refusal of St. John, subsequent to the novel.
Oddly, Taylor went to India). Like Sterne, whose influence was
toyed with in her Charles Townsend Angrian stories,[22] Charlotte
is acutely aware of mind-body interaction and conveys bodily
sensation with erotic undertones. In three famous letters (to
G. H. Lewes, 12 January and 18 January 1848, and to W. S.
Williams, 12 April 1850), she criticized Jane Austen for failing

to show flesh and the blood that mantles beneath it; she could
not believe that Jane Austen's characters had true emotions or
bodily functions.

The sense of 'passion' in Charlotte's writing comes from a
variety of sources. We first hear the word in *Jane Eyre* in
connection with Jane's violent outburst of rage ('Did you ever
see such a picture of passion?', Ch. 1). In its eighteenth-century
sense of something passively experienced, it is linked with
Charlotte's power of conveying physical, as well as emotional,
states: Jane suffers in her skin and nerve-endings as she is
lashed by cold winds and rain, walking two miles to church,
thrusting chilblained feet into thin shoes, starved of fire by the
great girls; expanding into joy when given seedcake by a warm
fire, caressed by warm winds and a sweet night in the garden at
Thornfield. There is the treatment of love and sex: Jane is in
love with Mr. Rochester before she has any indication of his
feeling for her; he tells her, an employee half his age, about his
mistresses; when Bertha sets Rochester's bed on fire and, on a
separate occasion, attacks her brother, Rochester and Jane are
running in and out of bedrooms together. When Jane writes,
after the interrupted marriage, that 'Conscience . . . held
passion by the throat', she means she is literally choking with
thwarted desire. Peter Cominos writes of euphemisms for sexual
repression in the Victorian 'Innocent femina sensualis'.[23]
Victorian readers would not have seen the image as a stale
hangover from the eighteenth century, a pallid abstraction; they
grasped the expression's implied physicality. Nineteenth-century
writers were adept at euphemism and circumlocution, writing
books that could be read aloud in the family circle, but which
clearly indicated to the grown-ups exactly what was going on
(think of Nancy in *Oliver Twist*). Our own generation, used to
plain, even obscene, speaking, must re-learn the art of decoding
innuendo if we are to get the full flavour of Victorian novels. It
is difficult to teach *Jane Eyre* to young people in the late
twentieth century, when a majority of marriages end in divorce,
and adultery is no longer considered shameful. That Jane's
lover has a wife is considered by the young no barrier to
cohabitation. For Charlotte Brontë, things were different.
Writing about the parting from Rochester, Charlotte was
describing the emotional crisis of her life: 'I think, however long

I live, I shall not forget what the parting with M. Heger cost me; it grieved me so much to grieve him, who has been so true, kind and disinterested a friend . . .', she wrote to Ellen, 23 January 1844. The parting with M. Heger was, in fact, due to his wife, though while the pain of separation is described in *Jane Eyre*, the sweetness of temptation offered can only have been imagined. (In *Villette*, Madame Beck is portrayed as the agent of attempted separation of Lucy and her lover.) But Madame Heger was, in real life, neither a madwoman nor a scheming widow: she was a happy wife, partner in a successful business, sane, calm, blooming and fertile. A beck is a stream: Madame Beck tries to 'throw cold water' over Lucy's romance with Paul Emmanuel. Charlotte, choked with anguish, wrote about separation and desire, in terms so frank, by the standards of her day, that contemporaries picked up the note of sexual frustration and winced at its nakedness. In the parting scene, as with the scene where Jane refuses St. John's offer of marriage, Charlotte was writing from her own emotional experience. St. John brings snow indoors with him, his kisses are ice, he is white marble: he freezes Jane (turning the girl who had been an 'ardent, expectant woman', in more than one meaning of the word, frigid). Barbara Hill Rigney thinks the marriage with St. John will be 'sexless',[24] but the text makes it plain that what Jane dreads is sexual relations without love: 'Can I receive from him the bridal ring, endure all the forms of love (which I doubt not he would scrupulously observe) and know that the spirit was quite absent?' (Ch. 34). The pair actually discuss it: St. John insists there must be the 'physical and mental union in marriage'. Jane scorns the marriage of convenience which was becoming, at the time, a middle-class norm. Doubtless this was the sort of frankness which offended readers in the 1840s, truthful and vital as it is. Charlotte had read Sterne and Richardson, who speak with a freedom Dickens and Thackeray regretted had been lost to the writers of their day.

Rigney writes that 'passion' was Charlotte's euphemism for sexuality,[25] but there was more to it than that. Charlotte owned a copy of Isaac Watts's *The Doctrine of the Passions*, now at the Parsonage Museum. Its subtitle runs:

> Explained *and* improved: OR, *A Brief and Comprehensive Scheme of the Natural Affections of Mankind*, Attempted in a plain and easy

Method; with an Account of their Names, Appearances, Effects, and different Uses in Human Life: to which are subjoined, MORAL AND DIVINE RULES for the Regulation or Government of them

by I. Watts, D.D.

He that hath no Rule over his own Spirit, is like a City that is broken down and Without Walls (Prov. xxv. 28)

The book is

> . . . a diligent inquiry into the nature of these *mingled powers of flesh and spirit* . . . a part of the *science of human nature*, or the knowledge of ourselves [giving] some assistance towards the forming proper *rules* for the better management, and the bringing these active and restless promoters, or disturbers of our happiness, under a moral and religious discipline; without this, we can neither be men of wisdom or piety. . . .
>
> Ungoverned passions break all the bonds of human society and peace. . . . Passion unbridled would violate all the sacred ties of religion. . . .
>
> But when these vehement powers of nature are reduced to the obedience of reason: it renders our conduct amiable and useful to our fellow creatures . . . the soul which governs its affections by the sacred dictates of reason and religion . . . is better prepared to part with all earthly comforts at the call of providence. Such a happy temper of mind will enable us chearfully to resign life itself . . . and to enter gloriously upon . . . the diviner joys that await us in the upper world.

These doctrines, then so widespread, now historical, help us grasp the dialectical framework of *Jane Eyre*; in the light of these one-time commonplaces, both the parting with Rochester and even the way St. John's glory is invoked at the end, look less strange. Jane's journey has given her, it is implied, some accommodation between the needs of flesh and spirit in marriage (perfectly orthodox Christian doctrine). Jane has chosen nature as her mother and her guide, and settled for 'earthly comforts', but she admires the holiness she has rejected in St. John. At least, that's what she tells us. Whether we believe her is another matter. Many readers agree with Richard Benvenuto[26] that in *Jane Eyre* nature and grace remain

45

unreconciled. While contemporaries complained that Jane Eyre was 'irreligious', modern readers find religion puzzlingly intrusive. Charlotte's work shows a life-long ambivalence about the clergy; unlike the other parsonage daughter, Jane Austen, she never rewards her heroines with clergymen as lovers or husbands: Lucy Snowe's choice is a teacher, while the brilliant and eligible Shirley marries a boring male-governess-figure.

Reconciling self-control and the need for love is a permanent feminine problem that Charlotte sweated over. Harriet Martineau objected to this preoccupation, which she considered unhealthy,[27] but Harriet was abnormally self-sufficient and strong-minded, with her cold baths and starlit walks before breakfast. Charlotte wrestled with the problem of love, human and divine, and in *Jane Eyre* struggled to defend human, fleshly love as part of God-created nature. The life-denying religiosity which threatens Jane is no longer part of our cultural climate, but needs to be understood if we are to grasp the book whole. *Jane Eyre* is a brave attack on perverted religiosity, and a defence of natural human 'passion' within the moral law.

The word 'passion' has shrunk since Charlotte used it. In the previous century, its range of meanings was comprehensive, and Watts defines his terms. (Definitions of the word 'passion' in the family dictionary at Haworth are similarly wide.)

> . . . the term *passion* sometimes signifies any *painful suffering of soul and body* [for example] 'the *passion* of Christ'. . . .
>
> *Passions*, in this discourse, signifie the same with *natural affections* in general, such as love, hatred, joy, hope, anger, sorrow, &c. . . . *passion* [is] . . . often used in conversation—to denote . . . *anger* or *sudden resentment*; as the word *affection* is used sometimes also in a limited sense, and signifies *love*. So we say *Moses was once in a passion*, whereby we mean *he was angry*; or *Jonah was a passionate man*, i.e., he was given to sudden and violent resentments; and in the same manner we say, *David had an affection for Jonathan*, i.e., he loved him: or St. *John was an affectionate man*, i.e., he was of a loving and kind disposition. But in this discourse we take *passion* or *affection* to mean the same thing [e.g.] love, joy, &c.

Watts raises a central problem:

> it is hard, if not impossible, for us precisely to distinguish how far the animal nature, and how far the mind or spirit, are concerned

... in raising these sensations or commotions which we call
passions ... those sensible commotions of our whole nature, both
soul and body. ...

In the first rank of passions are

admiration, love and hatred ... the second rank ... are the divers
kinds of *love and hatred*. ... If the object appear valuable, it raises
a *love of esteem*; if worthless, the hatred is called *contempt*.

Watts contrasts '*love of benevolence*, or *goodwill*' with '*malevolence*,
or *ill-will*'. We begin to understand Charlotte's moral categories
a little better, to think of Miss Temple's 'benevolence' contrasted with the ill-will of Madame Walravens, 'Malevola', the
evil fairy, who wishes to trample upon the love between
Protestant Lucy and Catholic Paul. As we all know, 'The
passion of love grows up to *desire*; hatred expresses itself in
aversion; or *avoidance* ...' [fear is also defined as 'insecurity'].
Treatises on 'the passions' had a long history.[28] They were
documents of moral psychology, teachings on the nature of
man. Watts goes on to discuss the physiological problems of
sensation and emotion, with reference to Descartes, and
rehearses the familiar eighteenth-century debate.

The eighteenth century and its phrenological heirs deeply
wanted to believe there was, must be, an art to find the mind's
construction in the face.[29] Watts tells us: '... most of the
passions have some effects on the colour or features of the
countenance, and especially on the eyes.' That the emotions
and character could be read from the eye is manifest nonsense,
possibly related to Plato's statement, which survives as folklore,
that 'the eyes are the windows of the soul.' They may be
windows we look out through; successful attempts at looking in
are doomed to failure. But Charlotte believed it, describing
Mrs. Reed's eye as 'cold, composed' (Ch. 3); she has 'an eye of
ice' (Ch. 4), 'a peculiar eye which nothing could melt' with an
'imperious, despotic eyebrow' and 'stony eye' (Ch. 21). This all
belongs to the pseudo-science of physiognomy, later to develop
into phrenology, a system which conveniently moralized
physical characteristics, and which interested Charlotte, who
had begun to analyse character when she was 5 years old. For
Watts, the innocuous word 'love' was double-edged: *Love*
'signifies *gluttony* and *friendship*; *ambition*; *concupiscence* or *lust*,

47

while *modesty* and the blush of *confusion* or *dishonour* were both called *shame*'. Other passions listed include 'jealousy, suspicion, envy, anger, wrath, fury'. We slide into eighteenth-century elocution theory[30] with this: '*Wonder*, or *amazement* or *astonishment* discovers itself by lifting up of the hands or the eyes. . . .' Charlotte's antithetical structures of plot and character are not a stylistic weakness, but a reflection of deep-rooted eighteenth-century habits of thought. '. . . Neglect is no passion. The rest of the passions, at least the most of them, go in pairs.' Georgiana Reed is an emblem of worldliness, who marries a 'wealthy, worn-out man of fashion' (Ch. 21), while her grim sister, who prefers the 'Rubric' to the spiritual treasures of the liturgy, becomes the Superior of a French convent; Georgiana, a schematic contrast, becomes the 'cynosure of a ballroom, the other the inmate of a convent cell'. Jane rejects both these extremes, worldliness and asceticism. Rochester, with all his faults, has warmth and wit, unlike those two complementary pillars of the church, black Brocklehurst and snow-white St. John. Brocklehurst is like Little Red Riding Hood's wolf (Ch. 4): 'what a great nose! and what a mouth! and what large, prominent teeth!' Instead of the good shepherd, we have a wolf-man, a bogy, an ogre. His perverted morality is no guide, but a snare. The morality of *Jane Eyre* echoes Watts:

> If we esteem ourselves and our own good qualities no higher than they deserve, it has been called by some writers *generosity*, which is a just sense of one's own worth. . . . A due *courage*, a just *fortitude*, and *magnamity*, a readiness to meet dangers, or to undertake great exploits, are the natural effects of this generosity [though '*humility*' is consistent with it].

Seen in this light, Jane's defiant claim to spiritual equality with her master, her decision to 'respect myself' and leave him, can be seen neither as social rebellion (though there is an element of revenge by the suppressed governess class in Jane's outburst) nor mere conventionality, but as morally and psychologically healthy.

Working as a governess (the female social equivalent, she writes bitterly in her fragment, *John Henry* or *The Moores*, of 'clerk'[31]) Charlotte had experienced '*haughtiness* and *insolence* in our carriage to our fellow-creatures, and *scorn* and *disdain* toward those whom we think much beneath us'. Charlotte possibly expected to find this sort of behaviour in the likes of Mrs. White of Upperwood, and the prophecy was self-fulfilled. In this context, Watts supplied Charlotte with one of her most suggestive symbols:

> We have so much of *pride, vanity* and *self-love*, that we take all occasions to borrow from everything that has any relation to us, some fine *plumes* [my italics] to dress ourselves in, and to advance our self-esteem.

Here we have a twist on the traditional expression, itself rooted in moral fable, of 'borrowed plumes'. Charlotte makes a moral symbol concrete, a characteristic of her art. We remember at once the party arriving at Thornfield, with 'fluttering veils and waving plumes' (Ch. 17), Blanche 'infatuatedly pluming herself on her success' with Mr. Rochester (Ch. 18), and the visiting Brocklehurst daughters, flaunting among the drab, uniformed Lowood girls (*Jane Eyre*, Ch. 7), 'splendidly attired in velvet, silk and furs'; their hats are 'shaded with ostrich plumes', apt emblems of vanity. Their hair is artificially curled, while Brocklehurst orders Julia's natural curls, defiantly red and springy, to be 'cut off' (a Procrustean image of mutilation). Brocklehurst wishes the Lowood girls not to conform to nature, but to become children of grace. Just as his worldly pride is emblematized by his daughters' ostrich plumes, so his hypocrisy is imaged by his wife's 'false front of French curls'. A 'false front' was a hair-piece, but there is also the overtone of dissimulation. Charlotte Brontë energizes language when writing most simply, sensuously and directly, with such resonances. *Jane Eyre* was considered 'coarse' and shocking because it satirically tested the conventional pieties of the time. Yet Jane's morality did not seem to Charlotte subversive; she had traditional authority for it at home. Watts warns against 'excessive love to creatures'. Charlotte uses this concept both in a youthful letter to Ellen ('we are in danger of loving each other too well—of losing sight of the *Creator* in idolatry of the *creature*', Mrs. Gaskell, Ch. 7) and in *Jane Eyre* (Ch. 24): 'I could not, in those days, see God for his creature: of whom I had made an idol.' Watts's remedy is stern, and relevant to the novel's plotting: 'Practise voluntary self-denial and absent yourself both in body

and in mind, from whatsoever you love to excess. . . .' Jane Eyre
tries this recipe, thus obeying morality, but is rescued from its
miserable effects by magical means, which she insists are
'powers of nature'. In leaving Rochester, however, she obeys
Watts's 'rules against unreasonable fear': 'Never rest without
some comfortable hope of the love of God. If you are . . . under
his protection, you need fear nothing.' And God does lead Jane
to her cousins at Marsh End. Readers remember her reliance on
'the universal mother, Nature' but tend to skip the passages
where Jane prays and feels 'the might and strength of God'
(Ch. 28). She continues:

> Sure was I of his efficiency to save what He had made: convinced
> I grew that neither earth should perish, nor one of the souls it
> treasured. I turned my prayer to thanksgiving: the Source of Life
> was also the Saviour of Spirits. Mr. Rochester was safe: he was
> God's, and by God would he be guarded.

Watts warns: 'Never think yourself sufficiently guarded against
the power and danger of any of your vicious passions, till your
nature be renewed by divine grace.' The maiming of Rochester
will be discussed below, but Jane believes Rochester when he
tells her:

> . . . my heart swells with gratitude to the beneficent God of this
> earth just now. He sees not as man sees, but far clearer: judges
> not as man judges, but far more wisely. I did wrong. . . . Divine
> justice pursued its course; disasters came thick on me: I was
> forced to pass through the valley of the shadow of death. *His*
> chastisements are mighty; and one smote me which has humbled
> me for ever. . . . Of late, Jane . . . I began to see and acknowledge
> the hand of God in my doom. I begin to experience remorse,
> repentance; the wish for reconcilement to my Maker. I began
> sometimes to pray. . . .

According to Watts, the person of a great soul '*disdains* . . . mean
and base practices, even under the strongest temptation'. Jane,
warned, flees temptation. As Watts's treatise witnesses, the
word 'passion', far from being limited to sexuality, embraced
the whole problem of right conduct, emotional control and duty
to God.

By the end of the century, it had become usual to ascribe the
Brontë 'frankness' to provincial innocence, the greater because

they lived in a backwater where Victorian prudery had not fully penetrated.

John Taylor wrote in the *Methodist Monthly* for January 1896,

> ... the so-called coarseness of her writings was merely the candour of an unsophisticated mind. Her deep, unchanging love of purity is shown in the reply of Jane Eyre to Rochester's immoral proposal, 'Mr. Rochester, I will *not* be yours.' She assailed society conceptions of virtue, but paid deepest reverence to those divine laws upon which life in the home and in the State is founded. She held, for example, that marriage which is merely a thing of the market or an affair of convenience, and therefore destitute of real love, is little better than prostitution. She spoke and wrote with perfect frankness out of an untainted heart of things which others feared to name because of their evil acquaintance with them. She gave no quarter to prudery, which is so often the mask of uncleanness; and would never for a single moment admit that she had betrayed true womanliness by anything she ever wrote. Hers was a life in which she knew much trouble and sadness, but she wrestled with and triumphed over the temptations to selfishness and sloth, and her experience will be an inspiration to all who care to live uprightly and to keep themselves unspotted from the world.

Grace Elizabeth Harrison, in *The Clue to the Brontës*, threw further light; she suggests persuasively that Wesley's images had burnt into the minds of the young Brontës:

> When Charlotte speaks of love she calls it quite naturally 'Living fire, seraph brought from a divine altar', and she had no idea that she was handling high explosive. This trick of hers of Methodising love would in the end make history, for it would introduce passion, for the first time, into the English novel.[32]

NOTES

1. W. A. Craik, 'The Brontës', in *The Victorians*, ed. Arthur Pollard, *Sphere History of Literature in the English Language*, Vol. 6 (London: 1969), p. 144.
2. Letter to W. S. Williams, 5 September 1850.
3. Charles Burkhart, *Charlotte Brontë: A Psychosexual Study of her Novels*, p. 12.
4. Miriam Allott, Introduction to *The Brontës: The Critical Heritage*, p. 25, and more fully in *Jane Eyre and Villette* (Casebook), pp. 22–4.
5. Tom Winnifrith, *The Brontës and their Background*, Ch. 7, p. 110.

6. Edith M. Weir, 'Contemporary Reviews of the First Brontë Novels', *B.S.T.*, 11 (1947), 89–96.

7. Eanne Oram and John Mitchell, separate notes printed together as 'The "Taste" of Charlotte Brontë', *B.S.T.*, 14 (1962), 20–3.

8. See E. M. Delafield, *The Brontës: Their Lives Recorded by their Contemporaries*, p. 189.

9. Ibid., p. 181.

10. Elizabeth Rigby, *Quarterly Review*, December 1848.

11. *Christian Remembrancer*, April 1848.

12. *Letters of Mrs. Gaskell*, ed. J. A. V. Chapple and Arthur Pollard, p. 410.

13. Margaret Smith, 'The Manuscripts of Charlotte Brontë's Novels', *B.S.T.*, 18 (1983), 189–205.

14. Winifred Gérin, *Charlotte Brontë: The Evolution of Genius*, p. 397.

15. See K. J. Fielding, 'The Brontës and "The North American Review"': A Critic's Strange Guesses', *B.S.T.*, 13 (1956), 14–18.

16. Elizabeth Hardwick, *Seduction and Betrayal*, p. 6.

17. See Gérin, *Charlotte Brontë*, p. 430.

18. George Steiner, *On Difficulty*, p. 101.

19. Lewes, 'Recent Novels, French and English', *Fraser's Magazine*, December 1847, repr. *Casebook*, ed. Miriam Allott, p. 54.

20. Lewes, *The Leader*, 12 February 1853, repr. *Casebook*, p. 79.

21. Lewes, 'Recent Novels, French and English', *Casebook*, p. 54.

22. See Valerie Grosvenor Myer, 'Shandy in Angria', *N.Q.*, n.s. 34(4), 232 cont. series (December 1987), 491.

23. Peter Cominos, 'Innocent Femina Sensualis', in *Suffer and Be Still*, ed. Martha Vicinus, p. 156.

24. Barbara Hill Rigney, *Madness and Sexual Politics in the Feminist Novel*, p. 25. Dale Kramer, 'Thematic Structure in *Jane Eyre*', *Papers on Language and Literature*, 4 (1968), writes that Jane is 'repelled by the idea of sexual relations with such a cold and selfish being as St. John' (292).

25. Rigney, p. 26.

26. Richard Benvenuto, 'The Child of Nature, the Child of Grace, and the Unresolved', *English Literary History*, 39 (December 1972), 620–38.

27. Review of *Villette*, *Daily News*, 3 February 1853.

28. See Valerie Grosvenor Myer, 'Tristram and the Animal Spirits', in *Laurence Sterne: Riddles and Mysteries*, ed. Myer (London: Vision Press; Totowa, N.J.: Barnes and Noble, 1984), p. 99.

29. See, e.g., Alan T. McKenzie, 'The Countenance You Show Me: Reading the Passions in the Eighteenth Century', *Georgia Review*, 32:3 (1978), 758–73.

30. Most eighteenth-century treatises on 'elocution' give lists of appropriate gesture for indicating emotion. See, e.g., John Mason, *An Essay on Elocution, or, Pronunciation* (1748).

31. *John Henry*, published with the Clarendon *Shirley*, p. 831. The speaker puts clerk, governess, mercer, milliner, all on one level. She is a snob and a target for satire, but Charlotte implies that such people hold the governess class in contempt. Under the title, *The Moores*, the fragment is published with *Jane Eyre*, in the Complete Edition of Charlotte's works,

with an introduction by W. Robertson Nicoll (London: Hodder and Stoughton, 1902). In *Deerbrook* (1839), Harriet Martineau's characters discuss women's earning prospects. Maria tells Margaret that for an educated woman 'there is no chance of subsistence but by teaching . . . or by being the feminine gender of the tailor or the hatter' (quoted Anthea Zeman, p. 45).

32. Grace Elizabeth Harrison, *The Clue to the Brontës*, p. 136.

4

'Mad Methodist magazines'

> I am a Calvinist and believe Jerry and Quamina and O'Connor and Gordon were predestined to the fire-grate.—Branwell Brontë

Harrison's book is pithy and arresting. She concludes that the truth was suppressed because Charlotte had a Puseyite husband and a Unitarian biographer.[1] Winnifrith criticizes Harrison for 'a reluctance to distinguish closely between the Brontës' adoption of Methodist ideas and their reaction against them',[2] but that surely does not matter: the Methodist motifs have been identified. I cannot agree with Winnifrith that 'it seems fanciful to derive the names Shirley and Huntingdon from the Brontës' knowledge of the family of Whitfield's [sic] patron.'[3] Why? Where else would Charlotte and Anne have got them from? While the Methodist influence cannot 'explain' the achievement of the Brontës, it gave them a language of enthusiasm and emotion, to be now mocked, now exploited, a language of ardour and rapture. Winnifrith makes an important point:

> religion channelled off sexual feeling in the same way that it channelled off political passion; this is particularly noticeable in Charlotte's letters to Ellen Nussey during her period of religious doubt when teaching at Miss Wooler's.[4]

It also provided the young Brontës with a vocabulary. I agree with Valentine Cunningham that writers on the Brontës 'have not given Mrs. Harrison due credit'.[5] Cunningham links Patrick's fear of fire with Methodist influence, though in the days of naked candle-flames and open fires, this fear was not abnormal. Exposed to the pulpit eloquence of their father, who almost always spoke extempore, surrounded by his printed works, the children grew up with models of utterance, joyful, unrestrained, sanctified. The moral and social influences in the household may or may not have been repressive, but there were no penalties for being articulate. 'The highest stimulus, as well as the liveliest pleasure, we had known from childhood upwards, lay in attempts at literary composition', said Charlotte.[6] In the juvenilia they experimented. They did not accept influences uncritically. The satire on Dissent in *Wuthering Heights* and *Shirley* demonstrates that. Cunningham reprints Charlotte's hilarious parody of the *Methodist Magazine*. With deadly accuracy Charlotte homes in on the politico-religious envy of the fanatic:

> Blessed be my maker I was not shaken either by the multitude or the Sodomitish appearance of my adversaries—I calmly advanced & taking out my pocket-bible & holding it forth in my right hand—I commenced with a loud clear voice—Go to now Ye rich men! Howl & cry for your miseries that are come upon you.[7]

This makes nonsense of the assertion that Charlotte lacked humour. The tale is a parody of the 'testimony' offered in the Methodist magazines, and a skit on Wesley's *Journal* itself. This manuscript is part of 'Julia', written when Charlotte was 21, now in the Miriam Lutcher Stark Library, University of Texas. Cunningham warns against Gérin's 'astonishingly inaccurate transcription of parts of this manuscript'.[8]

Charlotte writes in *Shirley* of 'mad Methodist Magazines, full of miracles and apparitions, of preternatural warnings, ominous dreams, and frenzied fanaticism' (Ch. 22).[9] Among Wesley's works is listed a book called *The Epworth Phenomena: to which are appended certain psychic experiences recorded by John Wesley in the pages of his Journal*, collated by D. Wright (London: 1917). Psychic experiences could be taken as signs from God. A typical example of what Caroline Helstone found in her uncle's library survives in the *Methodist Magazine* for 1799, which 'being a continuation of the *Arminian Magazine*, vol. xxii', was 'Printed for George Whitfield, City Road, and sold at the Methodist Preaching Houses in Town or Country, MDCCXCIX'. This George Whitfield is not to be confused with George Whitefield (pronounced Whitfield), whose conversion preceded that of Wesley, and who died in 1770.

The magazine tells the story of the visions and miraculous escapes of Eusebius.

> When he was an infant about four years of age, he was waked in the night, by something lying on his forehead, which felt like the impression of a cold hand. It continued some time after he was awake; when he perceived a tall man close by the bedside, who looked very sternly at him.
>
> Much about this time, he saw another person standing on the opposite side of the bed, drest in a very mean apparel whose aspect seemed earnest, serious and composed. However, what the design of either of these appearances might be, he pretends not to know. When he was between five and six years old, being upon a visit to some of his father's relations in Switzerland, he was travelling over some high mountains, on horse-back; but through the neglect of the guide who had the care of his horse, instead of pursuing the proper road, the horse directed his course towards a large lake; but before he entered, Eusebius saw very plainly one like a man in a white garment, coming upon the water towards him; upon which the horse turned away, and got into the right road again. . . . (Several other miraculous escapes, though not attended with any appearances, he has had since that time. . . .)

It should be noted that 'he pretends not to know' does not mean that Eusebius is being sly or deceitful; it means he 'makes no pretension, no claim, to knowing'. Charlotte made fun of this sort of thing, even though it erupted eventually into *Jane Eyre*. In her early womanhood, especially during the depressing period of teaching at Roe Head, Charlotte wrote to Ellen (precise date uncertain),

> I abhor myself—I despise myself—if the Doctrine of Calvin be true, I am already an outcast—you cannot imagine how hard, rebellious and intractable all my feelings are.

In another letter, she writes that she is 'smitten at times to the heart that —— ghastly Calvinistic doctrines are true. . . . If Christian perfection be necessary to Salvation, I shall never be saved. . . .' This letter (Bonn. 162), now at Haworth, presents problems: to save paper, it is heavily 'crossed', and somebody (believed to be Ellen) has scratched out certain words. Gérin follows the Shakespeare Head Brontë and prints '——'s ghastly', but Winnifrith argues convincingly that the erased word must be 'your'.[10] The manuscript shows one descender only and no trace of an apostrophe. Winnifrith points out that 'your' may refer not to Ellen's personal convictions: it may mean 'the ones you were just mentioning'. The question is, where did Charlotte get her religious gloom from?

Rosamond Langbridge takes it for granted that the religious atmosphere at Haworth was 'Calvinistic',[11] a by-product of Mr. Brontë's 'Black Protestantism', the embittered Protestantism of Ulster. She identifies Mr. Brocklehurst with Mr. Brontë. By Calvinism she seems to mean 'repressive religiosity'. However, the word 'Calvinism', which some writers bandy loosely, has a precise technical meaning. The *Concise Oxford Dictionary of the Christian Church* says:

> it shares with Lutheranism belief in the Bible as the only rule of faith, the denial of human free will after the Fall of Adam, and the doctrine of justification by faith alone . . . the gratuitous predestination of some to salvation and others to damnation.

Calvinism was at bottom a debate about reconciling the doctrine of God's sovereignty with the freedom of man's will. Its social effect was to give people nightmares about hell. If you were reprobate, not among those selected at birth for heaven, you could not avoid hell, however good you were or however much you believed. Some people, believing Calvin's doctrines in their hearts, whistled in the dark and became Antinomians, like Michael Hartley in *Shirley* (the name Hartley implied a materialist psychology, after David Hartley, the writer after whom Coleridge named his first child). The Antinomian does not obey the moral law, in the knowledge that, should you not be among the Elect, you are, as the saying goes, 'damned if you do and damned if you don't'. The Elect, on the other hand, sure of their future in heaven, can do what they like here below without affecting the outcome. The 'doctrine of perseverance' meant that those Elect could never lose God's favour whatever they did. Burns satirizes the certainty of Election in 'Holy Willie's Prayer'. Calvinism led to religious depressions, because it denied the hope that Methodism offered. Whereas in Calvinism, you had the duty of faith, but no certainty as to whether you were Elect or Damned, Methodists who truly repented of their sins and turned to Christ in love, could be confident of welcome in heaven. The good Methodist could get himself to heaven, if he surrendered his heart to God, especially to the Second Person of the Trinity, and led a sanctified life of Christian perfection. This accounted for Methodism's huge appeal to the English working classes, whose prospects in this life were restricted. Methodism offered a programme; Calvinism was a recipe for paralysis. Methodism had its roots in the teaching of Arminius (Jakob Hermans or Harmens, 1560–1609). Arminius taught that the divine sovereignty was compatible with free will; that Christ died for all men, and not just for the elect; and that doctrines of predestination were unbiblical.

In the standard work on the *Thirty-Nine Articles of the Church of England*,[12] E. J. Bicknell writes that Arminius

> taught that God predestines to eternal life certain men because He foresees that they will use their free-will aright and be faithful to the grace that is given them. . . . Predestination according to foreseen merit logically implies condemnation according to fore-seen failure . . . we need to bear in mind that Scripture insists upon three great thoughts (i) God has an eternal purpose of love for all nations and individuals whom He has made. (ii) Salvation and grace are from first to last the gifts of God's free bounty. (iii) Man is responsible to God for his conduct.

Although Article XVII has sometimes been made to bear a Calvinistic interpretation, rejected by Bicknell, Calvinism has been no part of Anglican orthodoxy since the troubled seventeenth century.

That the young Brontës knew about such matters is certain. The epigraph from this chapter comes from Gérin's biography of Branwell. In one of Branwell's stories, Montmorency is trying to form a choir, and says,

> 'I am sure from your chambermaid's pretty mouth . . . that she has a sweet treble. We'll make up 4 parts. . . . I am a Calvinist and believe Jerry and Quamina and O'Connor and Gordon were predestined to the fire-grate, so I won't call them in to join us.'
>
> 'Oh, but Hector,' expostulated Percy, 'I am not a Calvinist. I am as good a Wesleyan as was ever hatched and I insist that *all* shall be saved.'[13]

Caroline Helstone in *Shirley* (Ch. 12) recites Cowper's poem, 'The Castaway'.

Mary Taylor told Mrs. Gaskell

> Cowper's poem *The Castaway* was known to them all, and they all
> at times appreciated, or almost appropriated it. Charlotte told
> me once that Branwell had done so; and though his depression
> was the result of his faults, it was in no other respect different
> from hers. Both were not mental but physical illnesses. She was
> well aware of this, and would ask how that mended matters, as
> the feeling was there all the same, and was not removed by
> knowing the cause. She had a larger religious toleration than a
> person would have who had never questioned, and her manner of
> recommending religion was always that of offering comfort, not
> of fiercely enforcing a duty. . . . Charlotte was free of religious
> depression when in tolerable health; when that failed, her
> depression returned. . . . I have heard her condemn Socinianism,
> Calvinism, and many other 'isms' inconsistent with Church of
> Englandism. I used to wonder at her acquaintance with such
> subjects.

The word 'castaway', used by both Brocklehurst and St. John,
comes from St. Paul (I Cor., 9:27) and was important in
Calvinism. Stephen Cox writes that Cowper, who went mad
with religious melancholy, identifies himself, in poems and
letters, with a storm-tossed ship, a solitary pillar or crumbling
rock, a shattered and equally solitary tree; the conviction grew
on him that he had been cast off by God.[14] Margot Peters
blames Aunt Branwell's 'repressive brand of Calvinistic
Methodism' for religious gloom at the parsonage, but offers no
evidence, except that she was, according to Nancy Garrs, 'a bit
of a tyke'.[15]

There was Calvinistic Methodism and Wesleyan, or Arminian,
Methodism. Miss Branwell belonged to the Wesleyan, Arminian,
branch of Methodism whose doctrine of 'redemption for all' was
the opposite of Calvinism. She followed Wesley's Four Points:
an objection to orthodoxy; repentance and Gospel faith; justi-
fication by free grace; and faith that this life could offer a
foretaste to heaven to the believer.[16] Miss Branwell's collateral
descendants, incidentally, are still members of the Methodist
congregation in her native Penzance. There is a private museum
of the Branwell and Brontë families at 25 Chapel Street,
Penzance, one-time home of the family. Daphne Du Maurier's
Vanishing Cornwall (London: Gollancz, 1967) has a chapter on

Cornish Methodism called 'The Brontë heritage'. Mr. Brontë
has been blamed for repressive religion, but though he may
have been a 'half-crazy tyrant',[17] he did not preach Election and
Reprobation. Arthur Pollard discounts the possibility of extreme
Methodism: 'I see no evidence of a belief in Christian perfection
in the writings of Patrick Brontë.'[18] Although he was a protegé
of Thomas Tighe, a prominent Methodist, Patrick held no
extreme views. His Anglicanism was modified by the Presbyterian and Wesleyan patrons who helped him, but unlike his
wife and sister-in-law who belonged to separatist Methodist
congregations he remained orthodox.

John Wesley, whose heart was 'warmed' on a famous
occasion, was the father of Methodism, but remained all his life
an Anglican priest, as did his follower George Whitefield. After
their deaths, the movement split from the Church of England,
and worshipped exclusively in the buildings set up for meetings
of the Methodist societies within the church. Whitefield was
originally a servitor at Pembroke College, Oxford, where he
came under Wesley's influence and was invited to go out as
missionary to Georgia, the first of many American journeys.
Whitefield came back to England to receive priest's orders and
to raise funds for the establishment of an orphanage. As the
established clergy did not welcome him to their pulpits, he
began to preach in the open air, as did Wesley later. On
Whitefield's return he quarrelled with Wesley because Wesley
was an Arminian and repudiated Calvinism, to which Whitefield
adhered. Whitefield withdrew from the Wesleyan Connexion
(then still within the Church of England) and his friends built
the Moorfields Tabernacle for him. Eventually Whitefield fell
on hard times and was rescued by Selina, Countess of Huntingdon, who appointed him one of her chaplains. Lady Huntingdon
was a Calvinist, who set up her own theological college at
Trevecca, Wales, and the founder of a Christian Calvinist sect
with the picturesque name, the Countess of Huntingdon's
Connexion.

The 'revival' within the Anglican church in the eighteenth
century was in its origins Evangelical; Evangelical Christianity
required pure and zealous spiritual conviction. It held that God
and Satan were contending for the soul of man, which was
radically sinful but open to salvation through grace. Evangelicals

believed in hell-fire for the damned and eternal bliss for the saved. They believed firmly in the special intervention of providence in guiding the pilgrim's progress through life; we see this guidance in *Jane Eyre*. Some, but not all, Evangelicals embraced a puritanical morality which considered such diversions as dancing and card-playing to be sinful. Nineteenth-century puritanism was largely the work of Evangelicals.

The word 'Methodist' was originally a word of mockery applied to Evangelicals. Methodism required 'conversion', a whole-hearted commitment to Christ. A good summary of the social influence of Methodism is to be found in Annette Brown Hopkins's *The Father of the Brontës*, which explains how Wesley's aim, the spiritual revitalization of the Established Church, allowed clergymen with Methodist connections, like Patrick Brontë, to remain conscientious members of the Anglican communion. See also F. K. Brown, *Fathers of the Victorians* (Cambridge: Cambridge University Press, 1961). From Mr. Brontë we have the evidence of his sermons, which emphasize conversion (or, as we would say, 'commitment'), and the famous letter about not wanting a curate who

> would deem it his duty to preach the appalling doctrines of personal election and reprobation. As I consider these decidedly derogatory to the attributes of God, so, also, I should be fearful of evil consequences to the hearers from the enforcement of final perseverance, as an essential article of belief. . . . I want . . . a plain rather than able preacher; a zealous but at the same time a judicious man, one not fond of innovations, but desirous of proceeding on the *good old plan*, which alas! has often been mar'd, but never improved. I earnestly wish that some of the Clergy in our Excellent Establishment were as solicitous for improvement as they are for change. (To the Rev. J. C. Franks, vicar of Huddersfield, 10 January 1839.)

The curate he found was the Rev. William Weightman, the brilliant classical scholar and 'thorough male-flirt' whom Charlotte regarded with affectionate amusement and christened 'Miss Celia Amelia'. Charlotte wrote to Ellen on 7 April 1840: 'Miss Celia Amelia delivered a noble, High Church, Apostolical Succession discourse—in which he banged the dissenters most fearlessly and unflinchingly. . . .' Charlotte considered such opinions 'bigoted, intolerant and wholly unjustifiable on the grounds of common-sense—my conscience will not let me be either a Puseyite or a Hookist. . . .' A few years later she wrote to Ellen from Brussels: 'I consider Methodism, Quakerism and the extremes of High and Low Churchism foolish, but Roman Catholicism beats them all. '

Charlotte's views did not come to her easily, by inheritance— she had to struggle for them. In Brussels, her sense of social identity, never strong, was shattered. Provincial, unsophisticated, untravelled, she found the stimulus of a foreign language exhilarating, but her value-system, her personal integrity and whole being, were challenged by the deeply disturbing experience of being a foreigner. In the context of a norm of Belgian Catholicism, she was an anomaly, a heretic, an extravagant and erring spirit. England until recently was a profoundly Protestant country; our literature, with few exceptions, is embedded in Protestant assumptions. Catholicism, in England, has become a form of Dissent. Shocked to find herself marginalized, Charlotte operated a familiar mechanism of self-justification: defiant contempt for the natives, at ease in their own country and culture, who pitied her. She quickly developed a minority group psychology and clung to the idea that Anglicanism, which in world terms is a fringe sect in one corner of Europe, represented a mean between extremes, centrality of truth. One of her anxieties about the man she was eventually to marry was that he was 'a Puseyite and very stiff'.[19]

William Weightman won all hearts, and probably stole Anne's. When he died suddenly at the age of 26, Mr. Brontë took the unusual, for him, step of writing a funeral sermon for him and having it printed for distribution in the parish. (Only two of Mr. Brontë's sermons survive, because he usually spoke extempore.) Mr. Brontë's text was St. Paul, I. Cor., 15:56–8: 'The sting of death is sin, and the strength of sin is the law. But thanks be to God, who giveth us the victory, through our Lord Jesus Christ. Therefore, my beloved brethren, be ye steadfast, immoveable, always abounding in the work of the Lord, for as much as ye know that your labour is not in vain in the Lord.'

> Die we must, whether we will or no, judged we must be, though we should call on the hills and mountains to cover and hide us from the face of Him, who will sit on the great white throne of judgement. . . . through sin, and sin alone, death entered the

62

world . . . sin gave death a goad, a poisoned dagger, fatal and tormenting, and capable of destroying both body and soul in hell for ever. . . . Our obedience . . . must not be niggardly, . . . but must result from the overflowings of a heart changed by the renewing of regeneration—so shall we infallibly obtain the reward of our labour—a reward, indeed, not of debt, but of grace,—the free unmerited grace of him who was dead and is alive again. . . .

Of William, Mr. Brontë said:

> . . . his religious principles were sound and orthodox, his sermons were the key of scripture opened, through Christ, the door of salvation to all. . . . He thought it better and more scriptural to make the love of God rather than the fear of hell the ruling motive for obedience. He did not see why true believers . . . should create unto themselves artificial sorrows, and disfigure the garment of Gospel Peace with the garb of sighing and sadness. . . . We were ever like father and son. . . .

Describing William's peaceful death, Mr. Brontë said that such a death could only be the effects of divine grace in the regenerated heart; our own purpose as Christians was to look forward to a joyful resurrection.

This sermon survives because Henry H. Seymour of Buffalo 'had the pamphlets placed in his hands by Mrs. Brown, widow of the sexton and uncle of Martha', and Mr. Seymour had them bound and reprinted.

Abraham Holroyd, a local publisher, heard Mr. Brontë preach:

> Mr. Brontë gave an extempore sermon, devoid of all oratorical display, and remarkable for studied simplicity. He spoke to his hearers of the hollowness of all earthly pleasures, the uncertainty and brevity of human life, and advised everyone to seek religion. . . .[20]

The other surviving Brontë sermon is bound in the same volume with the funeral sermon and others by divers hands, published by the Society for the Promotion of Christian Knowledge. Mr. Brontë's 'bog sermon', which Mrs. Harrison says closely follows one of Wesley's in similar circumstances, came eighteen years earlier. There is less simplicity and feeling in it, but it has a certain epic grandeur. The type-founts of the cover are melodramatically Victorian-chapel-Gothic; the sermon is on

> Joys of Heaven, Power Infinite and Love Divine: A sermon preached in the church at Haworth on Sunday, the 12th day of September, 1824, in reference to an EARTHQUAKE and Extraordinary Eruption of Mud and Water, that had taken place ten days before, in the moors of the chapelry.... This was a solemn visitation of Providence.... Earthquakes have been, in different ages and countries, the most dreadfully effective instruments of vengeance, which God has employed against his guilty creatures.

Mr. Brontë gives a graphic description of the scene of the disaster, then explains:

> God sometimes produces earthquakes as manifestations of his power and majesty ... sometimes ... awful monitors to turn sinners from the error of their ways, and as solemn forerunners of the last and greatest day, when the earth shall be burnt up.

He describes the idle curiosity of the sightseers and their neglect of their immortal souls. He concludes:

> Happy are they, and they only, who attend to the voice of the Holy Spirit, who deny themselves, and take up their daily Cross, and follow Christ ... [to] ... victory that overcometh this world—they shall come off more than conquerors over death—and in perfect security on the last day, they shall fearlessly and triumphantly survey the wreck of universal nature, when the sun shall be turned into darkness, and the moon into blood,—when the stars shall fall from their orbits, and the heavens and earth shall dissolve in flames, and pass away.

Putting the fear of God into the parishioners was a parson's job in those days and Mr. Brontë shows an ear for the rhythm of a sentence. Hell-fire preaching is not Calvinism; the stress on regeneration is Methodist-Evangelical, with no trace of Calvinism. The issues were less muddied nearer in time to the Brontës. William Scruton wrote, in 1898, 'Mr. Brontë's theological views were much more Arminian than Calvinistic. The teaching of John Wesley had leavened the Church of England infinitely more than that of Whitefield....' Scruton adds, 'As a clergyman, Mr. Brontë was an Evangelical; as a politician, a Tory.' He explains that Evangelical people were, in the main, 'rigid Tories in matters political . . . haters of "popery". . . .'[21]

Mrs. Gaskell (*Life*, Ch. 2) writes about the Calvinist Rev. William Grimshaw, a predecessor of Mr. Brontë as Curate of Haworth, who 'devoted himself, with the fervour of a Wesley, and something of the fanaticism of a Whitefield, to calling out a religious life among his parishioners . . . in his preaching he was occasionally assisted by Wesley and Whitefield. . . .' Mr. Grimshaw used to horsewhip loiterers to church. Himself an Anglican parson, he built a chapel for the Wesleyan Methodists. Although his tenure was in the third quarter of the eighteenth century, his influence lingered in the parish, and something may have come down to the Brontë children through Tabby.

Winnifrith offers extended discussion of Calvinism, Methodism and Evangelicalism in *The Brontës and their Background*, issues taken up by Arthur Pollard in 'The Brontës and their Father's Faith'.[22] The identification of Mr. Brontë with Mr. Brocklehurst is against the evidence, though frequently made.

That Brocklehurst's portrait is a brilliant caricature of the awful truth is borne out by the surviving writings of the original, the Rev. William Carus-Wilson. They show a morbidity quite lacking in the writings of Mr. Brontë. No Brontë commentator can resist quoting as titbits for the astonished reader the remarkable Carus-Wilson writings for children. They demonstrate that the picture of Brocklehurst is, if anything, understated. Carus-Wilson's *Child's First Tales*, preserved at Haworth, illustrated with woodcuts, shows us on page 6 a picture labelled 'No. 6—The Gallows'. The text runs:

Look there! Do you not see a man hang by the neck? Oh! it is a sad sight. A rope is tied round his neck to what they call the gal-lows: and there he hangs till he is quite dead. See what a crowd there is round him, to see him hang! I daresay there is his mo-ther, and his friends. How full of grief they must be, to see him come to such a sad end. But you will want to know who it is. It is Dick Brown. When he was a boy, he would pick and steal small things. He would steal pence from his mo-ther when he could. When he grew to be a man, he went on to steal great things. He stole some hens and ducks, and was sent to gaol for six months. When he was let out, and got home, he went on in his bad ways. And he stole some sheep. So the Judge thought it was high time to hang him. . . . When they put the rope round his neck, he said ... 'good folks, take care how you steal small things. It led me to steal great ones. .... May Lord have mer-cy on my poor soul.'

Grim though this may be, it is doctrinally unspecific. The Rev. William Carus-Wilson's grandson, Clement Carus-Wilson Shepheard-Walwyn, M.A., wrote that Carus-Wilson

> had been ordained to the curacy of Whittington, near Kirby Lonsdale. But his Evangelical principles rendered him obnoxious to the then Bishop of Chester, by whom he was rejected on presenting himself for Priests' Orders, on account of his 'Calvinistic opinions'. (This was simply a contemptuous way of designating *Evangelical* views: he was not a 'High Calvinist' at all.)[23]

This shows that the term 'Calvinist' was used loosely, and even as a term of abuse, in the early nineteenth century. The word 'Calvinist' is never used, in *Jane Eyre*, in relation to Brocklehurst, though he says Jane should be grateful 'for the privilege of her election' (Ch. 4) to Lowood, which he describes as 'an evangelical, charitable establishment' (Ch. 7). As John Maynard says, Brocklehurst's Evangelical opinions are 'evaluated not as ideas but as masks for a brutal temperament'.[24] Neither Mr. Brocklehurst nor the Rev. William Carus-Wilson can be dismissed as isolated fanatics; they represent a trend that Charlotte hated. Parents bought Carus-Wilson's stories and gave them to their children. *The Children's Friend*, 10 (1833) has a story called, 'Some Account of Little Charles', signed at the end, 'G—, 14 July 1832. MALVINA'. It reads:

> Charles ... displayed many of those wicked tempers, and sinful propensities, which are so natural to every fallen child of Adam, and the bitter fruits of that corrupt nature in which 'dwelleth no good thing'.

The emphasis on the depravity of fallen nature is part of Evangelical belief (the point which Evangelicals shared with Calvinists), and is the object of Charlotte's satire. *Jane Eyre* is a fictional solution to the problem of reconciling nature and grace, though the success of this reconciliation is often doubted (see Benvenuto, and also Annette Tromly, who writes of 'Jane's lifelong inability to reconcile nature and grace'[25]). Carus-Wilson's tale continues:

His infant mind was early imbued with the first rudiments of Christianity, and as soon as his tongue could articulate a distinct sound, it was taught to lisp the words of prayer and praise, and pronounce with reverence the name of his God and Giver. He was generally very docile and obedient to the lessons of piety which were instilled into his mind, but did not seem to feel that lively interest in them which was shown by his brother, who was about a year and a half older than himself. He listened, however, with pleasure, and his innocent remarks were often both amusing and interesting.

When about two years old he was afflicted with the hooping [*sic*] cough, which left him so extremely weak that little hope was entertained of his recovery. A sea voyage, however, and change of air, together with the mode of treatment recommended by a skilful physician, were effectual, under the blessing of God, for his restoration.

Passing one day with his mother through a burial ground, little Charles observed the sexton digging a grave; and asked what it was for. On being told, he said with great earnestness, 'Pray, mamma, do ask the man to dig a grave for me also; for my God will soon call me to live with him, and I wish very much to go.' 'But, my dear,' said his mother, 'your papa and I would wish to have you a little longer with us, and we shall be very sorry when you are taken away.' The child raised his finger with an expression of great meaning, and looking earnestly in her face, replied, 'Oh mamma! it is naughty to wish for that; God wishes me to go, and I should be much better with him. Now, mamma, mind, you must not cry when I go away, for my God would be angry with you.'

This fearlessness of death was evident through all his conduct, and often broke forth in an almost triumphant manner. I asked him one day, when he had been saying something on the subject, in order to see what ideas he had of the grave;—'But, my love, are you not afraid to go down into the ground? the grave is very dark and cold, is it not?'. . . . Charles was then sitting, or rather lying, on my knees; with a look of confidence, he replied, 'But you know, Miss M——, that I shall not be there long; my Saviour has died for me, that I might not go to hell, and he will soon take me up out of the pit-hole.' Sweet child! Well might we say, 'O death! Where is thy sting? O grave!! Where is thy victory?'

Sometimes the dear child felt such a sinking of nature that . . . he would call all his friends around him, and desire them to sing hymns while he departed . . . [and] would entreat them to continue, in the hope that singing would hasten the summons; and when nature seemed again to revive, he also expressed great disappointment at the delay.

The death of Helen Burns owes something to this literary tradition as well as to Charlotte's traumatic experiences watching the death of her sister Maria. But Helen's death, in its unselfish resignation, is a critique of the morbidity we find here. Helen was idealized by some early readers, criticized by others as beautiful but untrue and an artistic failure. She is no model for Jane, who chooses to have life abundantly, but her influence is wholly good. Helen's lesson is forgiveness, a lesson Jane puts to use when she freely forgives the dying Mrs. Reed. Returning to Gateshead (Ch. 21), Jane reflects: '... I had left a hostile roof with a desperate and embittered heart—a sense of outlawry and almost of *reprobation*' (italics added). Jane had felt herself to be one for whom salvation was impossible. Brocklehurst (Ch. 4) tells Jane she has 'a wicked heart' and she 'must pray to God to change it: to ... take away your heart of stone and give you a heart of flesh'. Brocklehurst, that grim-faced black pillar, is quoting Ezekiel 11:19, echoed in the key document of Puritanism, the Westminster conference of 1647. Brocklehurst's public repudiation of Jane, in front of the whole school (Ch. 7), confirms her 'forlorn depression' (Ch. 2) by his categorization of her as 'a little castaway—not a member of the true flock, but an interloper and an alien'. He urges the teachers to 'punish her body to save her soul' and doubts whether 'such salvation be possible'. Brocklehurst uses the vocabulary, but does not preach the doctrines, of Calvinism. *Jane Eyre* is an impassioned plea against such perverse spiritualization, a plea for bodily health and bodily love, within the framework of 'the law given by God; sanctioned by man' (Ch. 27): 'Self-righteousness is not religion' (preface to second edition).

The case of St. John Rivers is more complex than that of Brocklehurst. Some have taken St. John to be a portrait of the Rev. Henry Nussey, Ellen's brother, who proposed marriage to Charlotte, though neither Ian Jack nor Arthur Pollard consider this likely.[26] For Pollard, Henry seems 'too dull a dog to prefigure Rivers, for whom Henry Martyn seems a better model'. Pollard argues, against Winnifrith, that Charlotte meant Brocklehurst to be considered as a Calvinist. I cannot agree; Brocklehurst and St. John represent dangerous, but different, trends within the Anglican Church.

There is no doubt that St. John is a Calvinist; we know from his sermon.

> The heart was thrilled, the mind astonished, by the power of the preacher: neither were softened. Throughout there was a strange bitterness; an absence of consolatory gentleness; stern allusions to Calvinistic doctrines—election, predestination, reprobation— were frequent; and each reference to these points sounded like a sentence pronounced for doom. . . .

It seems to Jane that

> the eloquence to which I had been listening had sprung from a depth where lay turbid dregs of disappointment . . . insatiate yearnings and disquieting aspirations. I was sure St. John Rivers— pure-lived, conscientious, zealous as he was—had not found that peace of God which passeth all understanding. . . . (Ch. 30)

Winnifrith suggests that many writers, including Gérin and L. and E. Hanson, are confusing 'the peculiarly Calvinist belief in predestination with a belief in eternal punishment, common in the nineteenth century to most sects outside and inside the Church of England'.[27] As the century progressed the Calvinistic emphasis lost ground, especially in the mainline churches as opposed to small, extreme groups; within the Church of England, Armininianism was the rule and Calvinists were the exception.

Brocklehurst represents the extreme Evangelical wing of the Church of England, while St. John, despite his superficial attractiveness, represents an even gloomier and more destructive form of Christianity. Evangelicals believed all mankind to be sinful and in danger of hell, but deliverance was possible. For the Calvinist, conclusions were foregone. St. John's religion is even more of a threat than Brocklehurst's. St. John 'believed his name was already written in the Lamb's book of Life' (Ch. 35): that he was one of the Elect. Like Brocklehurst's, St. John's attitude to nature is suspect:

> . . . nature was not to him that treasury of delight it was to his sisters. He expressed once . . . affection for the dark and hoary walls he called his home; but there was more of gloom than pleasure in the tone and words in which the sentiment was manifested. . . . (Ch. 30)

69

Marriage with the holy St. John would be hell on earth for Jane, just as Rochester's marriage to Bertha is. Rochester, trapped in the West Indies, contemplates suicide, as he tells Jane after the interrupted marriage ceremony: 'Of the fanatic's burning eternity I have no fear: there is not a future state worse than this present one—let me break away and go home to God!' A fresh wind from Europe restores Rochester to sanity. The speech shows that Rochester associates the fear of hell-fire with fanaticism. Eventually, after his punishment here on earth, Rochester does 'go home to God' in repentance, united in love with Jane, before they travel to their final resting place.

Hell-fire preaching is out of fashion today. Because Christian fanatics are now pushed to the fringes of our culture, modern readers react with boredom to St. John. His ruthless subordination of emotion to his chosen cause is often found incredible. But if we make a small imaginative leap and transfer St. John's compulsive proselytizing drive from Christianity to an obsession with today's social equivalent, revolutionary politics, we recognize the truth of his characterization. It may be worth pointing out that both Christianity and Marxism are millennial faiths, demanding sacrifice now to ensure a glorious future.

In an interesting paper, Betty H. Jones[28] points out that St. John is 'yoked . . . with images of decay and death. His patrimony will consist of a "crumbling grange" with "scathed" firs behind it and "yew-trees" in front.' Convincingly, she argues that the 'ice' of St. John is self-created, a perverse determination of the will, 'as false an attachment as that of Macbeth or Lucifer'. Describing St. John's fantasy about marrying Rosamond Oliver (indulged for precisely fifteen minutes) as 'the most erotic in the book', Jones says: 'Not content with . . . turning . . . himself to stone, St. John proposes to do the same to Jane.'[29]

It is worth noting that St. John's admitted attraction to the beautiful, but trivial, Rosamond takes place in high summer. St. John, tempted by her approach, perhaps a little like that of Dalila in *Samson Agonistes*, looks away from her to 'a humble tuft of daisies' and 'crushed the snowy heads of the closed flowers with his foot' (Ch. 30).

After St. John has proposed, Jane sees him as 'no longer flesh, but marble; his eye was a cold, bright blue gem; his tongue a speaking instrument—nothing more. . . . If I were his wife, this . . . man . . . could soon kill me' (Ch. 35). Surely hovering over this passage we are meant to hear the words of St. Paul, I. Cor. 13:1: 'Though I speak with the tongues of men and of angels, and have not charity, I am become as sounding brass, or a tinkling cymbal.' St. John lacks 'charity', which as Charlotte well knew, is *agape*, divine love; St. John has no true love, neither *eros*, which he has strangled, nor yet love which is charity. St. John is hard on humanity: he uses the language of Calvinism, despising his 'feeble fellow-worms'; he fears that Jane, if she does not submit to his pressure, will become a 'castaway'. He threatens her, indirectly, with the fate of 'the fearful, the unbelieving [who] shall have their part in the lake which burneth with fire and brimstone, which is the second death'. Yet marriage with St. John seems her only future. As the 'iron shroud' contracts around her, Jane is tempted to submit:

> Religion called—Angels beckoned—God commanded—life rolled together like a scroll—death's gates opening showed eternity beyond it: it seemed, that for safety and bliss there, all here might be sacrificed in a second. The dim room was full of visions. (Ch. 35)[30]

But the heavenly vision of St. John proves false: the voice of Nature (by which Jane means her true sexual instinct) leads her away from St. John back to Rochester, who has found salvation by repentance. By the time she wrote *Jane Eyre*, or perhaps by the very action of writing it, Charlotte had convinced herself that 'ghastly Calvinistic doctrines' were spiritual death.

That she read and thought about such subjects we know from Mary Taylor's account, Charlotte's own letters, in her maturity, to W. S. Williams, and the evidence of John Elliot Cairnes, who visited Haworth in 1858. Martha Brown showed him Charlotte's

> little library, not above sixty or seventy vols. in all, but . . . a most choice collection. Amongst others I noticed the Life of Sterling, Sartor Resartus, Newman on the soul, & books of that cast, her fondness for which shewed what a great revolution her religious views had undergone from that early time, when she used to correspond with 'E.' in the sickly pietistic strain—a

revolution, by the way, of the progress of which it wd. have been most interesting to have had some record, but which Mrs. Gaskell scarcely seemed to be aware of, leaving her readers to discover it only by its results. . . .[31]

Ian Jack, co-editor with Margaret Smith of the Clarendon *Jane Eyre*, argues, against Q. D. Leavis (see Introduction to Penguin edition, 1966), that it is 'a deeply Christian book'.[32] He writes:

> When Jane leaves Rochester it is not because of any 'collapse of will' resulting from an 'artificially trained "conscience" ': . . . it is the triumph of a religious training . . . she is a female Pilgrim who must follow the course ordained for her, heart-breaking as it is often to prove. It is revealing that Mrs. Leavis described the 'analysis' of the character of St. John Rivers as 'really profound'. It is nothing of the sort: he is in no sense a worthy rival to Mr. Rochester and the presentation of him at the end of the book only serves to underline the novel's greatest weakness.

While I feel the work of my old teacher, Mrs. Leavis, to be too often wilful and erratic, about St. John I agree with her and part company with Jack, though I do not accept Mrs. Leavis's reading in full. St. John's placing at the end of the novel is a framing device; he stands with Brocklehurst as an example, more attractive but equally deadly, of false light. He is a will-o'-the-wisp, like the ones in the song Bessie sings to Jane the child (Ch. 3), and quite unlike the true light Jane sees gleaming from the cottage at Marsh End where Providence has led her to her cousins after the 'poor orphan child' has struggled over the moors. The song foretells Jane's story: 'God is a friend to the poor orphan child.'

Charles Burkhart, whose attitude to Charlotte is on the whole one of tolerant male patronage, seeing *Jane Eyre* as 'an addled mixture of romantic spinster and Victorian blue-stocking',[33] observes that the Victorians did not skim or block out religious discussion as we do. Burkhart writes:

> Rochester begins as a Byronic hero; at the end he looks more like a Victorian gentleman. The kind of harmony that Charlotte Brontë achieves in her best novels is a union of what at first appear to be opposites. The energy of her ability to reconcile and transform is unique.[34]

(Presumably Burkhart is invoking *Biographia Literaria*, Ch. 13.) The question is whether Charlotte does truly 'reconcile and transform': many critics suspect her of putting her thumb in the scale, wrenching *Jane Eyre* to a forced conclusion. Is *Jane Eyre* a Christian book, or a paean to pagan forces? Rochester sees himself at the end as a Vulcan, 'blind and lame into the bargain', while he imagines the unseen St. John as an Apollo.

One critic thinks the true meaning is subterranean paganism. R. E. Hughes, in '*Jane Eyre*: the unbaptised Dionysos',[35] writes that the imps, fairies and leprechauns haunting the novel are 'stunted versions of the *chthonioi*, the ministering spirits of the underworld'.[36] Jane's 'fit' in the Red Room is a visionary trance, Miss Temple an Apollonian spirit, Helen Burns a priestess of Apollo, and Rochester is Dionysos, coming out from among the oak trees and getting cut down at harvest-time. Jane 'becomes a Bacchante' at Gateshead; unfortunately, she forgets to tell us about it. The idea on which so much of Hughes's argument rests is imported.

Hughes is yet another victim of the hypnotic fascination that Nietzsche's essay, *The Birth of Tragedy*, exerts on its readers. This may well be because it puts old wine in new bottles: it restates, in archaic terms, which are therefore felt to be more profound and inward than commonplace distinctions, the basic human conflict between emotion ('passion') and reason, body and soul, first articulated in the Western consciousness by Plato, developed by St. Paul. Faced with Rosamond, St. John

> looked nearly as beautiful for a man as she for a woman. His chest heaved once, as if his large heart, weary of despotic constriction, had expanded, despite the will, and made a vigorous bound for the attainment of liberty. But he curbed it, I think, as a resolute rider would curb a rearing steed. (Ch. 31)

Charlotte, daughter of the classics graduate Mr. Brontë, friend of classical scholar William Weightman, almost certainly knew about Plato's image in *The Phaedrus* of man as a charioteer driving two horses, one black and one white, one being desire and the other reason. Christians, including Charlotte, have been taught to look on this as a struggle between nature and grace. That Christianity has its roots in ecstatic dying-god and vegetation cults makes such interpretations as Hughes's

superficially attractive, but such fanciful arguments are unnecessary; they add nothing to our reading of *Jane Eyre*. The
Freudian model of the human soul, with id and ego reconciled
by the superego, also having its roots in classical thought, has
led to widespread acceptance of a metaphor as factual description. Freudian-inspired interpretations of *Jane Eyre* will be dealt
with in Chapter 7 and subsequently.

More convincingly than Hughes, Nina Auerbach is worried
that the book ends with 'St. John's self-immolating cry to this
implacable and unnatural divinity', despite 'the apparent victory
of Jane's fire over St. John's ice: everything that Rochester
represented was crushed at Thornfield.'[37] Here we have a real
problem. The maiming of Edward Rochester will be discussed
in Chapter 12.

Sarah Moore Putzell offers us a possible way out of our
difficulty; she argues that Charlotte's romantic faith in the
human heart and the rights of the individual

> is inconsistent with Calvinism. It is not, however, inconsistent
> with the Arminian bias of Brontë's Methodist aunt and Anglican
> father, nor is it inconsistent with the Neo-Platonism of the
> seventeenth-century importers of Arminianism, the Cambridge
> Platonists.[38]

(St. John himself hints at the Platonic ladder: 'From the
minute germ, natural affection [religion], has developed the
overshadowing tree, philanthropy' (Ch. 32).) For Putzell,
Charlotte's novels are neither anti-Christian nor inconsistent,
but typical of a major perspective within English Protestantism.
Writing to Mrs. Gaskell on 26 April 1854, Charlotte mentioned
'my latitudinarianism'. Putzell argues that whereas Calvinists
upheld the Augustinian view of fallen man as totally depraved,
Neo-Platonists saw him as still retaining a divine spark even in
his corrupt state. Reason is both man's true nature and his
moral guide. Putzell links Helen Burns's creed, which 'no one
ever taught her' to Cudworth's statements, and concludes that
Charlotte 'emphasises man's power to act rationally and thus
morally', minimizing the concept of original sin. Charlotte
shares with the Neo-Platonists their confidence in man's power
to co-operate in his own salvation. This argument seems to me
wholly just.

'Mad Methodist magazines'

Charlotte wrote to Miss Wooler on 14 February 1850:

> I am sorry the Clergy do not like the doctrine of Universal
> Salvation; I think it a great pity for their sakes, but surely they
> are not so unreasonable as to expect me to deny or suppress what
> I believe to be the truth!

> Some of the clergy will not like 'Shirley'; I confess the work has
> one prevailing fault—that of too tenderly and partially unveiling
> the errors of 'the curates'. Had Currer Bell written all he has seen
> and known concerning these worthies—a singular work would
> have been the result. (No. 8, Fitzwilliam Museum)

George Smith wanted her to cut the first chapter, but she wisely
refused. The harsh picture of the curates is truthful, very funny
and in a well-established literary tradition. Like Chaucer's
Friar, the curates are false shepherds. The workpeople in *Shirley*
are hungry sheep who look up and are not fed; Michael Hartley
falls prey to Antinomianism and alcoholism, rabid left-wing
politics and madness. The Luddites are led astray by self-serving
false lights like Moses Barraclough. (We may discount the
sentimental-leftist view of Terry Eagleton that the machine-
breakers, being working-class, were naturally in the right.[39])
The Yorkes (*Shirley*, Ch. 33) approve of John Wesley because he
was 'a Reformer and an Agitator'. But Charlotte's satire on
Wesley does not negate the possibility of his influence on her
language and habits of thought. As we have seen, she could
digest and combine to form new wholes. Early commentators
thought the Brontës were wild originals, with no literary
influences. W. Robertson Nicoll, addressing the Brontë Society
on 10 April 1898, said, 'They were not great readers. They
looked into their hearts and wrote.' Yet that same year, Mrs.
Humphry Ward, in her Introduction to the Haworth edition of
the Brontë works, made the famous observation:

> There were no children's books at Haworth Parsonage. The
> children . . . were nourished upon . . . The Bible, Shakespeare,
> Addison, Johnson, Sheridan, Cowper . . . Scott, Byron, Southey,
> Wordsworth, Coleridge, *Blackwood's Magazine*, *Fraser's Magazine*,
> and Leigh Hunt . . . newspapers . . . Lockhart's *Life of Burns*,
> Moore's Lives of Byron and Sheridan, Southey's *Nelson*, Wolfe's
> *Remains*; and on miscellaneous reading of old Methodist magazines

... Mrs. Rowe's *Letters from the Dead to the Living*, the *British Essayists*, collected from the *Rambler*, the *Mirror*, and elsewhere, and stories from the *Lady's Magazine*.

If Mr. Brontë's Evangelical bias had been of the grim, Puritan sort, his children would not have been allowed to read poetry and fiction, condemned as 'false' by, for instance, Carlyle's father.[40] Much of Charlotte's adult, as well as formative, reading has been traced. While we do not know what books arrived on loan from W. S. Williams, we do know that she received boxes of forty French books at a time. Florence Dry, in *The Sources of Jane Eyre*, has demonstrated the direct absorption of other writers, in particular Scott and George Sand, by Charlotte. Lawrence Jay Dessner picks on the weakest points in Dry's sober argument,[41] doubtless because he proceeds to do much of her work over again in *The Homely Web of Truth*.

Charlotte wrote to Mrs. Gaskell on 27 December 1853, 'The Church of England has faults—but I love her—....' To W. S. Williams, she had written in 1847,

I love the Church of England. Her ministers, indeed, I do not regard as infallible personages. I have seen too much of them for that, but to the Establishment, with all her faults—the profane Athanasian creed *ex*cluded—I am sincerely attached.

Charlotte's objection to the Athanasian creed was that it includes anathemas against those who do not believe its affirmations. Robert Bernard Martin explains: 'In general, as one would expect from the daughter of a Methodist, Miss Brontë tried to be as tolerant as possible of Dissenters who were sincere in their beliefs.'[42]

It is a point against the Rev. Matthew Helstone that he asks Shirley's assent to St. Athanasius's creed (*Shirley*, Ch. 11). Charlotte was hard on Church of England clergymen who fell short of her standards. She wrote to Ellen, 18 June 1845:

I have no desire at all to see your medical-clerical curate—I think he must be like all the other curates I have seen—and they seem to me a self-seeking, vain, empty race. At this blessed moment we have no less than three of them in Haworth Parish— and God knows there is not one to mend another.

She goes on to describe a teatime visit when

... they began glorifying themselves and abusing Dissenters in such a manner—that my temper lost its balance and I pronounced a few sentences sharply and rapidly which struck them all dumb—Papa was greatly horrified also—I don't regret it.

The three curates in *Shirley*, conscious of their social status, reflect this experience. (Charlotte also prayed God, in that novel, Ch. 16, to reform the Church.) The pilloried originals, far from being angered, were flattered, and adopted their fictional cognomens as mutual modes of address. A fourth, given one short paragraph to himself as the conscientious 'Mr Macarthey', likely, at the thought of tea with a Dissenter, to be 'unhinged for a week', roared with laughter as he read, clapping his hands and stamping on the floor. With gentle tact, he gave the woman he loved and eventually married a present she could not refuse—a book of Common Prayer.

Well used, it is inscribed in Charlotte's beautifully even, delicate script:

'Charlotte Brontë, Haworth. Presented by Mr. Nicholls on the publication of "Shirley".'

NOTES

1. Grace Elizabeth Harrison, *The Clue to the Brontës*, p. 210.
2. Tom Winnifrith, *The Brontës and their Background*, p. 28.
3. Ibid.
4. Winnifrith, p. 33.
5. Valentine Cunningham, *Everywhere Spoken Against: Dissent in the Victorian Novel*, p. 113n.
6. Charlotte Brontë, 'Biographical notice of Ellis and Acton Bell'.
7. Quoted Cunningham, p. 289.
8. Cunningham, p. 291n.
9. For fuller treatment, see Robert Bernard Martin, *The Accents of Persuasion*, esp. pp. 48–55.
10. Tom Winnifrith, 'Charlotte Brontë and Calvinism', *N.Q.*, n.s. 17, 215 cont. series (January 1970), 17–18.
11. Rosamond Langbridge, *Charlotte Brontë: A Psychological Study*, p. 153. Langbridge's theory is that Charlotte was suffering from 'suppressed personality'. Carol Ohmann, in 'Charlotte Brontë: The Limits of her Feminism', *Female Studies*, 6 (1972), 154, writes: 'What has passed as a religious crisis in Charlotte Brontë's life at the time she went to teach at Roe Head should, most probably, be viewed as a crisis caused by the necessity of conforming

to an uncongenial pattern of work and of personal identity.' While this may be true, Charlotte's despair and self-detestation were real, nevertheless.

12. E. J. Bicknell, *A Theological Introduction to the Thirty-Nine Articles of the Church of England* (London: Longman's, 1919; reference to third edition, 1955), p. 222.
13. Quoted Gérin, *Branwell Brontë*, p. 256.
14. Stephen Cox, *The Stranger Within Thee*, p. 124.
15. Margot Peters, *Unquiet Soul*, p. 18, paperback edn.
16. See Eanne Oram, 'Brief for Miss Branwell', *B.S.T.*, 14 (1964), 28–38.
17. Patricia Beer, *Reader, I Married Him*, p. 27.
18. Arthur Pollard, 'The Brontës and their Father's Faith', *Essays and Studies*, n.s. 37 (1984), 48.
19. Letter from Catherine Winkworth to Emma Shaen, 8 May 1854.
20. Abraham Holroyd, *Currer Bell and Her Sisters* (reprinted from the *Bradford Advertiser*, 1855), p. 10. Three copies of this pamphlet are held at Haworth and one in the Brotherton Collection, Leeds. Its dating is, however, dubious. See Valerie Grosvenor Myer, *B.S.T.*, 19 (Autumn, 1987).
21. William Scruton, *Thornton and the Brontës* (Bradford: 1898), p. 74.
22. See n. 18. Pollard criticizes the work of John Lock and Canon W. T. Dixon in their biography of Mr. Brontë, *A Man of Sorrows* (1965). He also disagrees with Winnifrith's interpretation of Anne's religious tenets, and argues that little profit can be derived from an attempt to apply Christian concepts to *Wuthering Heights*, an opinion I endorse. He summarizes Charlotte's comments on Roman Catholicism (pp. 56–8).
23. Clement Carus-Wilson Shepheard-Walwyn, M.A., *Memorials of a Father and a Mother* (London: Elliot Stock, 1882), quoted Herbert Wroot, *B.S.T.*, 2 (1902), 34.
24. John Maynard, *Charlotte Brontë and Sexuality*, p. 5.
25. Annette Tromly, *The Cover of the Mask*, p. 56.
26. For Jack's opinion, see Clarendon *Jane Eyre*, p. 624. The editors, Ian Jack and Margaret Smith, quote Clement Shorter's opinion that Nussey's diary is the work of a 'dull uninspired person, with no sufficient brains to be a high-souled fanatic' (*Charlotte Brontë and her Sisters*, 1905), 169–70.
27. Tom Winnifrith, *The Brontës and their Background*, p. 29.
28. Betty H. Jones, 'Moor House Revisited: Another Look at St. John Rivers', *English Record*, 32 (Winter 1981), 9–12.
29. Jones, p. 10.
30. Wayne Burns interprets the experience described in this passage as a 'form of orgasm . . . her body takes over . . . and at the height of her physical ecstasy she hears Rochester's voice—to which she responds with "I am coming" ' (Burns, 'The Critical Relevance of Freudianism', *Western Review*, 20 (1956), 310). It seems to me more like a rush of blood to the head.
31. T. P. Foley, 'John Elliot Cairnes' Visit to Haworth Parsonage', *B.S.T.*, 18 (1984), 293.
32. Ian Jack, 'Novels and those "necessary evils": annotating the Brontës', *Essays in Criticism*, 32:4 (October 1982), 334.
33. Charles Burkhart, 'Another Key Word for *Jane Eyre*', *N.C.F.*, 16 (1961), 177–78.

34. Burkhart, *Charlotte Brontë: A Psychosexual Study of her Novels*, p. 69.
35. R. E. Hughes, '*Jane Eyre*: The Unbaptised Dionysos', *N.C.F.*, 18 (March 1964), 347–64.
36. Ibid., 351.
37. Nina Auerbach, 'Charlotte Brontë: The Two Countries', *University of Toronto Quarterly*, 42:2 (Summer 1973), 335.
38. Sarah Moore Putzell, 'Rights, Reason and Redemption: Charlotte Brontë's Neo-Platonism', *Victorian Newsletter*, 55 (Spring 1979), 5–7.
39. Terry Eagleton, *Myths of Power: A Marxist Study of the Brontës*, p. 52.
40. W. J. Houghton, *The Victorian Frame of Mind*, p. 127. Carlyle's family was not Evangelical, but Presbyterian. However, the proscription of fiction and poetry characterized extreme Protestant sects in general.
41. Lawrence Jay Dessner, *The Homely Web of Truth*, p. 1. He mocks Dry, quite rightly, for seeing a likeness between the names 'Old Mother *Blood* and Grace *Poole*', but allows no credit for her careful demonstration that characters and plot incidents have parallels in Scott and George Sand. Dry suggests, for example, that Fergus MacIvor, in *Waverley*, influenced the character of Rochester (and see my Chapter 8 for the suggestion that he has affinities with Shakespeare's Antony in *Antony and Cleopatra*). See also Winnifrith, *The Brontës and their Background*, Ch. 6, and Clifford Whone, 'Where the Brontës Borrowed Books, the Keighley Mechanics Institute', *B.S.T.*, 11 (1950), 344–58. Andrew Lang, in a column called 'At the Sign of the Ship', in *Longman's Magazine*, June 1895, p. 210, observes that in the *Author* Robert Sherard had noticed that the case of Jane Eyre and Rochester is similar to that of Moll Flanders and Jemmy, who hears Moll's cry of distress forty-five miles away. Janet Spens is usually credited with noticing *Jane Eyre*'s affinities with *Pamela* (explicitly mentioned in *Jane Eyre* (Ch. 1)). Spens's essay, 'Charlotte Brontë', *Essays and Studies by Members of the English Association*, 14 (1929), 54–70, was preceded by Helen Shipton, in the *Monthly Packet*, November 1896. Leo Mason, in 'Charlotte Brontë and Charles Dickens', *Dickensian*, 43 (1947), 118–24, notes that Charlotte's Lowood appeared after the awful boarding school had been introduced into fiction with Dotheboys Hall. Mason notes: 'Unlike the child creations of Dickens, however, [Jane] was not the "angelic type" who suffered in silence. . . . Mr. Brocklehurst, the teachers and events at the school are portrayed with a Dickensian forcefulness' (p. 122). Mason believes that just as *Nicholas Nickleby* influenced *Jane Eyre*, so *Jane Eyre* influenced *David Copperfield*. I agree.
42. Robert Bernard Martin, *The Accents of Persuasion*, p. 53.

5

Patrick Brontë's
The Cottage in the Wood and the Plot of *Jane Eyre*

Be good, sweet maid, and let who will be clever.—Charles Kingsley

The Rev. Patrick Brontë's works are little read today. Their intrinsic interest is minimal, as he writes in clichés. However, one of his moral stories, intended as improving reading for the poorer classes and Sunday school pupils, contains many motifs which Charlotte seems to have taken over for the moral skeleton of *Jane Eyre*.[1]

The child of poor but virtuous Christian parents, Mary is invited by a rich, drunken and dissolute young man, Mr. Bower, to become his mistress. She declines with scorn. He 'was about to mount his horse and ride off; when his passions, which he had never been accustomed to control, kindled with increasing fury and impelled him towards the possession of the desired object . . .' He offers her marriage, pretending he was merely testing her 'integrity'. She proudly refuses to be 'yoked with an unbeliever', especially one who had shown her so little respect as to act the part of tempter. Her parents are proud of her '(unlike many professors of religion, who criminally dispose of their children for gain)', and say, 'Blessed be God, for giving us such a daughter.'

God, however, 'thinks fit to refine his children in the furnace of affliction', and Mary's parents die.

'She next went to the house of a poor relation, where she

80

obtained an asylum for a few weeks.' Mr. Bower renews his offer of marriage, but 'Her character remained unsullied, and her principles unshaken.'

Mary finds a job as companion to an 'old pious maiden lady'. Mary lives happily there for more than three years until the old lady dies and leaves Mary 'upwards of four thousand pounds', which she proceeds to give away to others 'in distress'.

Mr. Bower, meanwhile, has been influenced by Mary's virtue, but unable to resist his old bad ways. After a debauch one evening, his companions are shot dead by robbers, and he escapes, which turns his mind to religion.

Mr. Bower, having wasted his own money, has been shy of approaching Mary now she is rich, but he takes up good works and meets her when he is teaching Sunday school.

> Her conscience now told her that she might indulge the pure passion. . . . However polite and engaging the conversation and manner of sensual young men may occasionally appear to a graceless and unthinking woman, yet all who view them closely, and with spiritual discernment, will readily discover the . . . basic hypocrisy of their conduct. . . . Mr. Bower was once an agreeably accomplished rake, in full possession of these allurements that have inveigled so many to their ruin. At that time, Mary, though not without an effort, resisted and overcame all his temptations. But now his looks are humble, his manners unaffectedly kind, his conversation instructive, lively and spiritual, and his whole deportment far more pleasing to her than it ever had been. What once could be termed only a disallowed and transient passion, is now become pure and settled affection, founded upon the immoveable basis of friendship and esteem. . . . They lived many years together, not without some trials, but in the full enjoyment of as much happiness as can fall to the lot of humanity, in this changeable and uncertain world.

While this is unremarkable tract literature, the points of likeness are striking. Jane, like Mary, is tempted by a 'rake', who attempts to seduce her. Jane, like Mary, resists and goes away to relations and to earn her own living. Jane, like Mary, inherits a fortune, which she gives away. Rochester, like Mr. Bower, comes by Providence back to religion, and is fit for marriage to the proudly independent heroine. The fire at Thornfield may be seen as a literal reading of the standard religious metaphor, 'the furnace of affliction'. But the happiness of the Bowers is muted, as is that of Rochester and Jane at damp, unhealthy Ferndean, because true happiness can only be found in heaven.

Those who read *Jane Eyre* as a secular tale of feminist rebellion and nothing more may well be distorting the novel in the light of twentieth-century perceptions. The structure of *Jane Eyre* shows how, in a great and original novel, Charlotte Brontë incorporated many of her father's values, offering some support for the argument that Charlotte intended *Jane Eyre* to be read as a religious novel.

This summary is enough to clarify the question of Mr. Brontë's teaching. The message is self-control and the avoidance of vice (Branwell's conduct must have been torture to the man who wrote a story such as this one), repentance, redemption and good works. The belief in charitable work is Evangelical, in contrast to the Calvinists and Lutherans, who believed in salvation by faith. The emphasis is on leading a good life in this world, always in the consciousness that there is another one to come. The girl in the story is to be admired for her independence and her self-respect, and her firmness is rewarded eventually by a happy marriage. This is a long way from Carus-Wilson's obsession with death. The two clergymen demonstrate the extremes of Evangelicalism: Carus-Wilson its savage repressive Puritanism, Mr. Brontë its concern for right conduct.

NOTE

1. The Rev. Patrick Brontë, 'The Cottage in the Wood', repr. in *Brontëana: The Rev. Patrick Brontë, A.B., His Collected Works and Life. The Works; and The Brontës of Ireland*, ed. J. Horsfall Turner (Bingley: printed for the editor by T. Harrison and Sons, 1898), pp. 102–20.

6

'Hypochondria'

I put my headache in my pocket.—Charlotte Brontë, letter to
Mary Taylor, 4 September 1848.

John Todd and Kenneth Dewhurst note that

> Charlotte's religious depression was at its height in 1836, when
> she was—together with Branwell and Anne—greatly under the
> influence of William Cowper's religiously pessimistic poem *The
> Castaway*. This fact is of considerable psychiatric interest, since
> Charlotte, Branwell and Anne had a constitutional tendency to
> depression, whereas Cowper himself was prone to bouts of
> religious melancholia with suicidal impulses and a fixed delusion
> that he was irrevocably damned. . . .[1]

They conclude that Charlotte had 'more than her fair share of
ill-health, disappointment, and bereavement. . . . [she] suffered
from recurrent depression which was severe enough to impede
her work and detract seriously from the happiness of her life.'[2]
Doctors and psychiatrists are fascinated by the Brontës as
retrospectively speculative patients, and their assessments have
influenced critical opinion, as we shall see.

In a separate article, Todd writes that Charlotte was

> a martyr to migraine, insomnia, dyspepsia and depression . . .
> like all introverts, Charlotte tended to be gauche in company . . .
> the isolation of her childhood, and her physical unattractiveness,
> must have contributed. . . . Her books [seem] sounding boards
> for her own ideas and attitudes . . . she favours plain heroines
> who are financially and psychologically independent of their
> suitors . . . the unenviable and humiliating lot of the Victorian
> governess is vividly depicted in them. . . .[3]

83

This is an example of the clumsy generalization characteristic of amateur Brontë commentators. Charlotte makes Jane Eyre and Shirley Keeldar financially independent of their suitors, but Lucy Snowe accepts the gift of a school from hers. As to psychological independence, what Harriet Martineau objected to was its absence. For Kate Millett's view of the question, see the chapter on *Villette*.

Todd thinks it probable that Charlotte died from 'phthisis', as written on her death certificate, the consumption that had killed Emily and Anne. He supposes Charlotte, if born later, 'would have benefited from up-to-date drugs to relieve her sick-headaches, insomnia and periodical melancholia'.

In an undated letter which Professor Mildred Christian attributes to late 1852, Charlotte wrote to Miss Wooler:

> I pity Mr. Thomas from my heart. For ten years I have not, I think, been a sufferer from nervous complaints—For ten years he has felt the tyranny of Hypochondria—A most dreadful doom, far worse than that of a man with healthy nerves buried for the same length of time in a subterranean Dungeon—I endured it but a year—and assuredly I can never forget the concentrated anguish of certain insufferable moments and the heavy gloom of many long hours—besides the preternatural horror which seemed to clothe existence and Nature—and which made Life a continual waking Nightmare—under such circumstances the morbid Nerves can know neither Peace nor enjoyment—whatever touches—pierces them—sensation for them is all suffering—a weary burden nervous patients consequently become to those about them—they know this and it infuses a new gall—corrosive in its extreme acritude, into their bitter cup—When I was at Dewsbury Moor—I could have been no better company for you than a stalking ghost—and I remember I felt my incapacity to *impart* pleasure fully as much as my powerlessness to *receive* it. (Letter 3, Fitzwilliam Museum)

Charlotte's letter indeed describes clinical depression. 'Hypochondria' was the word for it used by the Victorians; it did not come to mean 'imaginary illness' until the end the century. Charlotte's mental state after the deaths of her beloved younger sisters, having lost their support as sympathetic critics and fellow-novelists, is recorded in her letters to W. S. Williams, as she struggled to get *Shirley* finished. Her plight as a lonely

84

single woman who felt herself to be unattractive (see Chapter 7) is explored in *Shirley*. Charlotte was undersized and never fit. On 17 February 1852, she wrote to Miss Wooler that her stay at Brookroyd with Ellen had

> proved beneficial, not only to my health but more especially to my spirits which were so prostrated by the debility consequent on my illness that solitude had become somewhat too trying. ... these long storms, these incessantly howling winds, depress the nervous system much. (No. 13, Fitzwilliam Museum)

She had almost permanent headaches, which she attributed variously to eyestrain and to 'an inert liver' (20 January ?1852, No. 12). She suffered, like Charles Kingsley, from neuralgia and toothache. Before we criticize the Victorians for being over-concerned with their ailments, we should remember that dentistry was primitive; there were no anaesthetics (Mr. Brontë's cataract was removed without them); the general pain-killer was opium; houses were cold and draughty and chilblains an annual misery. Although Mr. Brontë indignantly denied that he refused his children meat, according to Ellen's account of her schooldays at Roe Head, Charlotte 'had the greatest dislike to it', possibly due to an inability to digest fat. She fell ill on a visit to Ellen, after the excitement of her London trip, when she had been strained by alien mealtimes and the demands of strangers. On 12 July 1850, Mr. Brontë wrote to Ellen, saying, 'One thing comforts me, that in you she will have the kindest and best nurse. It may be that she is labouring under one of her usual bilious attacks. ...' Bilious attacks are still with us, only today we call them migraines. Migraine affects 'highly-strung' people, is associated with poor liver action, and the symptoms are headache and continuous vomiting for about twenty-four hours. Meat should be avoided during attacks. Treatment is difficult, as anything taken by mouth is likely to be vomited, causing dehydration. The Victorians also called migraines 'sick headaches' (which seems also to have been a euphemism for period pains). Clement Shorter writes that a member of the Sidgwick family told him that when Charlotte was governess with the family,

> Mrs. Sidgwick told me that Miss Brontë often went to bed all day and left her to look after the children at a time when she was much occupied with her invalid father, Mr. Greenwood, at Swarcliffe.[4]

In 'Studies, Time, the Author as Wife', Anne Hart notes that though Mr. Brontë and Mr. Nicholls had their studies at Haworth, there are no rooms marked 'Charlotte's study' or 'Emily's study' or 'Anne's study': 'In this home of great women writers only the men, it was apparent, had studies of their own.' Hart observes that to be a spinster daughter of a country parsonage, if one

> happened to be a genius—a Jane Austen or an Emily or Charlotte Brontë—and if one was spared the normal life of a middle-class woman (marriage at eighteen followed by twenty or thirty years of perilous childbirth and intense domestic preoccupations) then one had instead a rather precious compensation, time of one's own. . . .[5]

She notes that Charlotte sewed green and white curtains for her husband's study; why, asks Hart sensibly, was the peat-room never turned into a study before the advent of Nicholls? Hart concludes, sadly,

> Probably most of her biographers are correct in concluding that her husband did not deliberately or overtly prevent her from writing, but neither can I find any direct evidence to suggest that he encouraged her to continue.[6]

For extended discussion of this topic, see Gérin (pp. 553–55), and Peters, *Unquiet Soul* (pp. 400–5, paperback edn.).

After Charlotte's death, Mr. Brontë said he always knew Charlotte was not strong enough for marriage. Presumably the man whose own wife had had six children with a rapidity that shocked Mrs. Gaskell meant 'not strong enough for pregnancy and childbirth'. Philip Rhodes, Professor of Obstetrics and Gynaecology, University of London, St. Thomas's Hospital Medical School, in an influential paper, describes the whole family as 'neurotic'. He writes:

> Morning sickness in pregnancy . . . only seems to become excessive in those who display neuroticism. . . . Her neurosis was the ultimate cause of her death. . . . Some doctors have suggested that hypermesis gravidarium is an unconscious rejection of the baby, and this might have been so in Charlotte's case.[7]

Margot Peters believes that Charlotte feared pregnancy, which is indeed probable. Peters cites Jane Eyre's dream of a wailing child. As E. F. Benson points out in his biography, Charlotte's attitude to children was less than romantic.[8] Peters wonders 'was her death to be in a sense voluntary—an unconscious solution to an unsolvable conflict—as she felt it—between her art and her marriage?'[9] If it was, then Charlotte must have chosen, unconsciously, to starve herself to death.

John Maynard in *Charlotte Brontë and Sexuality* conveniently summarizes Rhodes: according to Rhodes, Charlotte's death was psychosomatic, due to sexual neurosis, unconscious rejection of the baby and failure to achieve satisfactory psychological relationships. . . . 'Peters and Helene Moglen accept this diagnosis (Moglen, p. 241) and so does Robert Keefe (pp. 43–4).'[10] Maynard's own view is that

> All three have by and large accepted the assumptions in Rhodes's article that the disease was cause and proof of severe neurosis. . . . Moglen calls Brontë's mortal sickness 'the last of her neurotic illnesses'; Keefe speaks of Brontë's 'death wish' finally overcoming 'her will to live'.[11]

Maynard consulted Dr. Gerson Weiss, Professor of Gynaecology and Obstetrics at New York University Medical Centre, who comes up with the theory that, although her own doctor thought she was, maybe Charlotte was not pregnant at all. He argues that the information available

> does not allow us to say she was pregnant . . . many possible illnesses could cause the two symptoms that were probably taken as indications of pregnancy at the time: morning sickness and stopping of menses. Nineteenth-century medical texts, based on the necessity of practising without any pregnancy tests, caution physicians against possibility of error . . . the most likely and simplest explanation of her death is that she died of a severe terminal wasting disease of some sort without pregnancy.[12]

(Nobody seems to have thought of this at the time.) Maynard concludes, in the light of Weiss's opinion, that Dr. Rhodes's account is not a careful look at the evidence but another attempt to read Charlotte's life according to a pattern of neurosis.

> . . . it is important to avoid the kind of circular reasoning so common in Brontë studies: that is, the theory of her acute neurosis leads to the diagnosis of death which in turn supports the theory of neurosis.

He adds that we can hardly

> justify romantic notions that her death was caused by her
> psychological revulsion from motherhood or marriage, whatever
> we may think of the suitability of a woman of genius for either
> rôle in the nineteenth century.[13]

Maynard's discussion is replied to by H. W. Gallagher,
Honorary Consultant Surgeon, Ards Hospital, Newtonards,
Co. Down, Northern Ireland, in 'Charlotte Brontë: A Surgeon's
Assessment'.[14] Gallagher thinks Charlotte had an inflamed
gall-bladder, misdiagnosed as liver disorder. She describes the
misery of mercury poisoning as a result of medicines prescribed
for her (letter to Miss Wooler, dated 20 January 1851, though
Professor Mildred Christian believes Charlotte wrote the
previous year's date, in mistake for 1852). Gallagher says

> there may not be sufficient evidence for a firm diagnosis but the
> probabilities surely allow us to agree with Mrs. Gaskell. . . . I am
> not an obstetrician but point out that Dr. Weiss's statement that
> hyperemesis gravidarium is not necessarily a psychosomatic
> illness does not contradict Professor Rhodes' conclusions.[15]

Charlotte's own doctor thought she was pregnant and so did
everybody around her. If Charlotte had a wasting disease, why
did her menses not stop before marriage? That she and her
doctor took cessation to be a symptom of pregnancy suggests
previous normal functioning. No autopsy was performed. Asked
her opinion, my own medical woman replied that Charlotte was
almost certainly pregnant, that her constitutional tendency to
vomiting would have been intensified by the hormonal changes
of pregnancy, and her inability to eat was 'purely physical'. As
to phantom pregnancy, she considered this improbable, as
Charlotte, unlike her sister Anne, gave no sign of yearning for
children of her own. Charlotte died of the weakness brought on
by starvation and dehydration. There is, however, some support
for the Rhodes–Peters thesis in that Jane Eyre thinks of starving
herself to death (Ch. 2), and Caroline Helstone develops
anorexia nervosa when Robert neglects her, but is saved by a
mother's love. And see Susan Gubar's brilliant paper, 'The
Genesis of Hunger According to *Shirley*',[16] reprinted in *The
Madwoman in the Attic* by Gilbert and Gubar (Ch. 11). That

Charlotte's tendency to throw up was linked with self-suppression tends to confirm the suggestion of 'neurosis' (see my Chapter 7).

John Reed, in *Jane Eyre*, 'habitually gorged himself at table, which made him bilious' (Ch. 1). Charlotte seems to have found the thought of 'gorging' disgusting, but she suffered from biliousness just the same. Was she, in fact, anorexic? She wrote to Ellen (24 January 1852):

> I am to live on the *very plainest* fare—to take *no butter*—at present I do not take tea—only milk and water with a little sugar and dry bread—this with an occasional mutton chop is my diet—and I like it better than anything else.

She told Mrs. Gaskell later that, during the desolate period when she was writing *Villette*, 'sleep almost forsook me, or would never come except accompanied by ghastly dreams; appetite vanished, and slow fever was my constant companion. . . .' We remember her reluctance, at school, to eat meat. Charlotte's relations with food and appetite seem to have been unstable, to say the least. Maynard seems to think that having found a doctor who casts doubt on Charlotte's pregnancy disposes of the question as to whether or not Charlotte was neurotic. It does nothing of the kind. One must, however, agree with him that 'out of the often terrible conditions of her life, Brontë found the strength to present a major impersonal vision of experience in her art.'[17]

Stevie Davies agrees: '. . . doesn't Charlotte's writing, both personal and public, give out an extraordinary sense of joy?' Charlotte's life 'mutinies against its conditions through the joy of authorship, with unique conviction'.[18]

While Charlotte's well-nourished intellect found pleasure in creating, the 'joy of authorship' is less conspicuous, to most readers, than female protest, pain and anger. The majority of Brontë critics, feeling this, have preferred to plumb Charlotte's psyche for hidden complexes.

Charlotte Brontë: Truculent Spirit

NOTES

1. John Todd and Kenneth Dewhurst, 'The Periodic Depression of Charlotte Brontë', in *Perspectives in Biology and Medicine*, Vol. 2 (Chicago: University of Chicago Press, 1968), 208–16.
2. Ibid., p. 215.
3. John Todd, 'The Brontë Children: Aspects of their Lives of Medical Interest', *Practitioner*, 198 (1967), 581.
4. Clement Shorter, 'New Light on the Brontës', *B.S.T.*, 1 (1898), 19.
5. Anne Hart, 'Studies, Time, the Author as Wife', *B.S.T.*, 16 (1975), 379.
6. Ibid., 378.
7. Philip Rhodes, *B.S.T.*, 16 (1972), 107.
8. E. F. Benson, p. 88.
9. Margot Peters, *Unquiet Soul*, p. 405 (paperback edn.).
10. John Maynard, *Charlotte Brontë and Sexuality*, p. 218.
11. Ibid.
12. Quoted Maynard, p. 223.
13. Ibid., p. 224.
14. H. W. Gallagher, 'Charlotte Brontë: A Surgeon's Assessment', *B.S.T.*, 18 (1985), 363–69.
15. Ibid., 369.
16. Susan Gubar, 'The Genesis of Hunger, According to *Shirley*', *Feminist Studies*, 3 (1976), 5–21.
17. Maynard, *Charlotte Brontë and Sexuality*, ix.
18. Stevie Davies, 'Recent Studies of the Brontës', *Critical Quarterly*, 27 (Autumn 1985), 38.

7

Charlotte and her Unconscious

> The mind knew but did not feel its existence. It was away. It had launched on a distant voyage. . . .—Charlotte Brontë, Roe Head Journal

An important strand in twentieth-century criticism has been the view of Charlotte as psychological cripple, a female Philoctetes. That she was frustrated and disappointed is undeniable. The 'little plain, provincial, sickly-looking old maid'[1] as Lewes called her to George Eliot, was, as Thackeray and others could see, sex-starved. Yet despite this, and the shattering deaths of her sisters, she struggled on, despite ill-health, loneliness and despair, to complete *Shirley* and *Villette*. That they tackle loneliness and despair head-on is their distinction. Charlotte, in these novels, wrote about the problems of the unloved. Charlotte made up her mind at 12 that she would be an old maid. From Brussels she wrote to Ellen (6 March 1843),

> Goodbye to you dear Nell when I say so—it seems to me that you will hardly hear me in all the ['heaving' erased] waves of the Channel heaving and roaring between must deaden the sound. Good-b-y-e, CB.

At the bottom of the letter is a sketch of herself, with a balloon coming out of her mouth. She calls 'Goodbye' across the waters (ship in the distance). Charlotte's picture of herself is of a plain, drably dressed woman with a bun, while Ellen, ringleted and shawled, dressed in the height of fashion, is accompanied by a tall, handsome man in a top hat, labelled 'The Chosen'. To

emphasize this difference in their imagined life-styles, Charlotte
has written 'C. Brontë' and 'Ellen Nussey' underneath the
figures, then crossed Ellen's name out. Charlotte had never
been petted as pretty little girls are. Her father's *Cottage Poems*
include the following stanza:

> Religion makes beauty enchanting
> But even where beauty is wanting
>   The temper and mind,
>   Religion—refin'd
> Will shine though the veil with sweet lustre.[2]

The heroine of 'The Cottage in the Wood' is outstandingly
good-looking. Charlotte's message from her father was that a
woman ought to be attractive, but if she could not manage it,
then religion would be some sort of pallid compensation.

Charlotte wrote a sad poem, 'Reason'. It is difficult to date.
Written in pencil, it is similar to the hand Charlotte used
when in Brussels, but it is in a volume of poems in which the
latest date given is January 1836. It is now in the library of the
State University of New York at Buffalo. In it Charlotte is
making up her mind to single wretchedness. It runs:

> Unloved, I love, unwept I weep
> Grief I restrain hope I repress
> Vain is this anguish fixed and deep
> Vainer desires or dreams of bliss
>
> My life is cold love's fire being dead
> That fire self-kindled—self-consumed
> What living warmth erewhile it shed
> Now to how drear extinction doomed!
>
> Devoid of charm how could I dream
> My unasked love would meet return?
> What fate what influence lit the flame
> I still feel inly, deeply burn?
>
> Alas there are who should not love
> I to this dreary band belong
> This knowing let me henceforth prove
> Too wise to list delusion's song

Charlotte and her Unconscious

No Syren-Beauty is not mine
Affection's joys I ne'er shall know
Lonely will be my life's decline
Even as my youth is lonely now

Come Reason—Science—Learning—Thought
To you my heart I dedicate
I have a faithful subject brought
Faithful because most desolate

Fear not a wandering feeble mind
Stern Sovereign it is all your own
To crush—to cheer to loose to bind
Unclaimed—unshared it seeks your throne

I hear your thunders forcing seas
Beyond whose waves I left all love

Soft may the breeze of summer blow
Sweetly its sun in vallies shine
All earth around with love may glow
No warmth shall reach this heart of mine

Vain boast & false even now the fire
Though smothered slacked repelled is burning
At my life's source—and stronger higher
Waxes the spirits natural yearning

It waits to be crushed again
Faint I will not, nor yield to sorrow
Conflict and force will quell the pain
Doubt not I shall be strong to-morrow

Have I not fled that I may conquer
Crost the dark sea in firmest faith
That I at last might plant my anchor
Where love cannot prevail to death

Charlotte learned early to bite on the bullet, to brace herself
for rejection and disappointment, and strenuously to seek relief
through disciplined work. When Mrs. Gaskell met her, she was
'constitutionally devoid of hope', but Mrs. Gaskell did not meet
her till after her sisters were all dead. Charlotte longed to see

the world, to meet clever people, but she also guarded her privacy. Pauline Nestor, in *Female Friendships and Communities*, usefully charts the evidence of Charlotte's ambivalences about solitude and society.[3] Nestor discusses Charlotte's abortive friendship with Harriet Martineau and her movement towards, and then away from, Julia Kavanagh.[4] Nestor notes:

> The two women were hardly fellow-thinkers, and Kavanagh's theories of a distinctively feminine prose with 'three great redeeming qualities . . . Delicacy, Tenderness and Sympathy', for example, would have been anathema to Brontë, who steadfastly resisted all notion of separate standards for male and female writers.[5]

Margaret Drabble, addressing the Brontë Society in 1974, observed that it was

> only in the nineteenth century that the notion of the writer as exile, out of key with his times, a misfit in the world of action, became popular. Byron, so much admired by the Brontës, was largely responsible for this concept. . . .[6]

Drabble adds, 'I would accept, personally, the Freudian view of art as a sublimation of the pains of life; very few writers are happy, and some, when they become happy, stop writing altogether.' If unhappiness be the food of fiction, Charlotte, who wrote to W. S. Williams on 31 August 1849, 'the deep, real tragedy of our domestic experience is yet terribly fresh', had plenty to chew on, though she complained in another letter to the same recipient (21 September 1849), 'It would be difficult to explain to you how little actual experience I have had of life, how few persons I have known, and how very few have known me.' To G. H. Lewes, she wrote on 12 January 1848:

> . . . my stock of materials is not abundant, but very slender; and, besides, neither my experience, my acquirements, nor my powers, are sufficiently varied to justify my ever becoming a frequent writer. . . . If I ever *do* write another book, I think I will have nothing of what you call 'melodrama'; I think so, but I am not sure. . . .

'One cannot doubt', says Drabble, 'that Charlotte felt she was unjustly denied the richness of experience that her talents demanded, and bitterly resented the denial.'[7]

One thinks of the list of painters whose work she wished to see drawn up by Charlotte at the age of 13: 'Guido Reni, Julio Romano, Titian, Raphael, Michael Angelo, Coreggio, Annibal Caracci, Leonardo da Vinci, Fra Bartolommeo, Carlo Cignani, Vandyke, Rubens, Bartolomeo Ramerghi.'

She got this list, of course, from her reading in the Annuals and literary journals, but it is still pretty impressive for a girl of 13. How many girls her age, today, with the advantages of colour television, art books, postcard reproductions, could produce a list anything like it?

Then there is the letter to Ellen, written while Charlotte was drudging as a governess at £20 a year (minus £4 for her laundry), while her brother Branwell was earning £130 a year as a railway clerk at Luddenden Foot:

> Mary's letters spoke of some of the pictures and cathedrals she had seen—pictures the most exquisite—and cathedrals the most venerable—I hardly know what swelled to my throat as I read her letter: such a vehement impatience of restraint and steady work. Such a strong wish for wings—wings such as wealth can furnish—such an urgent wish to see—to know—to learn—something internal seemed to expand boldly for a minute—I was tantalised with the consciousness of faculties unexercised—then all collapsed and I despaired ... I have no natural knack for my vocation ... it is the living in other people's houses—the estrangement from one's real character—the adoption of a cold frigid apathetic exterior that is painful. ... (7 August 1841)

In youth, she longed for wings. After her sisters died, she complained constantly in her letters about the isolation and monotony of her life alone with Papa, yet she clung to the walls of Haworth like an agoraphobic. It was her father who persuaded her to visit the Kay-Shuttleworths (Charlotte did not really like Sir James, but Papa felt he was a useful contact). She oscillated between the desire to escape and the making of excuses not to.

Charlotte's early struggle is pathetically revealed in her correspondence with Southey, who squelched her literary ambition (letter headed 'Keswick, March 1837') with the stern warning that 'the daydreams in which you habitually indulge are likely to induce a distempered state of mind ... literature cannot be the business of a woman's life, and it ought not to be.'

Her 'proper duties' when she became a wife would take up all her time. However, he encouraged her to go on writing poetry 'for its own sake' rather than for fame. Charlotte's initial letter to the great man is lost, but he thought the second one worth keeping.

Charlotte's reply is apologetic, squirming with the embarrassment of one who has shown her feelings too openly. She writes, revealingly, that she is careful to avoid any appearance of 'preoccupation and eccentricity'.

> Following my father's advice . . . I have endeavoured not only attentively to observe all the duties a woman ought to fulfil, but to feel deeply interested in them. I don't always succeed, for sometimes when I'm teaching or sewing I would rather be reading or writing; but I try to deny myself; and my father's approbation amply rewarded me for the privation.

Charlotte was 21, and still unhealthily dependent on her father's approval. She abases herself to Southey, thanking him for the punishment he has administered:

Roe Head, March 16th, 1837

> . . . I trust I shall never more feel ambitious to see my name in print; if the wish should rise, I'll look at Southey's letter, and suppress it . . . your advice shall not be wasted, however sorrowfully and reluctantly it may at first be followed.

So writing, for Charlotte, was an act of rebellion against the authority of Papa and of the Poet Laureate himself. Literature itself was part of the patriarchal pressure against the assertion of her true self in the exercise of her brilliant talents. The cost of breaking their prohibition was her migraines and her depressions.

It is time to consider, briefly, Charlotte's relationship to the male sex. It was Maria, the eldest child, whose cleverness engaged the affectionate attention of Papa. Charlotte, third in the family, never enjoyed that exclusive parental attention which is the privilege of the eldest. Soon she was supplanted by the unique son of the family, and significantly her only memory of her mother was a mental picture of Mrs. Brontë sitting with Branwell, the supplanter, on her lap. Branwell was followed by Emily ('the prettiest') and Anne, who grew up 'like twins', inseparable. When she was 9, Charlotte's elder sisters were swept away, and Charlotte, a 'middle child' if ever there was

96

one, had to assume motherly responsibility for the little ones, without ever having had the confidence-building idolization that is the birthright of the eldest child. She knew herself to be plain and puny. Nobody petted her; her aunt's favourite was Branwell. Charlotte could only hope to win approval by being good. M. Heger taught her that a woman could win approval by being clever (and this was perhaps his greatest gift to her). Charlotte's letters after her brother and sisters were all dead are full of solicitude for 'Papa', who showed her no gratitude for staying at home, instead of settling in London or emigrating to New Zealand, like Mary Taylor. Mr. Brontë made demands on Charlotte to cheer him when depressed, nurse him when ill. When threatened with the intrusion of Nicholls into the parsonage as Charlotte's husband, Papa behaved like the leader of the primeval herd. His veins stood out like whipcord and he swore he would allow no other man in the house while he was alive. As for Branwell, in their teens he was Charlotte's beloved collaborator, though her account of him as 'Patrick Benjamin Wiggins', written when she was 18, shows a shrewd insight into his weaknesses, which were soon to become hideously apparent. There were few young men for the girls to mix with; as John Maynard notes, the Brontë girls were expected, like their generation, to move from all-girl boarding schools into readiness for adult marriage. The lesson Charlotte learned was that to earn the approval of the male, a woman had to be domesticated and dutiful, and suppress her ambition. We have noted already the absence of studies for women in the parsonage, home of three women novelists.

Charlotte's unhappiness was compounded by guilt at being discontented, as her letters show. Resentful of woman's lot in her day, she did not find the current model of radical feminism, Harriet Martineau, congenial.

Many critics, including Malham-Dembleby (see p. 26), have believed Charlotte incapable of writing about men except to portray her father and her brother over and over again. The first person to 'psychoanalyse' Charlotte retrospectively was Lucile Dooley, who says 'M. Heger answered every requirement of the father-fixation'.[8] The Freudian Dooley was the first to suggest that Charlotte's death was the result of unconscious conflict.

97

Barbara Hannah, a Jungian, writes, in *Striving Towards Wholeness*, that like most girls with a strong father complex, Charlotte always experienced great difficulty in her relationships with men. More than one man wanted to marry her, but, as she wrote in a letter, her 'veins ran ice' at one such approach. Hannah agrees with C. W. Hatfield that M. Heger's being married made him a safe object for her affections. 'Not that Charlotte . . . was incapable of passion; on the contrary, passion was evidently such a burning force in her that she was terrified of it.'[9] Hannah believes that Charlotte's 'animus, or unconscious mind' was responsible for her writing as a man. Interestingly, Hannah sees Charlotte's early writing as 'archetypal', quoting Jung's 'Archetypes speak the language of high rhetoric, even bombast.' For Hannah, *Jane Eyre* is 'a happy mixture of Charlotte's earlier unchecked outpourings of the unconscious and the almost complete repression . . . in *The Professor*'.[10] Charlotte identifies with her plain heroines, Jane and Lucy, says Hannah, noting that Charlotte told Mrs. Gaskell that Jane's dream of carrying a restless baby in some gloomy place was a life-long recurring dream of her own, always preceding trouble. For Hannah, it is 'psychologically very interesting' that Charlotte died in pregnancy. Hannah also observes shrewdly that Charlotte was 'fond of power', though this was 'covered over . . . by a . . . modest and unassuming persona'.[11]

It was Adler, once as famous as Freud and Jung, now forgotten, who saw the will to power as the human motive force. A similar insight into the urge to power has been popularized by another channel, that of Marxist criticism. Terry Eagleton writes that Charlotte's characters want independence, but they also desire to dominate, and their 'desire to dominate is matched only by their impulse to submit to a superior will'.[12] The idea is developed in his *Myths of Power: A Marxist Study of the Brontës*:

> Because the heroine finds both solace and perverse stimulation in her superior, the final resolution contains a contention between them which fulfils several ends. It underwrites the heroine's impulse for independent identity in a depersonalising world; it allows her to vent a suppressed resentment of the other which is for the most part a function of class-bitterness; and it thereby partly purges her of the guilt of rebelliousness. . . . The heroine's

lonely *self*-reproval is replaced by a glad submission to the censorings of a soul-mate—censorings which stimulate rather than crush the spirit.[13]

Charlotte's novels thus embody rebellion, self-justification for that rebellion, and its reward. He overstates the 'submission', but is right in saying that embedded in Charlotte's work are two ambiguous, internally divided, sets of values, 'rationality, coolness, shrewd self-seeking, energetic individualism, radical protest and rebellion', against 'piety, submission, culture, tradition, conservatism'. For Eagleton, the novels are 'myths' working towards a balance or fusion of

> bourgeois rationality and flamboyant Romanticism . . . passionate rebellion and cautious conformity . . . and those interchanges embody a complex structure of convergence and antagonism between the landed and industrial sectors of the contemporary ruling class.[14]

Eagleton points out that the sisters were directly trapped in the educational machinery set up by the rich to exploit the sons and daughters of the 'genteel' poor. As governesses they moved as servants into the cultivated society to which they naturally should have belonged.

The bitter remarks of Mrs. Pryor, in *Shirley*, are Charlotte's revenge on the employers she felt had trampled on her. Mrs. Pryor quotes a Miss H.: 'WE,' she would say,—'We need the imprudencies, extravagancies, mistakes, and crimes of a certain number of fathers to sow the seed from which WE reap the harvest of governesses. . . . WE shall ever prefer to place those about OUR offspring, who have been born and bred with somewhat of the same refinement as OURSELVES.' (*Shirley*, Ch. 21)

Mrs. Pryor is quoting almost *verbatim* from the *Quarterly Review*, 84 (December 1848), '*Vanity Fair*—and *Jane Eyre*'. Charlotte's irony at the callousness which is complacent about family disaster as productive of a pool of cheap labour is savage. Caroline Helstone, who is not even allowed to go out to work as a governess, is bitterly conscious that she 'has no power' (*Shirley*, Ch. 13).

Freudian critiques, however, have predominated. Martin S. Day's essay, scorned by Burkhart as 'the abysses of psychological

criticism',[15] makes sense to me. Day points out that to the
proper Victorian mama with a nubile daughter, St. John Rivers
would appear as an 'ideal husband', but Jane has to choose
between the man who is 'wrong in all save love, and the man
who is right in all save love'.[16] Day interprets the conclusion of
Jane Eyre as an apology on Jane's part for not accepting the
'handsome, pious Rivers'. He notes that Rochester and St. John
are 'both domineering males'.[17] Day quotes Mrs. Fairfax
(Ch. 24), 'He might almost be your father.'[18] Rochester 'offers
the father's rôle. . . . The chief reason . . . for the existence of the
madwoman is to prevent Jane from entering into the wrong
partnership with Rochester'; the madwoman's existence is
Charlotte's 'excuse'.[19] Day points out that at the end, Jane is
the parent and Rochester the child,[20] which is patently true.

Peter Coveney, in *Poor Monkey* (1957), and Helene Moglen, in
Charlotte Brontë: The Self Conceived (1976), took up Dooley's and
Rosamond Langbridge's suggestion that Charlotte was a masochist. Coveney accuses Jane of 'enjoying masochistically, the
experiences of her persecution. . . . Everything is carefully prepared for the extended sado-masochistic relation between Jane
and Rochester. . . . [Jane] is indeed pathetic, a victim—but not
quite in the way Charlotte Brontë intended us to sympathise
with her.'[21] Mr. Coveney, whose own syntax is not beyond
reproach, accuses Jane of 'neurotic speech-rhythm'.

As others have done, Moglen notes Charlotte's attraction to
her employer, Mr. Sidgwick, in a letter to Ellen (8 June 1839):

> . . . I had orders to follow a little behind. As he strolled through
> his fields, with his magnificent Newfoundland dog at his side, he
> looked very like what a frank, wealthy Conservative gentleman
> ought to be.

Moglen's book is marred by mis-spellings (Sidgwick becomes
'Sedgewick', Bertha 'Berthe', for example). She concludes that
Charlotte married 'a father-substitute',[22] to which one might
reply that all marriages by women are to father-substitutes.
'Rejecting Branwell she could reject her own humiliation and
guilt';[23] Charlotte wrote 'priggish' letters about him. Moglen
shows no understanding of what life can have been like in the
cramped, poverty-stricken parsonage, with a crazed, drunken
opium-addict. What infuriated Charlotte was Branwell's refusal

to work or even to look for a job, in a household where money was short. Branwell was a parasite on his father (with a stipend of £200 a year) and on his sisters. As a man he could command far more than they could for the same work as household private tutor. He was 'a drain on every resource' and his tantrums were unbearable. Moglen elides these practical miseries into a psychological problem for Charlotte:

> Charlotte's renewal was made possible by Branwell's dis-integration. Her own obsession, her guilt, her humiliation were given concrete form in Branwell's illicit affair with Lydia Robinson. Heger's rejection was acted out in Lydia's denial. And in Branwell's long and terrible decline, *there* was the punishment which she would never have to accept.[24]

This is a plausible theory, which may be accepted or rejected. That Charlotte was given to self-laceration is indubitable. For Moglen, Charlotte's attachment to the unattainable Heger provided an 'outlet for [her] masochistic tendencies'. Why did not Charlotte leave Brussels? demands Moglen. One answer might be that in Brussels Charlotte had a job, though she did turn down an offer of £50 a year in order to stay there.

Geoffrey Wagner, in *Five for Freedom* (1971), finds *Jane Eyre* 'a profoundly and healthily s-m fiction'; he points out that Jane tells Rochester that he will not consent 'to cut your bonds till you have signed a charter',[25] and suspects that Charlotte had a more than passing interest in flagellation,[26] an opinion endorsed later by Elaine Showalter.[27] Neither critic mentions the fragment, *Willie Ellin*, which indeed reads like the pornography of flagellation: blows are repeatedly rained down on Willie's thin, quivering shoulders by his brutal brother. As has often been noted, brutal brothers (John Reed, Edward Crimsworth) recur in Charlotte's fictions. Whether or not Charlotte's interest in beatings was prurient or morbid, it must be remembered that ritual beating was the standard punishment in Britain until recently.

Frederick Karl (1976) saw the Brontës as 'voyeurs'.[28] Karl's comments are broad and general; he does not distinguish among the sisters or among the novels. For him Brontë characters 'live lives of enclosure and perpetual peering'.[29] Much of the action is 'interior-directed'. This expression is puzzling: is there some confusion with David Reismann's once-fashionable labels, 'inner-directed' and 'other-directed'? Karl believes that the action of 'Brontë novels' takes place

> in enclosed spaces, because they were, as females, themselves enclosed and restricted, limited in whatever social movement they were allowed to schools, houses, positions as teachers and governesses.[30]

This is to argue that because the lives were cramped, so are the novels; Karl's statements are nonsense. The action of *Wuthering Heights* is not enclosed; much of the action of *Jane Eyre*, *Shirley* and even *Villette* occurs in gardens, open country, streets, a park. Karl writes:

> Much of the Brontë ambiguity . . . lies in the oscillation between female identity, a fierce desire for a unique self, and the demands of the other side of the female appetite, the urgency of fulfilment by a male, and frequently not a particularly sympathetic or pro-feminist male.[31]

This has no application to Emily's or Anne's novels. Karl does not get us very far. The idea of the Brontës as 'voyeurs'[32] is, however, elegantly developed by Robert Keefe in *Charlotte Brontë's World of Death* (1979). Keefe also argues persuasively that Charlotte spent her life trying to expiate guilt for the deaths of her mother and sisters, and that her death, at the same age as her mother's, is significant.

Annette Schreiber, in 'The Myth in Charlotte Brontë', agrees with Moglen that her heroines marry father-surrogates.[33] In *Jane Eyre*, *Shirley* and *Villette*, each heroine 'rejects a sensible, stable, accessible suitor' and marries, or intends to marry, an irascible, tormented, ruthlessly masculine Byronic figure, 'all standing in paternal relationship by virtue of age or occupation'.[34] This is not true: Louis Moore is too colourless to be compared with Rochester and M. Paul; Robert is 'accessible' to Shirley, but is he sensible and stable? Lucy does not reject John Bretton: she is forced to recognize that she stands no chance. The heroines' marriages, says Schreiber, are 'blocked by other women'.[35] Jane's and Lucy's are, but nobody is blocking Shirley's choice (Schreiber takes it for granted that the eponymous Shirley must be the heroine). The heroines, says Schreiber, are all successful, independent and powerful:

the men reappear wounded and maimed, stripped symbolically of their manly rôle and sexuality, literally controlled and dependent on the heroine. . . . Frances refuses marriage until she is financially . . . independent. . . . Louis Moore gives up his job and moves in to his wife's house and money. . . . Paul emerges with the ultimate wound, the final castration, death.[36]

The endings all show 'a castrated submissive male subservient to a powerful and controlling female'.[37] Charlotte's vision is 'destructive, self-destructive and tragic'.[38]

Schreiber's carelessness is not confined to over-confident generalizations about plot; she writes of 'Rosalind' Oliver and the critic 'Richard' Heilman (literally, as the proverb has it, taking Richard for Robert).

Margaret Blom writes that while Charlotte depicts unmated women as psychically unhealthy and psychologically crippled, they can only respond to a male whose ability and willingness to control them, are in part sadistic, so that Jane Eyre, Caroline Helstone and Lucy Snowe rightly fear what they seek.

> The identification of passion with masochism and sadism is central to all of Brontë's works, appearing first in the juvenilia in the extended discussions of Zamorna's psychological brutalising of his wife and mistresses, and recurring in the violent battles of wills that characterise her adult novels.[39]

When Charlotte married, Mrs. Gaskell wrote to John Forster (23 April 1854) 'she would never have been happy but with an exacting, rigid, law-giving, passionate man. . . .' When she died, Peter Bayne wrote:

> But a few months ago we heard of her marriage. We learned, with a smile of happy surprise, that the merciless derider of weak and insipid suitors *had found a lord and master.* . . .

We may find ourselves wondering, with John Maynard, how could we ever have valued 'such a psychological freak for her art or insight'?[40]

NOTES

1. Cited Peters, *Unquiet Soul*, p. 289 (paperback edn.).
2. Patrick Brontë, '*Cottage Poems*', repr. in *Brontëana*, ed. J. Horsfall Turner, p. 56.
3. Pauline Nestor, *Female Friendships and Communities*, pp. 83–103.
4. Ibid., pp. 87–90.
5. Ibid., p. 87.
6. Margaret Drabble, 'The Writer as Recluse; The Theme of Solitude in the Works of the Brontë's, *B.S.T.*, 16 (1974), 259.
7. Ibid., 263.
8. Lucile Dooley, 'Psychoanalysis of Charlotte Brontë as a Type of the Woman of Genius', *American Journal of Psychology*, 31 (1920), 250.
9. Barbara Hannah, *Striving Towards Wholeness*, p. 131.
10. Ibid., p. 135.
11. Ibid., p. 121.
12. Terry Eagleton, 'Class, Power and Charlotte Brontë', *Critical Quarterly*, 14 (Autumn 1972), 233.
13. Eagleton, *Myths of Power*, p. 75.
14. Ibid., p. 4.
15. Charles Burkhart, *Charlotte Brontë: A Psychosexual Study of her Novels*, bibliography.
16. Martin Day, 'Central Concepts of *Jane Eyre*', *Personalist*, 41 (October 1960), 496–97.
17. Ibid., 498.
18. Ibid., 500.
19. Ibid., 503.
20. Ibid., 504.
21. Peter Coveney, *Poor Monkey* (repr. as *The Image of Childhood*, 1967), p. 107.
22. Helene Moglen, *Charlotte Brontë: The Self Conceived*, p. 238.
23. Ibid., p. 56.
24. Ibid., p. 75.
25. Geoffrey Wagner, *Five for Freedom*, p. 131.
26. Ibid., p. 132.
27. Elaine Showalter, *A Literature of their Own*, p. 116.
28. Frederick R. Karl, 'The Brontës: The Self Defined, Redefined and Reredefined', in *The Victorian Experience: The Novelists*, ed. Richard Lavine (Athens: Ohio University Press, 1976), p. 123.
29. Ibid., p. 124.
30. Ibid.
31. Ibid., p. 129.
32. Robert Keefe, *Charlotte Brontë's World of Death*, p. 4.
33. Annette Schreiber, 'The Myth in Charlotte Brontë', *Literature and Psychology*, 18:1 (1968), 48.
34. Ibid., 49.
35. Ibid., 50.
36. Ibid.

37. Ibid.
38. Ibid., 48.
39. Margaret A. Blom, 'Charlotte Brontë, Feminist Manquée', *Bucknell Review*, 21 (Spring 1973), 100.
40. John Maynard, *Charlotte Brontë and Sexuality*, p. 32. He writes that psycho-biographers have 'tended so often to a belittling fatalism . . . neurotic, psychotic, masochistic, sadistic, traumatized, obsessive, infantile, narcissistic: incurably this or that'.

8

Jane Eyre

> A book is more than a verbal structure or series of verbal
> structures; it is the dialogue it establishes with its reader and the
> intonation it imposes upon his voice and the changing and
> durable images it leaves on his memory. . . . Literature is not
> exhaustible for the simple and sufficient reason that no book is. A
> book is not an isolated entity: it is a relationship, an axis of
> innumerable relationships.—Jorge Luis Borges

The Brontë Museum at Haworth holds two versions of *Jane Eyre*
in comic strip form. The cover of one shows Bertha Mason,
barefoot and ragged, peering through matted black hair which
falls almost to her waist, lunging at Rochester, restrained by
Mason and Grace, while the other shows the faces of a demure
bonneted maiden and a glamorous top-hatted man. The violent
one, *Jane Eyre: Told in Pictures*, Thriller Comics, No. 31, 8d.,
starts with the arrival at Thornfield (though Gateshead and
Lowood are summarized as introduction). Adele's presence is
distorted ('I knew her dead mother, and so decided to adopt
Adele—as she was alone and penniless', these words being
spoken to Blanche Ingram). Jane wonders, 'Why, oh why is he
so sweet to me at times and yet so cruel at others?' After St.
John's proposal, we read, 'Meanwhile, back at Thornfield
Hall', which gives us the fire, death of Bertha, collapse, after
which 'Jane knew instinctively that Rochester was in trouble
and needed her. . . .' By contrast, the comic strip version which
offers a demure pair of faces to the world is presented in terms of
anodyne sweetness, and quaint 'period charm'. *Jane Eyre*,
No. 39 in Classics Illustrated, Featuring Stories by the World's
Greatest Authors, was issued twice, once in 1947, and reissued
(redrawn and retold) in 1968. The Museum has copies of both

editions. In the later one, Miss Temple looks like Bette Davis, Rochester like Robert Young, and Brocklehurst like David Niven. The different treatments are themselves critical acts, illustrating the two main ways this powerful story is perceived and received: as nightmare thriller and as consoling romance.

The dissemination of great literature in such debased forms argues its strength; a tiny handful of great works are known at popular, almost proverbial, level, to people who have not been 'taught' them in any formal way: the stories of Don Quixote tilting at a windmill, of Romeo and Juliet, of Oliver Twist asking for more (this was well known before the advent of Lionel Bart's musical, *Oliver!*), are recognizable to people who never read for pleasure. (*Frankenstein* and that by no means negligible work, *Dracula*, have taken on the qualities of nineteenth-century myth, but are special cases because of the endless film and television versions flooding the public consciousness. *Jane Eyre* is not so well known as they are.) To be among the number of those whose created works become living myth is itself prime distinction. We remember that Charlotte served her apprenticeship to literature from childhood onwards, and that she used to fascinate and terrify her fellow-pupils in the dormitory at boarding school with her nightly stories.

Queen Victoria wrote in her diary, 23 November 1880:

> Finished *Jane Eyre*, which is really a wonderful book, very peculiar in parts, but so powerfully and admirably written, such a fine tone in it, such fine religious feeling, and such beautiful writings. The description of the mysterious maniac's nightly appearances awfully thrilling. Mr. Rochester's character a very remarkable one, and Jane Eyre's herself a beautiful one. The end is very touching, when Jane Eyre returns to him and finds him blind, with one hand gone from injuries during the fire in his house, which was caused by his mad wife.

Many academic critics have written about *Jane Eyre* less sensibly than Queen Victoria, whose naïve reader response is endearingly direct. On a simple level, Victoria grasped the essentials. Modern critics have doubted the religious feeling,[1] elevated Bertha into the heroine of the novel,[2] and seen Jane Eyre as in search of, rather than in control of, her story.[3] As for the ending, critics have puzzled over it, pointing out that

Ferndean is damp, too unhealthy for Bertha to live there, but good enough for Rochester, Jane and their child.[4]

Rochester's stump of a hand (which Jane at one point says is his right, at another his left) is 'symbolic castration'.[5] All these points will be taken seriously. Lucky Queen Victoria, however, could read and enjoy, innocently, for the pleasure of the story. But she may have recognized some of its deeper meanings; she forgot that she had read the book aloud to Albert in 1858, when she found it a 'melancholy, interesting book'. What, one wonders, did she find 'peculiar'? The American feminist Adrienne Rich writes of the 'nourishment' *Jane Eyre* offers women. She quotes Q. D. Leavis's view that it is about 'how a woman comes to maturity' and quarrels with Virginia Woolf's assertion that Charlotte Brontë 'does not attempt to solve the problems of human life'.[6] Rich writes that a novel about how a man matures 'would not be dismissed as lacking in range'. I agree with Rich and other feminists that male critics have blundered over Charlotte, judging her by standards applicable to other kinds of fiction than hers. *Jane Eyre* is, in the fullest sense of the word, a woman's book. No longer need we apologize for loving it. Maurianne Adams, who has written finely on Charlotte, says adult re-reading is 'unnerving'; it is not the novel

> we were engrossed by in our teens or preteens, when we saw in Jane's dreadful childhood . . . our own fantasies of feeling unloved and forever unloveable, and of fearing that we were 'unpromising' girlchildren, whose lack of beauty and unpredictable tempers cut us off from an imaginable and acceptable future . . . the other side of that coin, which we latched on to with equal fervor and which also fed our fantasies, was the happy ending. . . .[7]

True, indeed, and important. *Jane Eyre* moulded, and moulds, expectations. (I can never go to a wedding without a tense anxiety that an impediment will be declared by a Mr. Mason-figure rushing down the aisle.) Jane Eyre has been an inspiration and example to generations of clever girls in a way which has remained unnoticed. She is the first defiantly intellectual heroine in English literature. Reading Jane Austen, we wanted to be nonchalantly brilliant like Elizabeth Bennet, whose wit seems to be a gift of fortune, not of study; we none of us wanted to be like dull pedantic Mary. (That Anne Elliot had cultural interests was a point too subtly made for me as a teenager.) But not only did Jane's story teach us that plain girls could win love; they could be swots and get away with it. The image of Diana and Mary Rivers reading German in their cottage has served as a beacon. Jane herself is literary, and Mr. Rochester, looking in disgust at his bestial, degraded wife, says to Jane that he has longed for an '*intellectual* (italics added), faithful loving woman' (Ch. 27). This consoling message that an erogenous zone might be found between the ears was counter-propaganda to the message of our culture, that men did not care for 'brainy' women. Diana and Mary and Jane found lovers; *Jane Eyre* liberated us to be bookworms and held out hope that intellectual tastes would not disqualify us from emotional fulfilment. Thank you, Charlotte, for giving us the courage to persist, to sustain our interests, often against the tide.

In *Jane Eyre*, Ch. 11, when Jane is settling in at Thornfield, she climbs up on to the battlements, quoting from *Macbeth*, looks down on the crows and surveys her world. She sees the wood 'dun and sere' (echoing Dunsinane and Macbeth's 'the sere, the yellow leaf'), turns from the outer world into the narrow garret staircase with its long passage, 'narrow, long and dim, with only one little window at the far end, and looking, with its two rows of small black doors all shut, like a corridor in some Bluebeard's castle'. A Bluebeard's castle it is indeed, but the image is also that of a prison, thrown into relief by the world outside, which Jane can only look at. Thinking of Bluebeard, she hears the laugh of the madwoman who has been locked up for ever. The next section introduces the note of feminist rebellion which has been considered 'irrelevant' to the narrative.[8] Jane complains of boredom, invites the reader to judge her case by asking, 'Who blames me?' (Ch. 12) and bursts out:

> It is vain to say human beings ought to be satisfied with tranquillity: they must have action; and they will make it if they cannot find it. Millions are condemned to a stiller doom than mine, and millions are in silent revolt against their lot. Nobody knows how many rebellions besides political rebellions ferment in the masses of life which people earth. Women are supposed to be very calm generally: but women feel just as men feel; they need exercise for their faculties, and a field for their efforts as

much as their brothers do; they suffer from too rigid a restraint, too absolute a stagnation, precisely as men would suffer; and it is narrow-minded in their more privileged fellow-creatures to say that they ought to confine themselves to making puddings and knitting stockings, to playing on the piano and embroidering bags. It is thoughtless to condemn them, or laugh at them, if they seek to do more or learn more than custom has pronounced necessary for their sex.

Charlotte has matured since the time, ten years earlier, when she felt compelled to lie to herself and to the pinnacle of the literary establishment that she tried to be 'deeply interested' in such humdrum things.

And in the next paragraph Jane tells us she often hears 'Grace Poole's laugh', the unwitting mockery of the madwoman locked up.

When Mr. Rochester erupts into Thornfield, bringing life and activity with him, the females are banished from the intellectual centre of the house, which is put to alternative use, taken over for trivial social purposes: 'Adele and I had now to vacate the library: it would be in daily requisition as a reception-room for callers.' A fire is lit in an upstairs apartment, and Jane has to carry their books up there. No wonder she has fears, during Mr. Rochester's possessive and domineering courtship, of losing her autonomy.

In a footnote to a paper called 'Deserts, Ruins and Troubled Waters: Female Dreams in Fiction and the Development of the Gothic Novel', Margaret Anne Doody writes:

> Conversations with women of various ages have led me to believe that dreams of fear are extremely common before marriage, and are quite separate from fear (if any) of sex. Young women who have had pre-marital sex, often for some years, with the men they intend to marry, seem to be just as much afflicted with nightmare prior to marriage as were women of a previous generation who went virgin to the bridal, and their fear-dreams embody the same images.[9]

Jane Eyre is 'smitten' and 'stunned' by 'almost fear' at the thought of becoming Jane Rochester. She wonders who 'Jane Rochester' is. Maurianne Adams writes that *Jane Eyre*, like other novels about women, 'traces the competing and possibly irreconcilable needs for perpetual love and perpetual autonomy'.[10]

She notes that the relationship with Rochester is characterized by a pervasive 'word-play' on 'master' and 'governess' in what appears to be, in part at least, Jane's struggle for self-mastery and self-governance at Thornfield. Even more, she struggles, after the engagement, not to have her identity submerged by his 'despotism' (Ch. 24). Engaged to Jane, Rochester tells her he has sent for the family jewels. Jane finds the idea 'unnatural and strange' (Ch. 24), but he refuses to listen, and talks about diamonds and bracelets and rings, talk which makes Jane squirm and protest she is 'your plain Quakerish governess'. He ignores her protests, and insists that the world shall 'acknowledge you a beauty' and promises he will attire her in satin: 'I will cover the head I love best with a priceless veil.'

Jane complains that this will turn her into a 'jay in borrowed plumes' (see my Chapter 3 for discussion of the significance of 'plumes' in the novel). Eventually, he takes her shopping and tries to buy her half a dozen dresses, which she manages to cut down to two. He chooses bright, fashionable garments, which she persuades him to change for a black satin and a pearl-grey silk, but he insists he will have her 'glittering like a parterre'. 'The more he bought me, the more my cheek burned with a sense of annoyance and degradation.' She regrets her own poverty, reflecting that she 'never can bear being dressed like a doll by Mr. Rochester, or sitting like a second Danae with the golden shower falling daily round me'. It is in this mood of resentment against possessive, insensitive, domineering male patronage that she sees his self-satisfied smile, 'such as a sultan might, in a blissful and fond moment, bestow on a slave his gold and gems had enriched'. She threatens to dress in gingham and her old Lowood frocks, which makes Rochester chuckle and rub his hands. 'I would not exchange this one little English girl for the Grand Turk's whole seraglio—gazelle eyes, houri forms and all!' The Eastern allusion stings Jane into retorting that if a seraglio is what he wants, 'away with you, sir, to the bazaars of Stamboul . . . and lay out in extensive slave-purchases some of that spare cash. . . .' She threatens, in jest, to go out as a missionary to 'preach liberty to them that are enslaved—your harem inmates amongst the rest'. She will 'stir up mutiny' and have him 'fettered' until he signs a charter 'the most liberal that despot ever conferred'. Jane insists that she must continue to earn her bread as Adele's governess until her marriage, though Rochester tells her, 'You will give up your governessing slavery at once.' He listens tolerantly, and says, 'It is your time now, little tyrant, but it will be mine presently.' Later, when he sings to her, she tells him she has no intention of 'dying with him': it is a pagan idea. All this sparring is linked thematically to Jane's assertion of spiritual equality with Rochester. He may accept spiritual equality, but unconsciously continues to assert social, sexual and economic superiority, oblivious of her humiliation. After the *débacle*, he tells her, 'Hiring a mistress is the next worse thing to buying a slave. . . .' (Ch. 27). He has learned enough wisdom to see Thornfield as 'this tent of Achan' (Ch. 27). The Clarendon *Jane Eyre* offers no gloss. The story of Achan, whose tent was found to be full of stolen gold and silver, is in Joshua 7:20–6. Thornfield is full of tainted gold, brought by Bertha. When Rochester is finally tamed and humbled, he tells Jane they will be married three days hence: 'Never mind fine clothes and jewels, now: all that is not worth a fillip.'

Peter A. Tasch, in an intriguing short paper, 'Jane Eyre's "Three-tailed Bashaw" ',[11] points out other thematic links: Charlotte was echoing a refrain of a song from an extravaganza *Blue-Beard* (1798), while the idea of an English girl in the 'Grand Turk's seraglio' asking for liberty comes from another stage comedy, 'The Sultan: or, a Peep into the Seraglio' (1775), performed in 1817 at Drury Lane.

R. J. Dingley notes that nobody has picked up the reference in Ch. 14, the incorporation of a phrase 'a man and a brother' in Rochester's speech to Jane about the 'Lowood constraint' still clinging to her. Dingley[12] points out that the expression 'alludes to the seal of the Slave Emancipation Society', which depicted a kneeling negro surrounded by the plea, 'Am I not a man and a brother?' This Wedgwood design was reproduced on various articles, including snuffboxes and ornamental hairpins. Dingley reads the reference as an implication that Rochester is Jane's slave, and that the use is tantamount to 'an avowal of his sudden passion for Jane'. Perhaps: it seems to me more likely an example of Rochester's theoretically liberal stance towards a paid employee, a stance he fails to maintain once he is in prospect of possessing her as his wife. Jane claims 'equality', but

Rochester is not yet liberated enough from the conventions of his sex and caste truly to grant it.

Anthea Zeman writes, 'Charlotte Brontë writes of love, they say, immune to her yearning for money and work.'[13] Richard Chase sees *Jane Eyre* as 'a feminist tract, an argument for the social betterment of governesses and equal rights for women'.[14] This is not altogether true: Charlotte shows no sign, in *Jane Eyre*, of wanting better treatment for governesses; she wants women to have enough money not to have to be governesses or village schoolmistresses (even lower socially, in Jane's opinion). Somebody else will have to do this dreary work, a problem Jane does not face. Jane's accession to an unearned fortune, made off the backs of slaves in the West Indies and therefore as tainted as Bertha's, is an admission of despair on Charlotte's part, and deeply reactionary. It signals recognition (as does the fairy-tale 'Puss in Boots') that hard work and thrift are not enough in themselves for upward mobility; only magic, fairy gold, a win on the pools, can raise the lowly to eminence. So long as she and her sisters (the real ones, Emily and Anne; the imaginary cousins, Diana and Mary, sister-substitutes) escape, Charlotte shows no concern for those left behind to toil in schoolrooms.

The questions to be asked about *Jane Eyre* are: is it a great novel, and, if so, what makes it so? Let us consider the question of impact. *Jane Eyre* is uniquely memorable in its detail and its plot. Two early numbers of the *Brontë Society Transactions* attest this. Sir Charles Eliot, Vice-Chancellor of Sheffield University, presiding at the meeting held on 18 January 1908, at Sheffield, said he was coming home to Europe from Uganda down the Nile on a gunboat when it broke down. Trapped in a swamp, he had nothing to do but read. Stuck there with Scott, Dickens, Thackeray, George Eliot and the Brontës, he read them all through. 'He had no doubt that the novel which stood out best in his memory was *Jane Eyre*', which he considered better than *The Mill on the Floss*. (Mrs. Leavis was to endorse this opinion later.) In *Transactions*, 5 (1913), we read that Mr. Thomas Seccombe recommended *Jane Eyre* as an 'anodyne' against the rheumatism of the hands he had recently suffered. Interestingly, he said he did not have such a high opinion of *Shirley*, but when he was living in Rome, a friend told him that while an Italian version was running as a serial in the evening papers, the servant girls found it so absorbing that 'they were becoming quite demoralised in regard to ordinary household duties'. (Dangerous stuff, this fiction of Charlotte's.) 'I know of no work of prose', said Mr. Seccombe, 'the rapidity of which is so marvellously sustained as in *Jane Eyre*.' This is perfectly true: neither *Jane Eyre* nor *Wuthering Heights* contains a word of padding.

The Gateshead and Lowood sections are read over and over again by children, because Charlotte evokes so wonderfully the feelings of being small, powerless, misunderstood, punished. *Jane Eyre* and its heir, *David Copperfield*, describe childhood feelings in a way children can understand, recognize and identify with. The immediacy of the descriptions and the speed of the action hold the attention, despite an extensive vocabulary. Notwithstanding the competing attractions of television, *Jane Eyre* is still read and deeply enjoyed by small girls.

Melvin R. Watson writes that it has a tighter plot structure than the other novels by Charlotte.[15] Its effect is one of epigrammatic concentration and stylized concreteness. Its palette suggests almost heraldic colours: indoors we meet black and white, red, gold and purple; outside the walls, the world of external nature is green. The view in the book of nature and its healing powers is Wordsworthian, but behind it is Shakespeare's 'great creating nature', the regenerative nature we find in *The Winter's Tale*, a fable which underpins, of course, both *Wuthering Heights* and *Silas Marner*. In *The Winter's Tale* a man's love is restored to him after he has sinned and repented; Jane's restoration to Rochester at Ferndean, when he recognizes her by sound and touch, owes something to Leontes's dazed and gladsome recognition of Hermione, the living statue. *Jane Eyre* is permeated with Shakespearean parallels, Shakespearean reference. Soaking through it is a submerged pattern of allusion to another Shakespeare play, dealing with lawless love and sexual passion.

Shakespeare's *Antony and Cleopatra* is a play about adultery. *Jane Eyre* is a novel about an attempted adultery. Antony, like Rochester, has a wife he does not love and another woman he does love. Antony, like Rochester, has made a marriage of convenience. Antony's conflict is between 'love' and 'duty', 'passion' and 'reason'. The conflict in *Jane Eyre* is transferred to the woman. Both play and novel contrast the hardness of the external world with the fluidity of emotion. In *Jane Eyre* we have seen the images of fire and air and water contrasted with marble, rock and stone. The phrase 'fire and air' comes from Cleopatra's dying speech (Act 5, sc. ii):

> I am fire and air; my other elements
> I give to baser life.

Committing suicide in the 'high Roman fashion', Cleopatra describes herself as having nothing

> of woman in me: now from head to foot
> I am marble-constant.

Cleopatra's love for Antony is heavily sensual and sexual; when Antony has returned to Rome, after Fulvia's death, Cleopatra, after the fashion of women, frets at his absence:

> Oh Charmian:
> Where think'st thou he is now? Stands he, or sits he?
> Or does he walk? Or is he on his horse?
> Oh happy horse to bear the weight of Antony!
> . . . Now I feed myself
> With most delicious poison. . . . (Act 1, sc. v)

Charlotte would not have allowed herself the frank physicality of 'happy horse to bear the weight', but at their first meeting Jane does bear Rochester's weight, when he falls from his horse. Later, he is always taking her hand between both of his, and he finally recognizes her at Ferndean by *feeling* her body to confirm that it is really she. St. John's sensual dream of Rosamond is dismissed by him as 'delicious poison' (Ch. 32). Rochester, like Antony, is a mature virile man, with many affairs behind him. Jane teases Rochester as Cleopatra teases Antony; while Cleopatra is a queen and Jane a poor governess, they are both anxious to keep their lovers on the boil. Cleopatra's sexuality is split off on to Bertha, while Jane remains ethereal and virginal, a sprite, an imp, an elf: anything but a real woman, in Rochester's eyes. But Jane is Rochester's temptation, just as Cleopatra is Antony's. The adultery motif is subtly signalled in Ch. 24, after the engagement. Rochester says, 'I lay that pleasant unction to my soul, Jane, a belief in your affection.' Hamlet warns his mother, the adulteress, not to lay the 'pleasant unction' of self-deception to her soul 'that not your trespass, but my madness speaks'.

Many of Charlotte's allusions are submerged. For example, only after the rejection of Rosamond (who loves him), does St. John become associated with ice. He first starts persuading Jane (who is still tormented at night by dreams of being in Mr. Rochester's arms (Ch. 32)) towards learning Hindustani in preparation for missionary work at Christmas time, when there are snowdrifts outside. Looking back, we remember the blighting of Jane's true love as if by:

> ... a Christmas frost ... at midsummer; a white December storm had whirled over June; ice glazed the ripe apples, drifts crushed the blowing roses; on hayfield and cornfield lay a frozen shroud; lanes which last night blushed full of flowers, today were pathless with untrodden snow; and the woods, which twelve hours since waved leafy and fragrant as groves between the tropics, now spread, waste, wild, and white as pine-forests in wintry Norway. (Ch. 26)

This remarkable metaphorical passage is on the same scale as the Homeric similes familiar to Charlotte from Milton. We may hesitate over ripe apples in June, but the image is of fruitfulness blighted by unseasonable weather. Concrete and specific, it is also highly literary, carrying echoes of *A Midsummer Night's Dream* (Act 2, sc. ii), where, due to a failure in married love between the nature-spirits Oberon and Titania,

> The seasons alter: hoary-headed frosts
> Fall in the fresh lap of the crimson rose,
> And on old Hiems thin and icy crown
> An odorous chaplet of sweet summer buds
> Is, as in mockery, set.

The full complexity of Charlotte's poetic imagery in this novel has never been fully examined: C. A. Linder's book, *Romantic Imagery in the Novels of Charlotte Brontë*, did not dig deeply.[16] So rich and thick are motifs that *Jane Eyre* must be read as we read a Shakespeare play: we must attend to the narrative, but we must also respond to a rich and powerfully controlled poetry. Scott made description, formerly confined to poetry, a part of the novel. It is easy for us to forget how important literary description was in the days when most people (unlike us, who

116

are bombarded with images in full colour) were starved of pictures, when woodcuts and black-and-white engravings were treasures. Charlotte was the first novelist to introduce to her descriptions detailed accounts of the weather and the skies, a technique learned from Bernardin de St. Pierre. Her originality is undervalued. Virginia Woolf's grudging appreciation comes to a true conclusion:

> It is the red and fitful glow of the heart's fire which illumines her page. . . . We read Charlotte Brontë not for exquisite observation of character—her characters are vigorous and elementary; not for comedy—hers is grim and crude; not for a philosophic view of life—hers is that of a parson's daughter, but for her poetry. (*The Common Reader*)

NOTES

1. See Annette Tromly, *The Cover of the Mask*, p. 53; cf. Benvenuto, Margaret A. Blom, R. E. Hughes.
2. Gail S. Griffin, 'The Humanisation of Edward Rochester', *Women and Literature*, n.s. 2 (1981), 118–29.
3. Rosemarie Bodenheimer, 'Jane Eyre in Search of her Story', *Papers in Language and Literature*, 16 (1980), 387–402, a brilliant essay.
4. See Annette Tromly, *The Cover of the Mask*, p. 57; Nina Auerbach, 'Charlotte Brontë: The Two Countries', *University of Toronto Quarterly*, 42:2 (Summer 1973), 335; Maurianne Adams, '*Jane Eyre*: Woman's Estate', in *The Authority of Experience*, ed. Arlyn Diamond and Lee R. Edwards, p. 139.
5. Richard Chase, 'The Brontës: A Centennial Observance', *Kenyon Review*, 9:4 (Autumn 1947), 487–506. Repr. in *The Brontës*, ed. Ian Gregor (Englewood Cliffs: Prentice-Hall International, 1970), p. 25.
6. Adrienne Rich, '*Jane Eyre*: The Temptations of a Motherless Woman', in *On Lies, Secrets and Silence*, pp. 89–91. Incidentally, in Rich's view, 'the thrill of masochism is not for' Jane Eyre: it is a temptation resisted (p. 96).
7. Maurianne Adams, '*Jane Eyre*: Woman's Estate', p. 137. Adams writes: 'Now that the burden of trying to pretend to a totally objective and value-free perspective has finally been lifted from our shoulders, we can all admit, in the simplest possible terms, that our literary insights and perceptions come, in part at least, from our sensitivity to the nuances of our own lives and our observations of other people's lives.'
8. Virginia Woolf, for instance, cited Anthea Zeman, *Presumptuous Girls*, p. 50. Zeman's book is a wry, witty and original account of women's plight as reflected in women's fiction.

9. Margaret Anne Doody, 'Deserts, Ruins and Troubled Waters: Female Dreams in Fiction and the Development of the Gothic Novel', *Genre*, 10 (Winter 1977), 539n.

10. Maurianne Adams, '*Jane Eyre*: Woman's Estate', p. 140. See also Nancy Pell, 'Resistance, Rebellion and Marriage: The Economics of *Jane Eyre*', *N.C.F.*, 31 (1977), 397–420, and John Halperin, *Egoism and Self-Discovery in the Victorian Novel*, p. 50.

11. Peter Tasch, 'Jane Eyre's "Three-tailed Bashaw"', *N.Q.*, n.s. 29, 227 cont. series (June 1982), 232.

12. R. J. Dingley, 'Rochester as Slave: An Allusion in *Jane Eyre*', *N.Q.*, n.s. 31, 229 continuous series (March 1984), 66.

13. Anthea Zeman, p. 181.

14. Richard Chase, 'The Brontës: A Centennial Observance', p. 26.

15. Melvin R. Watson, 'Form and Substance in the Brontë Novels', in *From Jane Austen to Joseph Conrad*, ed. Robert C. Rathburn and Martin Steinmann, Jr., p. 109.

16. Livelier work on imagery was done by Eric H. Solomon, 'Jane Eyre: Fire and Water', *College English*, 25 (December 1963), 215–17; David Lodge, 'Fire and Eyre: Charlotte Brontë's War of Earthly Elements', in *The Language of Fiction*, pp. 114–43; and Donald Ericksen, 'Imagery as Structure in *Jane Eyre*', *Victorian Newsletter*, 30 (Fall 1966). Lodge brilliantly analyses the thematic and moral significance of 'fire' in the novel, and notes that Charlotte's language moves from the 'quasi-metaphorical to the fully metaphorical to the literal without any sense of strain'. Analysing the passage I have quoted, he writes: 'The central passage, by its astonishing audacity of conceit, its elegiac rhythms, its fluent but controlled syntax—in short, by its verbal intensity on every level—conveys the response of a keen sensibility to an extreme emotional crisis. But this essentially poetic flight grows naturally out of the literal staples of the novel' (p. 129). Lodge also opposes the argument of Robert B. Heilman's 'Charlotte Brontë, Reason and the Moon'. See also Michael D. Wheeler, *The Art of Allusion in Victorian Fiction*.

9
Fairy Tale and the Imagination

> If you knew my thoughts—the dreams that absorb me—and the fiery imagination that at times eats me up and makes me feel society, as it is, wretchedly insipid, you would pity me and I dare say despise me.—Charlotte, letter to Ellen, 10 May 1836

Writing on 'Fairy-tale elements in *Jane Eyre*', Paula Sullivan quotes Rochester after Jane has saved him from being burned alive (Ch. 15): 'People talk of natural sympathies; I have heard of good genii:—there are grains of truth in the wildest fable.'[1] She cites Michael C. Kotzin, *Dickens and the Fairy Tale* (Bowling Green, 1972), as pointing out that 'Jane Eyre is both a Cinderella figure and the girl whose love releases a beast-bridegroom from his spell.'[2]

Actually, Jane, returning to Rochester, is both the Prince waking Sleeping Beauty with a kiss, and Beauty who has learned to love the Beast. Sullivan notes that Jane's initial perspective on Brocklehurst is not only Little Red Riding Hood's on the wolf, but that of Gulliver in Brobdingnag. Thus Charlotte 'creates a child's subjective perception of a world largely unknown and perilous, controlled by huge grownups'.[3] Sullivan relates Jane's story to Jack and the Beanstalk, David versus Goliath, and the films of Charlie Chaplin and Woody Allen, in which the intelligent protagonist overcomes the giants. She relates Ferndean to the mirror in the Red Room (Ch. 2) which throws back at Jane a 'visionary hollow'. Sullivan suggests that with 'Reader, I married him', Jane shuts the book of fairy tales and settles down to reality. For Sullivan, however, the 'enduring appeal of *Jane Eyre*' is that 'intense personal daydreams conform to fairy-tale patterns in storytelling which are universally satisfying'. She finds in the novel 'an egocentric dream-world in which everything is made to conform to the individual will',[4] agreeing basically with Armour Craig and with Chase. Dale Kramer observes that the inherent unity of *Jane Eyre* lies in 'age-old narrative expectations'.[5]

Samuel Pickering's analysis, 'Using and Controlling the Imagination in *Jane Eyre*', refuses to take the fairy-tale elements at face value. Pickering quotes Jane's reflections before the wedding: 'to imagine such a lot befalling me is a fairy tale—a daydream'.[6] Ultimately, her fairy-tale expectations are disappointed, and 'right religion governs her actions'.[7] Rochester is a 'sultan-figure' and his horse, Mesrour, is named after the executioner at the court of Haroun Al-Raschid.[8] 'The Arabian nights depicted a rich world of fleshly and imaginative delights . . . associated with passionate and imaginative experience.' Rochester 'fur-collared and steel-clasped' appears 'not as a homely, aging man, but as a Corsair figure from Byron or the Arabian nights'. Pickering sees the horse's fall as an emblem of Rochester's inability to 'control the flesh'.[9] Yet for Jane, Thornfield is 'a fairy place'. For Pickering, Rochester's love for Jane parodies the fable of Beauty and the Beast: 'Beauty's love could not turn Beast into a Prince, but would instead make Beauty bestial.'[10] True, but ultimately, having resisted the temptations of bestiality, Beauty returns and makes a prince out of the 'wronged and fettered wild beast, dangerous to approach in his sullen woe' (Ch. 37).

Pickering's reading of the religious motifs counterpointed against the fairy-tale daydreams is observant: it is the church bell that calls Jane to Marsh End; the cabinet outside Bertha Mason's room 'disciplined Jane's imagination, kept her from becoming a Bertha Mason and enabled her to reject Thornfield and be satisfied with Ferndean'.[11] But is it Jane's 'imagination' which is likely to make her into a Bertha? For Pickering, fairy tales help Jane grow up, but are something she must grow out of. Persuasive as Pickering's account is, I feel it over-moralistic, a framework which cramps and crushes the paradoxes and tensions of the novel into a too coherent pattern. The voice of Jane Eyre's imagination, when her inward ear is opened to 'a tale that was never ended—a tale my imagination created, and narrated continuously . . .' echoes in our own ears. It is her enduring gift to us. Its acknowledgement is followed by Jane's demand for 'action' (Ch. 12): are we to discount it as immature discontent, or recognize it as the vital principle of Jane's and Charlotte's being? As Patricia Meyer Spacks observes, 'Imagination is a slippery term, designating a power that penetrates the inner meaning of reality, but also a power that creates substitutes for reality.'[12]

Robert K. Martin, in '*Jane Eyre* and the World of Faery', offers a reading opposed to Pickering's. His argument is subtle and suggestive, although he describes Mrs. Reed as a 'phallic mother'.[13] Jane is 'first a childhood Cinderella, then a Sleeping Beauty, a wife in Bluebeard's castle, and finally Beauty wed to Beast, Rapunzel healing the prince'.[14] Martin concludes that R. E. Hughes's Nietzschean analysis is wrong: 'When Charlotte Brontë opposed the natural world of spirits to the artificial world of God, she was not opposing Dionysos to Apollo, but rather the fairy tale to the Bible.'[15] Martin tells us that only in the fairy tale was Charlotte likely to find traces of a non-patriarchal world. He posits 'the women's world of fairy tale, and the men's world of Christianity'.[16]

Margaret Blom argues in an early essay that 'Jane is incapacitated for Christian faith by her reliance on her vital, autonomous imagination.'[17] Jane, as Blom points out, never changes the belief underlying her response to Brocklehurst: 'I must keep in good health and not die.'[18] Jane triumphs 'as a result of her ruthless egoism' and 'selfish wishes'.[19] Blom points out that Jane's petition to God to grant her a new servitude leads only to discontent and restlessness when she finds one at Thornfield.[20] Blom draws on R. E. Hughes and R. B. Heilman for her interpretation that Rochester is a kind of 'sun-god', whereas Jane's planet is the moon. 'The richness and beauty of the Thornfield garden is "Edenlike" ',

> evocative not only of fruitfulness, but also of fatality and betrayal, and as Rochester torments Jane with fresh hints that he is soon to marry Blanche, a nightingale—symbol of male betrayal and of the violent potential of sexual passion—is 'warbling in a wood'.[21]

Blom concludes that Elizabeth Rigby was 'remarkably

accurate' in appraising *Jane Eyre* as ' "pre-eminently an anti-Christian composition" '.[22] Blom rejects Christian readings of the novel by Robert B. Martin, Barbara Hardy, David Lodge and Earl Knies. However, Blom accepts too easily Armour Craig's extraordinary notion that St. John is 'the full, official and authentic representative of religion' and reads Jane's refusal to be crushed by St. John as a rejection of God. Charlotte showed us plainly enough that St. John's brand of religion would have led only to death for Jane, spiritual as well as physical.

Daniel Margoliouth believes Charlotte tries to 'reconcile the spirit and the flesh by deifying both. What she actually deifies is her own subjective, dichotomized vision which domesticates both God and Nature to its own unholy fantasies'.[23] 'Seeking to objectify both her passionate nature and her narrow principles, Charlotte ... creates an outward Nature and fashions a God....'[24] Margoliouth seems angry with Charlotte for her 'distorted, bigoted judgemental inventions of narrowly presented opposites (such as the woman of the world and the nun)'.[25]

Elaine Showalter points out that as opposites Helen Burns and Bertha Mason function at realistic levels in the narrative, but are also used to present 'three faces of Jane'.[26] Charlotte 'resolves her heroine's psychic dilemma by literally and meta-phorically destroying the two polar personalities to make way for the full strength and development of the central con-sciousness'.[27] Showalter also notes that whereas Jane Eyre achieves a full and healthy womanhood, George Eliot's heroine, 'the gifted and loveable Maggie Tulliver represses her anger and creativity, and develops a neurotic, self-destructive personality.'[28]

Jennifer Gribble, in 'Jane Eyre's Imagination', writes that we see a mind actively creating its experience. Charlotte's interest in the imagination is 'less coherent than Coleridge's (whose poetry she certainly absorbed—there is no evidence of her reading his prose), but her novels show an increasing insight into its vagaries and powers'.[29] Gribble continues,

> It is only by confronting Jane with those aspects of society and identity that resist the controlling, synthesising activity of the observing and perceiving mind that she can represent the power of her own imagination to tell a tale that comprehends more than Jane's, and, as well, the validity of other versions of the facts.[30]

We all know, now, thanks to Iser and others, that reading is a creative, interpretative act; we cannot be lazy lookers-on, but must interpret our input. We always have known it, that we had to colour in, as it were, the black and white of the page before us. And, knowing this, each critic (except for those who have been seduced into total theoretical solipsism) hopes to offer, if not to impose, her own set of meanings, however contradictory, even fragmented, they may be. Somewhere, in the mud at the bottom of the well, there must be, we feel, a residue of deeper truth which has escaped other fossickers; this is the faith that underlies the critical enterprise, however disaffected the critic may be about traditional approaches and procedures. If writing is, like Jane Eyre herself, an orphan, who dare, today, take on the rôle of fostermother? It behoves critics to be humble. We should admit that creative writers are cleverer and subtler than we are; we stumble to thread our paths through the worlds they intuit, those glittering bubbles we try to catch in our hands, peopled with phantoms who haunt us. We are inside and outside fictions. The text of *Jane Eyre*, for all its hallucinatory vividness, is fluid and shimmering with images, visions, mirages, half-glimpses of things hinted, just out of sight.

'Imagination', two centuries after Europe was stirred and refreshed by Romanticism, is a stale, weary concept; we no longer believe in the imagination as an agent of redemption, a means to grace. What did Charlotte mean by imagination? As a child, Jane believes *Gulliver's Travels* to be literal truth, that Lilliput and Brobdingnag are parts of the earth's surface. This is clearly untrue, but books, the travels of the imagination, are Jane's comfort in a world where she is excluded from the Reed family, sitting behind a curtain, looking out on a frozen world. The world indoors is physically warm, but emotionally frozen; Mrs. Reed shares with Madame Beck the quality of coldness, and while it may be true, as Helene Moglen believes, that the Reeds are the Haworth family seen through 'the distorting glass of sibling rivalry',[31] Jane's plight at Gateshead, an interloper on the fringes of the family circle, reflects Charlotte's jealousy of the self-sufficient and happy family in Brussels. Imagination, and the world of books which enlarge and satisfy it, are consolatory for Jane. Charlotte wrote to W. S. Williams, after Emily and Anne were dead, when she had struggled to finish *Shirley*,

The faculty of imagination lifted me when I was sinking, three months ago; its active exercise has kept my head above water since . . . it is for me a part of my religion to defend this gift and to profit by its possession. (21 September 1849)

The Roe Head journal, written thirteen years earlier, 11 August 1836, shortly before she wrote to Southey in a bid for encouragement, is equally significant (italics added):

The thought came over me am I to spend all the best part of my life in this wretched bondage forcibly *suppressing my rage* at the idleness the apathy and the hyperbolical and most asinine stupidity of those fat-headed oafs and on compulsion assuming an air of kindness patience and assiduity? . . . Stung to the heart with this reflection I started up and *mechanically walked to the window*—a sweet August morning was smiling without. . . . I shut the window and went back to my seat. Then came on me *rushing impetuously all the mighty phantasm* that we had conjured from nothing *to a system strong as some religious creed*. I felt as if I could have *written gloriously*— I longed to write . . . if I had had time to indulge it I felt that the vague sensations of that moment would have settled down into some narrative better at least than anything I had ever produced before. But just then a Dolt came up with a lesson. I thought I should have *vomited*.

This revealing document gives us the themes that emerged in *Jane Eyre*: rage, the confined woman pacing 'mechanically' and looking out of a window, beset by 'mighty phantasms', like the 'rushing of wings' Jane hears in the Red Room, the visions that fill the room when she is tempted, against the bent of her nature, to marry St. John. In both these instances, the intolerable pressure of 'visions' is followed by escape, release. And in her rage and frustration at not being able to exercise her imagination, Charlotte wants to vomit. She vomited frequently all her life, and finally died of it. Yet she did suppress her rage when she received Southey's letter and decided such punishment was good for her, just as she told Mary Taylor it 'did her good' to be told, at 15, that she was 'very ugly'. Charlotte's need to earn a living, her Papa, the Poet Laureate, all told her that she must accept reality and 'suppress her rage'. Castigating herself, she 'internalised her society's oppression of women, deciding that the main faculty of women was self-control, while the primary masculine charac-teristic was self-assertion'.[32] But her imagination, working underground like a volcano, took its revenge on her body. She vomited.

Finally she spewed up the mighty phantasms in images of fire and destruction, disaster and maiming. Rage left the infant Jane feeling like a 'black and blasted' heath 'after the flames are dead', but when Jane seeks the relief of tears, Bessie might just as well have said to the fire, 'don't burn' as get her to stop.

Tears, anger, imagination all need 'outlets'. We see that for Charlotte the suppression of her imagination meant the slow smouldering of rage, while to cherish it was part of her 'religion'. Jane Eyre nurtures her imagination and stays sane: Lucy Snowe suppresses hers and has a breakdown. Mary Taylor, after reading the *Life*, told Mrs. Gaskell, 'Though not so gloomy as the truth, it is perhaps as much so as people will accept without calling it exaggerated', adding that the reviewers do not seem 'to think it a strange or wrong state of things that a woman of first-rate talents, industry and integrity, should live all her life in a waking nightmare of poverty and self-suppression'. Mary had emancipated herself by exile. Charlotte, oppressed by self and circumstances, found consolation; in common with other Romantics, she made Imagination into a religion. Unlike Shelley, who became a Platonist and atheist, Charlotte's religious interpretation of Romantic 'Sympathy' enabled her to reconcile it, to her own satisfaction at least, with Christianity.

NOTES

1. Paula Sullivan, 'Fairy-tale elements in *Jane Eyre*', *Journal of Popular Culture*, 12 (1978), 62.
2. Ibid., 73n.
3. Ibid., 63.
4. Ibid., 72.
5. Dale Kramer, 'Thematic Structure in *Jane Eyre*', *Papers on Language and Literature*, 4 (Summer 1968), 290.
6. Samuel Pickering, 'Using and Controlling the Imagination in *Jane Eyre*', *Illinois Quarterly*, 42:1 (1979), 18.
7. Ibid., 25.
8. Ibid., 18.
9. Ibid., 21.
10. Ibid., 23.

11. Ibid.
12. Patricia Meyer Spacks, *The Female Imagination*, p. 6.
13. Robert K. Martin, '*Jane Eyre* and the World of Faery', *Mosaic*, 10 (1977), 88. This spectral oxymoron stalks through Brontë criticism. Tom Winnifrith, reviewing J. H. Kavanagh's *Emily Brontë* in *Notes & Queries*, n.s. 33:4, 231 continuous series (December 1986), 559, writes: 'He is helped by adopting from Gallop the concept of the phallic mother, and by seeing phallic symbolism everywhere.' In a private letter, Winnifrith suggests it may simply mean a woman is 'bossy'.
14. Robert K. Martin, 94.
15. Ibid.
16. Ibid., 95.
17. Margaret A. Blom, '*Jane Eyre*: Mind as Law unto Itself', *Criticism*, 15 (1973), 353.
18. Ibid., 363.
19. Ibid.
20. Ibid., 356n.
21. Ibid., 359.
22. Ibid., 350.
23. Daniel Margolioth, 'Passion and Duty: A Study of Charlotte Brontë's *Jane Eyre*', *Hebrew University Studies in Literature* (1979), 187.
24. Ibid., 186.
25. Ibid., 194.
26. Elaine Showalter, *A Literature of their Own*, p. 113.
27. Ibid.
28. Ibid., p. 112.
29. Jennifer Gribble, 'Jane Eyre's Imagination', *N.C.F.*, 23 (1968), 281.
30. Ibid., 282–83.
31. Helene Moglen, *The Self Conceived*, p. 109.
32. Robert Keefe, *Charlotte Brontë's World of Death*, p. 30.

10

Signs, Presentiments and Sympathies

> Presentiments are strange things! And so are sympathies; and so
> are signs. . . . Sympathies, I believe, exist (for instance, between
> far-distant, long-absent, wholly estranged relatives asserting,
> notwithstanding their alienation, the unity of the source to which
> each traces his origin), whose workings baffle mortal compre-
> hension. And signs, for aught we know, may be but the
> sympathies of nature with man. (*Jane Eyre*, Ch. 21)

Barry Qualls writes, 'For Brontë nature and the truly religious
are inextricably connected: they constitute an alliance which
does not oppose, as do all of the novel's "religious" figures, a
genuinely human and creative life lived in this world.'[1] This
statement is unjust to Miss Temple, who 'mothers' Jane and
gives her seedcake. But Charlotte's 'alliance' of nature and
religion is crucial. In Jane's belief in a connection between
sympathies and signs, there is more than the mere 'superstition'
Jane rejects in her new maturity (Ch. 35). Samuel Jackson
Pratt's poem, *Sympathy* (1781) goes:

> Hail, sacred source of sympathies divine
> Each social pulse, each social fibre thine;
> Hail, symbols of the God to whom we owe
> The nerves that vibrate, and the hearts that glow.

There is a peculiarly eighteenth-century view at work here,
Cartesian mind–body interaction moralized. The age was
aware of, and receptive to the conscious acknowledgement of,
bodily rhythms: hearts, pulses, nerves, are all felt to be active,
in constant motion, giving as well as receiving sensation.

127

Charlotte's own writing, with its awareness of pulses and the motion of the blood, warm in anger or running ice, has absorbed this pervasive sense of the body in perpetual motion within itself, and its interaction with the external world, bound by 'sympathies'. Pratt's poem implies the body politic, or at least the body social; God gives us our perceptions and our powers in order to love Him and one another. The medieval 'correspondences' survived into the scientific age. Stephen Cox writes that for writers influenced by the cult of eighteenth-century 'sensibility', 'sympathy' was more than mere fellow-feeling: it was a mystical force.[2] Adam Smith exalted the 'sympathetic imagination',[3] and his *Theory of Moral Sentiments* put forward an idea taken over by Wordsworth and Shelley, that the moral life is founded not in the will but in the imagination.[4] Marthalene Atkinson, in an unpublished dissertation, summarizes as follows:

> Although used diversely in nineteenth-century literature, the term 'imagination' most consistently refers to that associating, synthesising mental power which provides the ultimate means of perception. Through the *sympathetic* function of imagination, an individual is able to know and identify with life outside self in a way that would be impossible through the senses or the intellect. This sympathetic imagination operates on a metaphysical level by allowing man to see himself as part of a unified whole, on an aesthetic level by allowing the artist to merge with his creation, and on the ethical level by allowing the individual to identify with other human beings.[5]

Rousseau, too, had written of 'sympathy of soul'.

So what, in the light of all this, do we make of the mystical voices heard by Jane and Rochester? For Joseph Prescott, they are a 'thumping piece of Gothic claptrap'.[6] Ruth Bernard Yeazell argues, against Barbara Hardy,[7] that 'the magic is grounded in the world of the novel': its truth is 'the truth of the psyche'.[8] John Maynard argues that 'Because the romance plot serves throughout primarily as a way of providing symbolic interpretation of Jane's psychology, it really matters little how this unresolved odd event is understood.'[9] John Halperin writes that the 'physical impossibility' is 'the symbolic and logical result of the development of her protagonists. They are only recreating physically a spiritual condition.'[10] True, but what is

this spiritual condition and how does Charlotte establish it?
The episode of the voices seems to offer a clue to Charlotte's
deeper meanings. In the Methodist fictions she read as a girl,
portents, signs and voices were messages from God. Jane and
Rochester, talking of remorse, before Jane knows what he has to
be sorry about, discuss spiritual messengers (Ch. 14).

Rochester tells Jane she has a kind of 'innate sympathy'
which will attract confessions. He tells her his impulse towards
pleasure is 'no devil, I assure you; or if it be, it has put on the
robes of an angel of light. . . .'

Jane replies, 'Distrust it, sir; it is not a true angel.'

'. . . By what instinct do you pretend to distinguish between a
seraph of the abyss and a messenger from the eternal throne—
between a guide and a seducer?'

This passage characteristically reverberates. Jane looks to
Rochester as guide, but discovers him to be a potential seducer.
She is the voice of his conscience, but conscience for Jane is not
externally imposed; it is identified with 'instinct'. After the
disrupted marriage ceremony, he says, 'I believe you felt the
existence of sympathy between you and your grim and cross
master'; a page later, he says, 'You are my sympathy, my better
self; my good angel.' Her answer is that she must leave him; she
tells him to trust in God and live sinless. Leaving him, she longs
to go back, but finds she cannot. 'God must have led me on'
(Ch. 27). Slipping in and out of the historic present, Jane
writes, 'I have no relative but the universal mother, Nature'
(Ch. 28). This recalls Byron's *Childe Harold*:

> Dear Nature is the kindest mother still;
> Though always changing, in her aspect mild:
> From her bare bosom let me take my fill,
> Her never-weaned, though not her favoured child.
>
> (Canto 2, 37)

Childe Harold informs much of *Jane Eyre*: Rochester's wanderings
derive from those of Harold rather more than from those of Don
Juan. Byron's theory of imagination was also important to
Charlotte:

> 'Tis to create, and in creating live
> A being more intense, that we endow
> With form our fancy, gaining as we give

129

The life we image, even as I do now.
What am I? Nothing: but not so art thou,
Soul of my thought! With whom I traverse earth
Invisible but gazing, as I glow
Mixed with thy spirit, blended with thy birth
And feeling still with thee in my crushed feelings dearth.

Yet must I think less wildly: I *have* thought
Too long and darkly, till my brain became
In its own eddy boiling and o'erwrought,
A whirling gulf of phantasy and flame:
And thus, untaught in youth my heart to tame,
My springs of life were poisoned. (Canto 3, 6–7)

The influences here on Charlotte's vocabulary and the presentation of Rochester are obvious. Rochester talks about his 'spring of life' (Ch. 27), meaning his heart.

Providence leads Jane, when she is once more starving (physical starvation is an emblem, throughout the novel, of emotional and spiritual starvation), to Moor House. It is the sympathy of kindred, under Providence, which draws Jane there, where she finds the true kinship, physical and spiritual, that her orphaned state and the wicked-stepmother activities of Mrs. Reed had denied. In the song Bessie sings to the child Jane, we read:

There is a thought that for strength should avail me;
Though both of shelter and kindred despoiled;
Heaven is a home and a rest will not fail me;
God is a friend to the poor orphan child.

(Despoiled, incidentally, would have been pronounced to rhyme with 'child' at the time.) Although the song is a hymn, its prophecy comes true in this world. Love, on earth, offers a foretaste of heaven, as the Methodists believed. God brings the 'poor orphan child', Jane, to 'shelter and kindred', whose sympathies with her evince the unity of their source. When Jane first sees the light streaming from the Rivers' cottage, she is afraid it might be a will-o'-the-wisp, one of the 'false lights' of the song, a running image throughout the novel. Like all great literature, *Jane Eyre* is concerned with spiritual quest. Jane finds a temporary home in the bosom of her cousins, before finding her true home with Rochester, as a result of a spiritual message, which, like the earthquake which shook Paul and Silas's prison, 'opened the doors of the soul's cell' (Ch. 38) and confirms she has grown up. She has found her true self.

Does this message come from God? Jane's God is indeed closely identified with nature: the orphan has supernatural parents, a mother in nature and a father in God, and the two are linked by sacred bonds. The voice Jane hears does not come from outside, in the air, or in the room, but from the spark of divinity within herself, in which both the Cambridge Platonists and Coleridge believed. Romanticism has been absorbed into *Jane Eyre* not at the trivial level of magic, but as Providential. Charlotte has digested the spirit of Romanticism, as well as its diction; she believes in the impulse from the vernal wood, totally opposed to the religion of Brocklehurst, who did not wish to conform to nature, and that of St. John, who wishes to 'turn the bent of nature'. For St. John love is 'a fever of the flesh, not a convulsion of the soul' (Ch. 35). His lip is 'bloodless'. In an exhilaratingly subtle and scholarly argument, Qualls relates Charlotte's novel to that patriarch of Victorian creative writers, Carlyle, and identifies St. John as a 'Diogenes–Teufelsdröckh determined not to acknowledge the "Demon-Empire" of feeling . . . his notion of "duty", like Helen's "doctrine of endurance", Jane Eyre's autobiography at once scrutinizes and redefines'.[11]

When Jane hears the voice, she makes several key statements, offered in the manner of dialogue, but it is more a dialogue of self and soul, a dialogue which takes place within the heroine as she communes with herself:

> 'Down superstition. . . . This is not thy deception, nor thy witchcraft: it is the work of nature. She was roused, and did—no miracle—but her best.'
>
> I broke from St. John, who had followed and would have detained me. It was *my* time to assume ascendancy. *My* powers were in play and in force.

Jane prays and 'seemed to penetrate very near a Mighty Spirit; and my soul rushed out in gratitude at His feet.' Qualls points out that Jane's God is not identical with nature; bad news for the feminists this may be, but I must agree with Qualls that 'the movement from feminine to masculine pronoun is decisive.'[12] However, he and I interpret Jane's meaning differently; he

131

writes, 'her daylight revaluation of that voice removes it from nature: "it seemed in *me*—not in the external world." '[13]

To think of 'nature' as merely in the external world is, I believe, mistaken. Jane's story has been a journey towards reunification with the 'universal mother' (Miss Temple and Mrs. Fairfax have been mother-surrogates along the way). Jane is connected to the world of nature, which, like the Kingdom of God, is within and around her (Luke 17:21), by a web of sympathies. She is both a separate entity and an integral part of nature, bound by links like those between every child and its flesh-and-blood mother. Returning to Gateshead after the nurturing process at the reformed Lowood, Jane 'experienced firmer trust in myself and my own powers, and less withering dread of oppression'. The Romantic search is the search for one's own subconscious powers, that in quiet moments give us echoes of infinity, voices speaking to the inner ear, pictures on the cinema screen within the skull. Jane, having found her true kindred, her natural family, has found integration and maturity. The web of sympathies which connects Jane to nature and to her kindred enables *her* powers to come into play, so that she hears that voice from within herself, as a function of that mystical connection. *Jane Eyre* is a fable about the growth and integration of the psyche. God and nature deeply interfused, as guiding principles of the universe, have led Jane to healing at Moor House which gives her strength to leave it again for Rochester. She goes out from the family into marriage. She has recognized that St. John would never 'make a good husband' (Ch. 34); she has found the confidence to listen to her own instincts, her own subconscious.

William H. Marshall, in 'The Self, the World and the Structure of *Jane Eyre*', writes about the connection between sympathies and the voices, but his discussion is invalidated by that theological illiteracy which bedevils the work of so many twentieth-century commentators. Marshall assumes that because life is seen as a journey, *Jane Eyre* is a Calvinist work.[14] Helen is one of 'the Elect'. St. John and Jane are 'rewarded' at the end for having chosen 'pain and suffering'. This would, of course, imply salvation by 'works', a doctrine specifically rejected by Calvinism, which believed in salvation by faith and election. Marshall's article is thoroughly confused. He does, however, perceive that only after she has fulfilled the demands of Helen's Christianity does Jane return to the grave in Brocklehurst churchyard to place there 'a grey marble tablet . . . inscribed with her name, and the word "Resurgam" '.[15]

(Does he mean Lowood churchyard?)

Philip Momberger writes perceptively:

> . . . each of Charlotte's protagonists begins his [*sic*] career as a guilty outcast, a 'placeless person' estranged from everything outside himself and thus in doubt about his identity. . . . This inmost sense of self must somehow be declared in interaction with the opposing world and, if it is to be fulfilled, must be recognized and supported by something in that world. . . .[16]

William R. Siebenschuh has traced 'The Image of the Child and the Plot of *Jane Eyre*'.[17] Jane's dream that Thornfield Hall is a 'dreary ruin, the retreat of bats and owls' comes true, and so, when she rescues Adele and has a real baby of her own, the spectral child of the dream 'rolled from my knee: I lost my balance, fell and woke'. All these themes and images, as Siebenschuh analyses them, have to do with reintegrating the self.

Qualls reminds us that for the early Victorian reader, 'preaching' was not considered an artistic flaw, as it came to be considered later in the century, but was part of a novelist's responsibility to his readers.[18] Qualls demonstrates that the morality and precepts of the seventeenth-century emblem books survived into Victorian religion. He argues that even if Charlotte's contemporaries read secularism into the novels, Charlotte never substitutes the 'self' for the 'soul', that 'crucial difference between Romantic and Puritan self-scrutinies'.[19] This seems to me to be the point at issue, not one to be taken for granted. Qualls's commentary should be read in full, though I do not, myself, totally accept it.

The question to be asked about *Jane Eyre* is: is the resolution true and satisfying, or is it a vengeful fantasy of wish-fulfilment? Only by attending to the fine religious discriminations within *Jane Eyre* can we hope to decode it. We may find some answer to this question if we look at the symbolic patterns.

NOTES

1. Barry Qualls, *The Secular Pilgrims of Victorian Fiction*, p. 46.
2. Stephen Cox, *The Stranger Within Thee*, p. 44.
3. Kenneth MacLean, 'Imagination and Sympathy: Sterne and Adam Smith', *Journal of the History of Ideas*, 10:3 (1949), 404.
4. Ibid., 400.
5. Marthalene Atkinson, *The Sympathetic Imagination in the Fiction of Mary Wollstonecraft Shelley*, D.A., Vol. 41, No. 6 (December 1980). See also Nora Crook and Derek Guiton, *Shelley's Venomed Melody* (Cambridge: Cambridge University Press, 1986), p. 70: ' "Sympathy", which of course is originally a medical term, was the point at which Romantic medicine touched on physics, chemistry, philanthropy and literature; sympathy related man to nature and man to man.'
6. Joseph Prescott, '*Jane Eyre*: A Romantic Exemplum with a Difference', in *Twelve Original Essays on Great English Novels*, ed. Charles Shapiro, p. 90.
7. Barbara Hardy, *The Appropriate Form*, p. 70.
8. Ruth Bernard Yeazell, 'More True than Real: Jane Eyre's Mysterious Summons', *N.C.F.*, 29 (1974), 128.
9. John Maynard, *Charlotte Brontë and Sexuality*, p. 136.
10. John Halperin, *Egoism and Self-Discovery in the Victorian Novel*, pp. 58–9.
11. Qualls, p. 46.
12. Ibid., p. 65.
13. Ibid.
14. William H. Marshall, 'The Self, the World and the Structure of *Jane Eyre*', *Revue des langues vivantes*, 27 (1961), 417–18.
15. Ibid., 421.
16. Philip Momberger, 'Self and World in Charlotte Brontë's Works', *English Literary History*, 32 (September 1965), 421.
17. William R. Siebenschuh, 'The Image of the Child and the Plot of *Jane Eyre*', *Studies in the Novel*, 8 (1976), 304-17.
18. Qualls, p. 51. See also Richard Stang, *The Theory of the Novel*, p. 67.
19. Qualls, p. 52.

11

Female Inner Space and Moral Madness

I'll be like the first Mrs. Rochester. I'll go mad behind the panelling.—Alan Ayckbourn

Robert Heilman, in 'Charlotte Brontë's "New" Gothic' writes:

In the novel it was the function of Gothic to open horizons beyond social patterns, rational decisions and institutionally approved emotions; in a word to enlarge the sense of reality . . . it became the great liberator of feeling. It acknowledged the non-rational . . . it released [Charlotte] from the patterns of the novel of society and therefore permitted the flowering of her real talent—the talent for finding and giving dramatic form to impulses and feelings which, because of their depth or mysterious-ness or intensity or ambiguity, or of their ignoring or transcend-ing everyday norms of propriety or reason, increase wonderfully the sense of reality in the novel.[1]

Seen another way, *Jane Eyre* can be read not as liberated but as a fiction which seeks to impose rational decisions and institutionally approved emotions on the passions. Rochester, disguised as a gipsy 'mother', tells Jane that her

Reason sits firm and holds the reins, and she will not let the feelings burst away and hurry her to wild chasms. The passions may rage furiously, like true heathens, as they are; and the desires may imagine all sorts of vain things; but judgement shall still have the last word in every argument, and the casting vote in every decision. . . .

His words are fulfilled when Jane conquers her passions and runs away.

Yet despite the high value set on judgement, despite the fact that Jane leaves the man she loves, only to return when he has been chastened, readers have felt that the book's emotions burst through the bonds of rational restraint. The impression left by *Jane Eyre* seems to be that it is a story of lawless passion. Many people recognized at the time that Charlotte Brontë was writing about sex. But Victorian frankness was not twentieth-century explicitness, and Charlotte's treatment of sex is largely symbolic, cloudy and suggestive.

Her symbols have been variously interpreted. For example, Joseph Prescott believes that Charlotte is 'under cover of her epicene pseudonym, thumbing her nose at conventional constraints upon feminine expression'.[2] The example he gives in support of this assertion is dubious in the extreme. Jane is telling Rochester about Rivers' proposal of marriage: 'He asked me more than once, and was as stiff about urging his point as ever you could be.' This may seem highly suggestive, even risible, to the male Prescott, and other male writers have endorsed this weirdly prurient opinion. Charlotte, however, is extremely unlikely to have been aware of any improper meaning. For her to be conscious of a physical import in the words would mean that she, a Victorian virgin without benefit of enlightened sex education, who had never even been kissed, knew about male erections before she was married. I do not believe it.

David Cowart writes in 'Oedipal Dynamics in *Jane Eyre*' that Jane

> occupies herself by netting, and the hands busy in her lap hint at one outlet for her sexual frustration. The purse she nets, in other words, is a genital symbol. . . . 'Bridewell', the word that Blanche and Rochester enact in their charade, is the name of an infamous prison; it suggests that Rochester is soon to be immured in a vaginal prison—a bride's well—that is the antithesis of Jane's netted purse.[3]

The vagina as antithesis to a purse? Are we talking about concavity or convexity? (Is he confusing a netted purse, the handiwork of many a Victorian gentlewoman, with a sporran?) If the 'genital symbol' is male, then Jane, sitting quietly at her needlework, is busy netting herself a set of male sex organs.

(And much could be made out of that word 'netting', I daresay.) What will she do with them when she has created them?

Margot Horne, in 'From the Window-seat to the Red Room: Innocence to Experience in *Jane Eyre*', imagines that when John Reed commands that Jane stand before him, 'thrusting out his tongue, then about to strike her with a book, the action . . . suggests a rape'.[4]

Geoffrey Wagner writes that

> Rochester loses his hand which, at a crucial moment in the relationship, Jane surely feels, without too much equivocation, as a surrogate penis ('a hand of fiery iron grasped my vitals'). In another part she sees a hand coming through a cloud in the sky. So sex and religion can be said to cohabit in her fantasies clearly enough. . . .[5]

Why should a 'hand of fiery iron' round Jane's 'vitals' be equated with a penis? The 'vitals' are the parts on which survival depends, the lungs, heart, brain. The hand coming out of the sky belongs to a female, a warning mother-figure. What sort of equipment is a *prehensile* penis? All Wagner offers is a gallop of false analogies.

The Marxist Feminist Literature Collective, despite some interesting analysis, fall into similar a-historical error; they write of Charlotte's

> metonymic discourse of the human body—hands and eyes for penises, 'vitals' or 'vital organs' for women's genitalia—often to comic effect:
>
> > I am substantial enough—touch me. . . . He held out his hand, laughing. Is that a dream? said he, placing it close to my eyes. He had a rounded, muscular and vigorous hand, as well as a long, strong arm. (Ch. 24)
>
> The tale told of women's sexual possibilities is a halting, fragmented and ambivalent one. The libidinal fire of Jane Eyre's 'vital organs' is not denied, not totally repressed, as the refusal of St. John Rivers suggests:
>
> > At his side, always and always restrained, always checked— forced to keep the fire of my nature continually low, to compel

137

it to burn inwardly, and never utter a cry, though the
imprisoned flame consume vital after vital. (Ch. 34)[6]

The confusion here is almost total. The reductionism that can
see only sexual meanings is damaging. While *Jane Eyre* is full of
metonymies and synecdoches, Jane's 'vitals' are by no stretch of
the imagination her genitalia; the primary meaning of 'vitals',
as in the seventeenth-century oath, 'Stap me vitals!', is the
lungs (i.e., 'may my breath be stopped!'). As I have pointed out
(Chapter 3), the image of 'Conscience' turning tyrant and
seizing 'Passion by throat' is an image of a woman choking with
the pressure of conflict; the 'hand of fiery iron' that clutches
Jane's vitals is the asthmatic's reaction to emotional stress: an
inability to breathe. Jane is hyperventilating. Her 'vitals', a
word used with such beautiful expressiveness in context, are her
lungs, her breath, her vital spark, her principle of life, and by
one of those daring extensions of literal meaning which create
the densely suggestive text that is *Jane Eyre*, her spiritual energy.
St. John's demands will quench Jane's *being*. St. John threatens
her that if she becomes a missionary without marrying him,
God will not be satisfied. 'Will he accept a mutilated sacrifice?'
St. John, in his arrogance, presumes to speak for God and
demand that Jane must sacrifice her soul on the altar and
sacrifice her body to be grilled alive in Calcutta (thus conjuring
up memories of the torture of St. Lawrence on his gridiron and
Calcutta's notorious Black Hole). That Rochester's hands are
sexually stimulating for Jane is perfectly true (male hands,
hairy and muscular, *are* sexually exciting), and if Charlotte falls
into innocent obscenity it is when Rochester draws his 'stump'
from his clothing and shows it to Jane. As recent commentators
have noted, *Jane Eyre* is rich in that which is *not* said. But to see
only in that sub-text the narrowly sexual is to distort. *Jane Eyre*
is much possessed by death and by socio-economics. The novel
is about the struggle to stay alive in a world where schoolgirls
died in epidemics every day, to stay physically and mentally
healthy: what are the conditions, asks the novel, in which a
woman can find life-enhancing satisfaction? Helen's religion is
benign, like her forehead, but Helen is doomed by disease to an
early death, and is not really fit for this world; she is a dreamy
muddler, trapped in a school where her intellectual and

spiritual gifts go unrecognized, in a setting where intellectual and spiritual development, theoretical desiderata, are neglected under a régime of petty tyranny. Helen accepts tyranny and looks forward to the next world. Jane has already turned against tyranny like a revolted slave, and she will later revolt against Rochester's sultan-like propensities. Jane's punishment in the Red Room is a foretaste of death. In Christian thought, death is the prison from which the faithful shall be freed by the merits of the Redeemer. Margot Horne sees the Red Room as 'a magnificent emblem of the interior of [Jane's] own mind'.[7] For Elaine Showalter, the Red Room is 'a paradigm of female inner space': 'with its deadly and bloody connotations, its Freudian wealth of secret compartments, wardrobes, drawers, and jewel-chest, the red-room has strong associations with the adult female body.'[8] The wound on Jane's head, and Jane's violent outburst, suggest to Showalter an 'emotional menarche', though Jane is only 10.[9] The idea is seductive, if only after so many reductionist critiques of *Jane Eyre*. Herman Rapoport, drawing on the work of Lacan, Abraham and Torok, searches the text for hidden associations, the *mot tabou*, and finds it in *haine-mère*: Mrs. Reed is a 'night-*mère*', in line with the 'sound-shape' which gives us ere, air, aware, beware, nightmare, glare, terror, eye, ire, Ireland.[10] For him the family name is associated for Jane with 'horror' and her fantasies of the 'voice' in that 'red room' are accompanied by a dissolution of the ego, a dispersion of the 'I' into all that terrifies her. Rapoport is much concerned with cryptograms as revelations of unconscious meaning.

It is not difficult to play with names in this way: redroom, bedroom, wedroom, redwomb. But for me the echo is with 'tomb' rather than with 'womb'. Jane hears voices and sees visions in the Red Room, which almost frighten her to death. She knows this is 'superstition'. The Red Room experience is paralleled by her vision when St. John's proposals threaten her with a living death in India; but this time Jane, mature, controlled and independent, can reject superstition and listen to the powers of nature, her own spring of life, and hear the true voice of love from Rochester.

For Jane at 10 years old, her incarceration in the prison of the Red Room is a foretaste of those things brought so vividly before Charlotte every Sunday in her father's sermons, death, judgement and hell. It is the abode of ghosts and spectral lights: the bed is 'like a tabernacle', the windows are 'shrouded', the room was 'chill, because it seldom had a fire; it was silent . . . solemn'. Insofar as the Red Room represents a body, that body is a corpse, 'a little quiet dust' like that the housemaid removes once a week from the room itself. The secret drawer has a jewel-casket and parchments: that is, a box of stones and dead, flayed animal skin; it represents material wealth without warmth or love. All that remains to Mrs. Reed of her dead husband is a 'miniature'; dead, he is diminished. She has finished with him, and by relegating Jane to the room in which Jane's only (or so we believe) blood relative breathed his last, she is relegating Jane to his fate: wishing Jane dead, she locks her up alive, like Antigone. Jane will be like Antigone again, leading her blind husband , 'old enough to be her father', about at Ferndean. Much has been made of Jane's vision of herself, 'half fairy, half imp', in the mirror in the Red Room, but her terror is not so much terror at her own physical development as the fear of the dead and death itself.

When Jane wakes from her fit, she sees before her 'a terrible red glare, crossed with thick black bars'. It is only the nursery fire, but fires, for Victorian children, were firmly associated with hell. And I believe we have here an 'Ancient Mariner' echo:

> And straight the sun was flecked with bars
> (Heaven's Mother send us grace!)
> As through a dungeon-grate he peered
> With broad and burning face. . . .

> Are those *her* ribs through which the Sun
> Did peer, as through a grate?
> And is that Woman all her crew?
> Is that a DEATH? and are there two?
> Is DEATH that woman's mate? . . .
> The Night-mare LIFE-IN-DEATH was she,
> Who thicks man's blood with cold.

On a subliminal narrative level, Jane has died and woken up in hell. Bertha's room is described by Rochester as 'the mouth of hell' (Ch. 26). It is time to take a closer look at the figure of Bertha Mason Rochester. After Bertha's nocturnal visit, Jane

takes refuge in Adele's crib, recalling the way she had snuggled
up to Helen. But Bertha represents aspects of reality far
removed from the innocent beds of little girls.

Bertha has the wordless voice 'now of a mocking demon, and
anon of a carrion-seeking bird of prey' (Ch. 20). Jane, hearing
these sounds, has not yet seen Bertha, only her deeds, that make
her wonder,

> What crime was this, that lived incarnate in this sequestered
> mansion, and could neither be expelled nor subdued by the
> owner?—what mystery, that broke out, now in fire and now in
> blood, at the deadest hours of night?

Well might Jane ask. Bertha is Rochester's 'crime', in that he
married her without really loving her, but a few pages later, he
denies to the ignorant and innocent Jane that he has committed
any crime; he admits only to 'error'. Did Charlotte know the
Greek word *hamartia*? The construction of *Jane Eyre* suggests that
she did.

'A new chapter in a novel is something like a new scene in a
play', writes Charlotte/Jane at the start of Chapter 11, forgetting the pretence of documentary autobiography and drawing
attention to art and artifice. Two acts of her drama have
already been played out, those at Gateshead and Lowood; she
is about to enter the climactic act of her five-act drama, the
one set at Thornfield. During this act we get the recognition,
or anagnorisis, of Greek tragedy, just as the reunion with
Rochester is the peripeteia. The screen falls, the cupboard is
opened, and the madwoman is revealed in all her pitiable
horror. The revelation of her appalling existence has been
carefully prepared, so that when she is revealed on the inner
stage, we know that we suspected something like her all along.
The first time we meet her face to face, apart from the
evidence of her deeds, is in Jane's tale to Rochester of a
'dream'. The woman is 'tall and large, with thick and dark
hair hanging long down her back': her dress is 'white and
straight; but whether gown, sheet or shroud, I cannot tell'.
The dress is totally removed from fashion, from that self-
grooming which is the mark of self-respect, which Jane,
despite her meagre wardrobe, is scrupulous to observe. In this
vaguely described white drapery, Bertha is like a ghost, but

she has substantial physical life. Jane sees the image of Bertha reflected in her mirror.

> It was a discoloured face—it was a savage face. I wish I could forget the roll of the red eyes and the fearful blackened inflation of the lineaments . . . purple: the lips were swelled and dark; the brow furrowed: the black eyebrows widely raised over the blood-shot eyes. Shall I tell you of what it reminded me? . . . Of the foul German spectre—the vampire.

Pickering, as we have seen, saw the cabinet outside Bertha's room as the emblem of 'right religion'. Barbara Hill Rigney sees a possible identification 'with the scapegoat aspect of the dying Christ',[11] while Mark Kinkead-Weekes writes (with an unconscious pun, perhaps, on 'story'):

> . . . it is essential to realise what the 'story' level of the book does not clarify until later: that the mad woman does not simply represent an external impediment, but also something within Rochester himself which he tries to deny, to escape, to imprison. When Jane finally enters that attic she is penetrating the most secret chamber of Rochester's own heart—an inner dimension in which the chained bestiality growls like a Yahoo, held in check by the sardonically named 'Grace', while the candlelight plays across the antique carvings of Christ's apostles, and the face of the betrayer, the Judas.[12]

Bertha is *not* chained, merely restrained. Kinkead-Weekes does not explore the question, either, as to who is betrayer and who is betrayed. Modern criticism increasingly sees Bertha as scapegoat and victim of capitalist society.

Bertha, that monster of the id, dominates the novel, yet she occupies only a few brief pages. Jane's remarkable description combines rich suggestiveness with lack of specificity: there is an undertone, somewhere, that Bertha is negroid, with her thick lips and blackened, 'savage', face. The picture is vivid, but deliberately blurred at the edges. Bertha is a 'Creole', an ambiguous word. The label 'Creole' was given equally to settlers of aristocratic French extraction and to people of colour.

Bertha's eyes are 'fiery' (which suggests fiend-like), her visage 'lurid', and for a second time Jane faints from terror. When Jane looks at herself in the mirror before going to church next morning, she sees herself a 'robed and veiled figure', almost the image of a stranger. These ghostly women, Bertha and Jane, not in proper clothes but vaguely draped, have no identity of their own: one is Mrs. Rochester, the other wonders who 'Jane Rochester' will be. Attempts to find real-life originals for Bertha are beside the point. The mad wife is not a Gothic fiction; many men, even today, have mad wives (an estimated one woman in nine receives treatment for mental illness at some time in her life). The Victorians had no tranquillizers or psychotherapy; mad people were locked up at home, if the house was large enough. (My own great-grandmother, at the end of the last century, married a widower whose first wife had spent her days under restraint, strapped to a sofa.) There is a large literature on female madness and its treatment in the period. If, as Scargill says, 'The mad woman of the Gothic novel has been put to allegorical use',[13] just what does she allegorize?

For David Smith, Bertha is an image of the mother-figure whose place Jane wishes to take,[14] Robert Bernard Martin sees her as an image of Jane's soul,[15] while others see Bertha as an embodiment of unrestrained sexual licence, a symbol of Rochester's misspent youth, or even the female in himself that he must, as it were, kill or cure. She has been interpreted as the embodiment of sexuality, but critics are not sure whether what she represents is male or female. As Barbara Hill Rigney conveniently summarizes:

> Terry Eagleton ... for example sees Bertha partly as a projection of Jane's psyche, yet 'since Bertha is masculine, black-visaged and almost the same height as her husband, she appears also as a repulsive symbol of Rochester's sexual drive'. Moglen ... describes Bertha [as] '... an androgynous figure, she is also the violent lover who destroys the integrity of the self; who offers the corruption of sexual knowledge and power—essentially male in its opposition to purity and innocence'.[16]

Charlotte herself told W. S. Williams (letter of 4 January 1848):

> I agree ... that the character is shocking, but I know that it is but too natural. There is a phase of insanity which may be called moral madness, in which all that is good or even human seems to disappear from the mind, and a fiend-nature replaces it. The sole aim and desire of the being thus possessed is to exasperate, to molest, to destroy, and preternatural ingenuity and energy are often exercised to that dreadful end. The aspect, in such cases,

assimilates with the disposition—all seem demonised. It is true that profound pity ought to be the only sentiment elicited by the view of such degradation, and equally true is it that I have not sufficiently dwelt on that feeling: I have erred in making *horror* too predominant. Mrs. Rochester, indeed, lived a sinful life before she was insane, but sin is itself a species of insanity—the truly good behold and compassionate it as such.

That Bertha Mason represents Jane's (and Charlotte's) *rage*, a *doppel-gänger* who attacks with knives and teeth, who destroys a house with fire, maims her husband and destroys herself, was first put forward in a scholarly argument by Sandra Gilbert and Susan Gubar in their feminist revision of literary history, *The Madwoman in the Attic*. For Virginia Woolf, Charlotte's anger had deformed her art; for Gilbert and Gubar, it is Charlotte's fuel. Their reading is so persuasive that it has gained wide acceptance. They have profoundly influenced the way we all, now, read *Jane Eyre*. Of course, we think. Why did not we see it before? Jean Rhys had given poor Bertha a novel to herself, in *Wide Sargasso Sea*, but while this was praised as a work of art, it was not taken seriously as a critique of *Jane Eyre* until the feminists took another look at the novel. For Gilbert and Gubar, all Charlotte's work is about 'hunger, rebellion and rage'.[17]

For Karen Chase, however, although they are 'right to stress the importance of confinement', they 'simplify just where the novel complicates'.[18] Chase points out that while confinement is a grave peril in *Jane Eyre*, so is exposure. Chase questions the tendency to identify characters as 'doubles' or 'parts' of Jane:

'If Rochester represents one aspect of Jane's personality,' writes Moglen, 'St. John represents the other.' Gilbert and Gubar regard Bertha as Jane's 'truest and darkest double'. Both suggestions are useful, but they risk transforming a process into hypostatised categories. . . . Bertha reflects Jane only at certain angles and at certain times. If, as various critics have claimed, St. John Rivers is Jane's super-ego, then one must explain why her super-ego is so slow to appear, and so quick to disappear. It is more illuminating, I think, to regard such characters, not as parts of, or doubles for, Jane, but as *phases*, temporary and extreme manifestations. . . . Since Jane's position changes as the plot changes, Bertha and Rivers appear *first* as reflections and *later* as alternatives.[19]

Robert Keefe recognizes that *Jane Eyre* 'is only superficially
concerned with ethics: at bottom it is concerned with the
psychology of survival'. Yet even so sensitive an observer as
Keefe imagines that Bertha makes 'vengeful attacks on Jane'.[20]
Barbara Hill Rigney[21] and Gail Griffin, among others, have
pointed out that Bertha only attacks men. Griffin praises Bertha
for her 'gentleness' towards Jane and sees her night visitation
not as destructive, but as a warning from

> one Mrs. Rochester to another; from one who has been sold in
> marriage to one who has been feeling she is about to be bought,
> like a 'slave' or a 'jewel' by the same buyer[22]. . . . Jane sees
> herself in Bertha's place—as the discarded plaything, as a
> madwoman. . . .[23]

Judging by her letter, it seems unlikely Charlotte meant us to
think of Bertha as 'gentle'. On one level Bertha is the hated
wife, the rival, Madame Heger, degraded into a being like
Branwell, somebody who makes life a misery for all around him
and sets fire to the bedclothes. H. W. Gallagher writes that
Branwell set his bed on fire and Emily rescued him 'about a
year after [*Jane Eyre*] was written'.[24] But the source is John
Greenwood's diary, which is not so much a diary as a series of
jottings, and all John Greenwood has to say about the date is
that it was 'in the latter end of [Branwell's] life'. Branwell's
degeneration was the open secret at the Parsonage, which made
it impossible for Charlotte to entertain Ellen there.

At Thornfield, the party of sightseers climb to the third storey
where Mr. Rochester opens the 'low, black door with his
master-key, admitted us to the tapestried room with its great
bed and its pictorial cabinet'. Mr. Rochester continues the
unveiling process, by lifting 'the hangings from the wall,
uncovering the second door; this too he opened.' Bertha is
incarcerated in a room 'without a window', trapped like an
animal in the zoo. A

> figure ran backwards and forwards. What it was, whether beast
> or human being, one could not, at first sight tell: it
> grovelled, seemingly, on all fours; it snatched and growled like
> some strange wild animal: but it was covered with clothing, and
> a quantity of dark, grizzled hair, wild as a mane, hid its head and
> face.

There is more than a hint, here, of a bearded lady. Bertha is, we are told, 'covered with clothing' (not dressed, like a human being), but that image is obliterated by the superimposition on our mental retina of that wild, grizzled hair, like an animal's pelt. Bertha lives in our memories as a hairy beast, precariously poised on her back legs. She is the 'clothed hyena' who 'rose up and stood tall on its hind feet', desexed by her narrator's pronouns. Parting her 'shaggy locks', the maniac 'gazed wildly' at her visitors. Jane 'recognized well that purple face—those bloated features'. Bertha goes for her husband, showing 'virile force', almost throttling, until he overpowers her and ties her to a chair with a rope. Jane remonstrates with Rochester for speaking so cruelly of Bertha, but the words of alienated disgust are Jane's. As Showalter says, Bertha is 'the female Yahoo in her foul den.'[25] Bertha is also a Nebuchadnezzar figure, running about on all fours, become an animal, rather than a human being. Nebuchadnezzar, we remember, 'was driven from men, and did eat grass as oxen, . . . till his hairs were grown like eagles' feathers and his nails like birds' claws' (Daniel 4:33). When Jane finds Rochester at the end, she says, 'You have a *faux air* of Nebuchadnezzar about you . . .' (Ch. 37). Nebuchadnezzar is man dehumanized.

There are several strange allusions and semi-allusions which add to the mystery. Jane, after her engagement, which promises a delusory paradise on earth, tells Rochester,

> I was thinking of Hercules and Samson with their charmers . . . you don't talk very wisely just now; any more than those gentlemen acted wisely. However, had they been married, they would no doubt by their severity as husbands have made up for their softness as suitors. . . . (Ch. 24)

There is something strange about this passage, as if Charlotte were laying a false scent. Samson and Hercules were both married, and both were destroyed by their wives. Paula Sullivan, in 'Rochester Reconsidered: *Jane Eyre* in the Light of the Samson Story', writes that

> Charlotte Brontë must have had the relationship of Samson and Delilah somewhat in mind as she developed that of Rochester and Jane. . . . As an admirer of Milton, who headed her list of 'first-rate poets', she had probably read *Samson Agonistes* . . . the repeated description of Rochester's physical appearance as

'athletic' may even stem from an understanding of the word *agonistes* as meaning an athlete struggling for a prize in the Olympic games.[26]

If Sullivan had reread *Samson Agonistes* before writing, she would have found ample proof that Charlotte knew it; *Jane Eyre* is saturated in Miltonic echoes, many of them directly from *Samson*, and throwing light on *Jane Eyre*. Bertha Mason, 'infamous daughter of an infamous mother', is described by her husband as 'intemperate, unchaste' (Ch. 27). The Chorus in *Samson Agonistes* explain how Samson has been prompted

> To seek in marriage that fallacious Bride,
> Unclean, unchaste. (ll. 320–21)

When Dalila arrives, Samson screams, 'Out, out, hyaena!' (l. 748).

Charlotte took up Milton's equation of a wicked wife and a 'hyaena' literally, and linked the ideas by means of the mad woman's laugh. Writing to her father from London, 4 June 1850, she described a visit to the London Zoo:

> The most ferocious and deadly-looking things in the place were these [large foreign rats nearly as large and fierce as little bull-dogs], a laughing hyena (which every now and then uttered a hideous peal of laughter such as a score of maniacs might produce) and a cobra di capello snake. . . .

Her imagination seized on words and images which she recombined. Rochester's marriage, like Samson's, is a degradation. Milton's Samson tells his father, Manoa, that the slavery of grinding, blinded, at the mill is preferable to the misery of his marriage:

> The base degree to which I am now fall'n,
> These rags, this grinding, is not yet so base
> As was my former servitude, ignoble
> Unmanly, ignominious, infamous,
> True slavery, and that blindness worse then this
> That saw not how degeneratly I served. [ll. 415–20]

His father replies, 'I cannot praise thy Marriage choises, Son. . . .' Samson's wife, say the Chorus,

> Seeming at first all heavenly under virgin veil,
> Soft, modest, meek, demure,

147

Once join'd, the contrary she proves, a thorn
Intestin, far within defensive arms
A cleaving mischief. . . . (ll. 1035–39)

This 'cleaving mischief' is generally accepted as an allusion to
the story of Hercules. Hercules had given his death-blow to
Nessus, the centaur; as Nessus died he told Deianeira, Hercules's
wife, to keep some of his blood as a love-potion. Deianeira soaked
a shirt in this blood and when Hercules fell in love with somebody else, gave the shirt to Hercules, hoping to recover his love.
But the centaur's blood was poisonous and clung to Hercules,
killing him. Rochester's blinding which brings enlightenment is
not only like Samson's, it is like Gloucester's in *King Lear*. And
the centaur turns up in *Lear* as a hideously negative image of
female sexuality, as Lear raves about female sexual appetite:

> Down from the waist they are Centaurs, though women all above:
> but to the girdle do the gods inherit, beneath is all the Fiend's.
> There's hell, there's darkness, there is the sulphurous pit; burning,
> scalding, stench, consumption. . . . (Act 4, sc. 6)

As a girl I found this passage acutely distressing, and other
female readers must have felt the same. To think of one's own
underparts as stinking, dangerous, an analogue of hell, a source
of disease, is hardly conducive to mental health in adolescence.
There seems to be built into the human psyche, along with the
surge of desire, an undertow of revulsion. Men fear engulfment,
the loss of precious bodily fluids, the *vagina dentata*. Women long
for the male, yet fear the dissolution of identity, the surrender of
independence, the 'sacrificial' element in penetration, which
involves submission to mastery which may be both desired and
feared. Normal sex can easily assume, in the mind of a virgin
female, the proportions of violation. Charlotte, whose virginity
was prolonged until she was 38, was both fascinated and
anxious. She had few rôle-models for married sex, till she was
faced with her rival, Zoe Parent Heger, who cheerfully conceived by the man Charlotte was pining for, and rounded apace
under Charlotte's very eyes. There was not one sexually satisfied
person in Haworth Parsonage: Papa was a widower, Aunt
Branwell and Tabby were spinsters, and four of the five sisters
died virgin. Charlotte certainly believed that Branwell had
committed adultery with his Lydia. The idea was both exciting

and appalling. Charlotte and her sisters had been brought up in a culture where sex was not talked about.

Before we confidently 'interpret' Charlotte we should bear in mind the backbone of Protestant literary culture (the Bible, Shakespeare, Bunyan, Milton) she shared with her readers, and the repressive morality dinned into girls, with its insistence that sex outside marriage was wicked and degrading. A lady must exhibit constant self-control and never show her emotions, though licensed to feel.

In the Parsonage Museum is a copy of Mrs. Chapone's *Letters on the Improvement of the Mind*, inscribed, 'Prize for good and ladylike conduct adjudged to Miss Nussey and presented with the Miss Woolers [*sic*] kind love Roe Head June 21st 32'. This presentation shows that Mrs. Chapone's precepts, then more than half a century old, were still current. In it we read lessons that Charlotte had taken to heart, and which she tests in *Jane Eyre*. For example,

> It is as unbecoming to [a young woman's character] to be betrayed into ill behaviour by *passion* as by intoxication . . . gentleness, meekness and patience are her peculiar distinctions; and an enraged woman is one of the most disgusting sights in nature. (p. 71)

Mary Wollstonecraft is credited with coining the phrase 'legal prostitution' for a money-marriage, but Mrs. Chapone anticipated the idea: we read (p. 65), 'A mercenary marriage is a detestable prostitution'. Letter 4, 'On the regulation of the heart and affections', tells us:

> There are no virtues more insisted on as necessary to our future happiness, than humility and sincerity or uprightness of heart; yet none more difficult and rare. Pride and vanity, the vices opposite to humility, are the sources of almost all the worst faults, both of men and women.

Future happiness, of course, means 'in the next world'. (By this standard, Blanche and even Rochester stand condemned.) Modesty-training was strict, and vanity, which poor Charlotte had such a small chance of indulging, was severely condemned, both by the Methodists and the secular moralists. Mrs. Chapone tells us:

> Whilst men are proud of power, of wealth, dignity, learning, or abilities, young women are usually ambitious of nothing more than to be admired for their persons, their dress or their most trivial accomplishments. The homage of men is their grand object: but they only desire them to be in love with their *persons*, careless how despicable their *minds* appear, even to ... their pretended adorers ... vanity ... always corrupts the heart. ... [It] requires all the efforts of reason, and all the assistance of grace, totally to subdue it.

Jane is on the watch against these moral dangers; it is the man who has 'wealth and power' to be proud and vain about. The world was full of dreadful temptations and pitfalls if one was not constantly alert. Rocheser allowed himself to be tricked into a marriage with Bertha, because his 'senses were excited'; married, he recognizes she has a 'pigmy intellect' and 'giant propensities'. He tells Jane, 'Your mind is my treasure' (Ch. 27). In the previous chapter, Rochester has described Jane as 'this young girl, who stands so grave and quiet at the mouth of hell, looking collectedly at the gambols of a demon'. The educated reader is immediately reminded of Milton's Satan, visiting his daughter, Sin, and their incestuous offspring, Death, in *Paradise Lost*, Book II. For Rochester, Bertha is a 'witch' with a 'familiar', a 'hag'. Jane reproves him for his cruel words, but Charlotte seems to endorse them. She writes to Williams, justifying herself, of 'moral madness', a current euphemism for that largely imaginary disease Victorian doctors were so afraid of, 'nymphomania'. Bertha carries for Charlotte an emotional loading of physical sexuality, and of a foul sort: the sexual relations of Sin and Death. That Charlotte, who provided her most vital heroines, Jane Eyre and Lucy Snowe, with father-figures as lovers, had a surreptitious interest in father–daughter incest has often been noted. While Bertha represents the rage of a woman, cabin'd, cribb'd, confined, she also represents sexual abandon. Jane, like anorexics and like Charlotte herself, is undersized, elfin, a sprite, a fairy, undeveloped, prepubescent in appearance. Bertha, by contrast, has the size and strength of a man; she is hairy, muscular and sex-crazed. Rochester's attractive, but threatening, muscularity has already been noticed; when Jane and Rochester come together again, 'the muscular hand broke from my custody; my arm was seized, my shoulder, neck, waist—I was entwined and gathered to him' (Ch. 37). This must be the most erotic grope in literature; Rochester's muscularity takes control and Jane willingly submits. But until she has a fortune of her own, and he has repented his errors, full physical intimacies are terrifying to Jane. Charlotte was horrified to think of clergymen in whom 'the animal predominated over the intellectual' (see my Chapter 3). By animal, she meant 'sexual'.

Jane Eyre is a virgin's horrified fantasy of adult sex: Rochester lifts the curtain, penetrates to the heart of the house, opens the door to Bertha's room with his 'master-key'. The 'marriage' cannot take place because Jane is terrified of being mastered, of being 'opened' with that male 'master-key' and turned into a 'clothed hyena', growling and sniffing about on all fours. Burkhart writes that 'Bertha's final descent from the attics, to rip up Jane's bridal veil, seems to represent Jane's natural terror at the loss of maidenhead.'[27] And Bertha's attacks with knife and teeth possibly represent the power of the male to penetrate Jane and make her bleed. Sexual experience, it is implied, can degrade a woman so that she becomes a brute beast, like a man; height, hairiness and strength symbolize, for Charlotte, male sexual appetite, an inflamed and enlarged version of her own. Bertha is an 'Indian Messalina', an awful warning of what an adulteress can degenerate into. Bertha's degradation is a warning against drunkenness and promiscuity, proof of how they can bring you down.

But her existence is not, as several have pointed out, the only obstacle to Jane's marriage. Jane is afraid and uneasy about the marriage before she knows of any impediment; many have noted her bitter resentment of Rochester's economic domination. I believe nobody has noticed that she is terrified of what she tells herself will be 'the bliss of union'. She cannot imagine, without anxiety, anything more physical than kisses. Bertha is an image of her virginal terror. Richard Chase makes an idiotic comment which I have not seen anywhere challenged: 'Bertha represents the woman who has given herself blindly and uncompromisingly to the principle of sex and *intellect* (italics added).'[28] Bertha's trouble is that she has no intellect; she has destroyed what brain she had with drink and debauchery. The link seems to be with Lawrence's Bertha Mellors, another hated wife; Lawrence took a great deal from Charlotte, but repudiated her feminism to embrace a repressive machismo. Lawrence did not think women had any business being intellectual and Chase has, in muddled fashion, projected Lawrentian prejudices back on to Charlotte. There is, objectively, nothing wrong with a woman giving herself to the principle of 'intellect', the very principle Charlotte endorses in Jane. Charlotte's fable took its shape, as fictions do, from the writer's own emotional pressures. Unregenerate sex is imaged by mad Bertha because Charlotte's own sexual wishes were focused on a married man, a father-figure. It was all too much like the union of Satan and Sin, productive of Death. Somehow, to make the fantasy come out right, the married lover had to become unmarried, so the heroine could enjoy him without guilt. The solution to the dilemma was very expensive.

NOTES

1. Robert Heilman, 'Charlotte Brontë's "New" Gothic', in *From Jane Austen to Joseph Conrad*, ed. R. C. Rathburn and Martin Steinmann, Jr., pp. 118–32; repr. *Twentieth Century Views*, ed. Ian Gregor, p. 108.
2. Joseph Prescott, '*Jane Eyre*: A Romantic Exemplum with a Difference', in *Twelve Original Essays on Great English Novels*, ed. Charles Shapiro, p. 100.
3. David Cowart, 'Oedipal Dynamics in *Jane Eyre*', *Literature and Psychology*, 31 (1981), 35.
4. Margot Horne, 'From the Window-seat to the Red Room: Innocence to Experience in *Jane Eyre*', *Dutch Quarterly Review*, 10 (1980), 206.
5. Geoffrey Wagner, *Five for Freedom*, p. 105.
6. Marxist Feminist Literature Collective, in *1848: The Sociology of Literature*, ed. Francis Barker *et al.*, p. 192.
7. Margot Horne, 'From the Window-seat to the Red Room', 206.
8. Elaine Showalter, *A Literature of their Own*, pp. 114–15.
9. Ibid., p. 113.
10. Herman Rapoport, '*Jane Eyre* and the *Mot Tabou*', *Modern Language Notes*, 94 (1979), 1098.
11. Barbara Hill Rigney, *Madness and Sexual Politics*, p. 27.
12. Mark Kinkead-Weekes, 'The Place of Love in *Jane Eyre* and *Wuthering Heights*', in *Twentieth Century Views*, ed. Ian Gregor, p. 83. The original of this apostles' cabinet is now in the Parsonage Museum at Haworth.
13. M. H. Scargill, 'All Passion Spent', *University of Toronto Quarterly*, 19 (1950), 122.
14. David Smith, 'Incest Patterns in Two Victorian Novels', *Literature and Psychology*, 15 (Summer 1965), 140–41.
15. Robert Bernard Martin, *The Accents of Persuasion*, p. 77.
16. Cited Barbara Hill Rigney, *Madness and Sexual Politics*, p. 26.
17. Sandra Gilbert and Susan Gubar, *The Madwoman in the Attic*, p. 339.

18. Karen Chase, *Eros and Psyche*, p. 62.
19. Ibid., p. 73.
20. Robert Keefe, *Charlotte Brontë's World of Death*, p. 127.
21. Barbara Hill Rigney, *Madness and Sexual Politics*, p. 26.
22. Gail B. Griffin, 'The Humanisation of Edward Rochester', *Women and Literature*, n.s. 2 (1981), 125.
23. Ibid., 127.
24. H. W. Gallagher, 'Charlotte Brontë: A Surgeon's Assessment', *B.S.T.*, 18 (1985), 364.
25. Elaine Showalter, *A Literature of their Own*, p. 115.
26. Paula Sullivan, 'Rochester Reconsidered: In the Light of the Samson Story', *B.S.T.*, 16 (1973), 192–93.
27. Charles Burkhart, *Charlotte Brontë: A Psychosexual Study of her Novels*, pp. 72–3.
28. Richard Chase, 'The Brontës: A Centennial Observance', repr. *Twentieth Century Views*, ed. Ian Gregor, p. 24.

12

The Maiming of
Edward Rochester

I suppose I should now entertain none but fatherly feelings for
you.—Mr. Rochester (*Jane Eyre*, Ch. 37)

Does *Jane Eyre* have a happy ending? Jane seems to think so, but
readers find it sad and puzzling: what has St. John's martyrdom
to do with married love at Ferndean? Donald Stone believes
that 'A Victorianised romance celebrating the virtues of home
and duty is the reward for the rejection of the excesses of
romance and Romanticism'[1] ... 'the brief but climactic
Ferndean section of *Jane Eyre* represents one of the earliest and
most satisfying of Victorian fictional attempts to balance the
opposing claims of the individual and society.'[2]

Annette Tromly, however, has doubts:

> Despite Jane's self-proclaimed sense of fulfilment, the final
> paragraphs of the novel reveal that her psychic equipoise is
> tentative. ... Something within her compares the epic scale of
> Rivers' mission with her pedestrian existence at Ferndean and an
> abyss of uncertainty opens before her—despite her protestations
> to the contrary.[3]

Tromly thinks life at Ferndean offers 'dismal prospects'[4]:
'... by means of [Jane's] inflationary rhetoric, she inadvertently
undercuts her own fictive Eden. The perfect concord she claims
to have found is inconceivable outside the gates of Paradise.'
Tromly points out that in her attitude to Adele, Jane has
become rather too much like Mrs. Reed. 'And as Brontë
implies, such happy endings occur only in fiction—in imaginary
prelapsarian worlds which are unacquainted with life's

unavoidable ambiguity. Through her art, Jane has deluded herself.' For Tromly, Charlotte gives the last word to St. John as a corrective to facile acceptance of Jane's 'happiness': 'Brontë implies that the last door will remain ajar; Jane cannot lock up her truth in fiction.'[5] This deconstructionist reading implies that Jane's happiness is a delusion and that Charlotte knows it. This is probably a fair answer to the worrying question as to why we revert to St. John at the end. Is his religion, so hateful to Jane, meant to be endorsed as right after all? Does Charlotte approve of the martyrdom Jane so healthily rejects? Lawrence Jay Dessner argues that the novel embodies a faith

> in a just although sometimes incomprehensible God, and a Puritan belief in the inexorable consequences of sin. The characters ... through the agency of plot, reap reward or punishment[6]. ... *Jane Eyre*'s coincidence-ridden plot makes a moral point and directs us to a moral rather than a psychological analysis.[7]

Dessner raises an important point:

> The mature Jane is insufficiently known and characterised; she intrudes her voice and her consciousness too faintly for us to know her, like her, and believe her when she criticises young Jane. The novel's plot and its message are not supported by the emotional reactions the book produces on the reader. Its intended unity is askew. ... An area of thought that has shifted dramatically since 1847 is the attitude toward the moral responsibilities of children. ...[8]

Dessner argues that Jane is at fault at Gateshead, and that we, the reader, are meant to see it; but 'we are not convinced that, however hard pressed, Jane's early rebellion was not only sin, but a sign of true spiritual calamity to come.' Many readers have felt this, but this may be due, as Dessner suspects, to historical shift. When Jane hears the voice, she is at last enabled to reconcile reason and feeling, but readers have found the 'magic' unconvincing. This may be less Charlotte's fault than the fading of Romantic ideals in our own minds.

Charlotte's own ambivalences provide the chief energizing tensions of her story: rage and violence in children are no doubt deplorable, as she tells us; she calls in Helen Burns to emphasize this lesson: but how understandable they are! What are we to do with our turbulence? Is religion really the answer? Brocklehurst's, false, worldly and hypocritical, definitely is not; Helen's might be, but Helen is destined for death, not for life; and St. John's brand of religion implies self-immolation, martyrdom and the fear of the pit. Charlotte is not certain, as George Eliot claimed to be, that 'all self-sacrifice is good.'⁹ Dessner writes of Jane's 'spiritual calamity to come': what spiritual calamity? Jane looks like the self-sacrificing Victorian wife ministering to her blind husband, but it is not Jane who has been sacrificed; it is Rochester. Critics frequently assert that Charlotte was a masochist and that her female characters, like her, need to be dominated by the male. If this is so in *Jane Eyre*, then Charlotte has a funny way of showing it. Mr. Rochester arouses Jane's resentment by trying to dominate her economically, socially and sexually. So what does Charlotte do to him? Taking her images from the Bible story of Samson and the gospel of Matthew 5:29–30 ('If thy right eye offend thee, pluck it out . . . if thy right hand offend thee, cut it off . . .') and 5:28 ('. . . whosoever looketh on a woman to lust after her hath committed adultery with her already in his heart'), little Charlotte arranges for a beam to fall on his head, knocking out an eye and crushing his hand flat, so that it has to be surgically chopped off. Jane has asked Conscience to tear her away from Thornfield, but Conscience has replied, '. . . none shall help you: you shall yourself pluck out your right eye; yourself cut off your right hand: your heart shall be the victim, and you the priest to transfix it' (Ch. 27). But in Jane's case this fate is merely metaphorical; in Rochester's it literally and hideously comes true. We are uncertain whether his amputated hand is the right or the left, because Jane contradicts herself. Whichever it is, such damage is an unkinder cut than the sacrifice of Julia Severn's red topknot in the interests of repressive religion. Actual sin brings with it swingeing punishment: Rochester is literally beaten over the head as his house collapses in flames. It is Rochester, not Jane, who becomes a 'mutilated sacrifice', and hence, like Samson, truly repentant. It is of course Charlotte, Chief Genius of Angria, who wreaks this vengeance on her puppet; Jane thinks only kind and loving thoughts, just as it is she who shows humane compassion for Bertha, while Rochester

rails in disgust. Charlotte's hostility to the madwoman is
expressed indirectly, both by description and by Rochester's
reactions; Jane's hostility to Rochester is imaged as divine
vengeance, which absolves Jane (and Charlotte) of responsibility. For Elizabeth Hardwick,

> The large gaping flaws in the construction of the stories—mad
> wives in the attic, strange apparitions in Belgium—are a
> representation of the life she could not face; these gothic subter-
> fuges represent the mind at a breaking point, frantic to find any
> way out. . . . They stand for the hidden wishes of an intolerable
> life.

As Hardwick notes, 'All of the Brontë sisters carried about with
them the despondency of their class and situation. . . . Jane
Eyre is always saving Mr. Rochester. . . . this is the circuitous
path to dominance imagined by a luckless girl.'[10] Charlotte's
fantasies are the common ones of making oneself indispensable
to the loved one, saving him/her from drowning. Yet she has
made her daydreams our own. How?

Adrienne Rich notices that although in childhood Jane's
images of love are those of willing submission to violence, she
later

> displays an inner clarity which helps her distinguish between
> intense feelings which can lead to greater fulfillment, and those
> which can only lead to self-destructiveness. The thrill of
> masochism is not for her. . . .[11]

Rich has already noticed that the first chapter establishes the
political circumstances of Jane's life: she is 'exposed to male
brutality and whim; as an economically helpless person she is
vulnerable in a highly class-conscious society.'[12] Mr. Rochester
is, in many ways, an old-fashioned hero for a novel of the 1840s.
Fathered by Carlyle's Plugson of Undershot, a new hero, the
self-made entrepreneur, was beginning to emerge. Charlotte
gave us this ambivalent hero in Robert Moore, in *Shirley*. As
Raymond Williams writes,

> the aristocrat who had seemed the natural figure for a romance
> was beginning to be affected . . . by the new bourgeois ethic of
> self-making and self-help. Indeed, a strong emphasis on work, as
> distinct from play, carried with it, actually as one of the main
> incentives of this class of fiction, a clear diagnosis of poverty,

which it included as a fact directly related to lack of personal effort or indeed to some positive vice.[13]

In *Jane Eyre*, however, the rising bourgeois figure, armed with intelligence and self-discipline, is a girl. And girls have no place in industrial society except as useless ladies, the consumers, like dolls on top of the Christmas tree, or as labourers. Industrialization offered opportunities for the man of talents to make his way in the world. But, as the Marxist Feminist Literature Collective point out,

> the meritocratic vision of 'individual self-reliance' . . . *cannot* be enacted by a woman character in the same way as it can be by a male. For a woman to become a member of the 'master-class' depends on her taking a sexual master whereby her submission brings her access to the dominant culture.[14]

Charlotte recognized the problem, and tackled it by becoming a writer. She won by making a fable in which Jane wins. As Hardwick notes, 'The romantic aspects of [the Brontë sisters] achieving anything at all have been inordinately insisted upon and the practical, industrious, ambitious cast of mind too little stressed.'[15] Charlotte's solution for Jane is a magical one: Jane, who is Rochester's equal in birth, though this advantage is obscured by her poverty, becomes his full social equal by inheriting a fortune. (Charlotte had to earn the small fortune she brought her own husband by self-help, but she lets Jane off this disagreeable necessity.) Lord David Cecil writes that in Charlotte's work

> the gale rages under the elemental sky, while indoors, their faces rugged in the fierce firelight, austere figures of no clearly defined class or period declare eternal love and hate to one another in phrases of stilted eloquence and staggering candour.[16]

Lord David could hardly be more wrong. While the period is vague, the class-relationships are anything but; they are finely etched. Jane's first friend is Bessie, but Bessie has indifferent ideas of principle or justice, because she has not been taught the morality of a gentlewoman; these ideals, of course, are conspicuously lacking in the Reed family. Bessie is surprised to find Jane, on her return to Gateshead after Lowood, 'quite a lady', and Jane is quietly pleased to report that 'I was a lady.' There is irony at the expense of Bessie's ideas of what constitute a lady: playing the piano, painting water-colours, knowing French, and embroidering on muslin and canvas (Ch. 10). The pathetic inadequacy of these accomplishments does not escape Charlotte's observation. We know what she thought of 'making puddings and embroidering bags'. The hierarchy among servants, so important to those within it, is finely discriminated, from Mrs. Fairfax down to Leah. The bite of *Jane Eyre* and an important part of its appeal to women come from its wish-fulfilling reversal of socio-economic, as well as sexual, dominance, so that a frail girl who starts with nothing but her intelligence and her determination comes to dominate and control a male of the employer class. Jane's membership of a 'good' family which leads to her becoming an heiress is pure romance. Jane, like so many self-made Victorian heroes, turns out to be a princess in disguise, for while the Victorians admired the self-made hero for his energy, no amount of social change and new channels for enterprise could quench their inherited love for a lord. The Victorians, even the most progressive, wanted to have it both ways. We know that Becky Sharp will come to no good because she is the daughter of Bohemians. Her mother is that far from respectable figure, a French 'opera dancer'. With such a background, we may wonder whether a good English education really eradicates Adele's hereditary weaknesses, as Jane hopes, or whether we should tremble for her future. Charlotte, grand-daughter of an Irish peasant farmer, was careful to bestow the distinction of 'good birth' on the Rivers family, her idealized image of sisterhood. Jane thus turns up trumps, being not only Rochester's spiritual equal but his social and economic equal as well, for despite Jane's brave words, Charlotte knew that spiritual equality is not recognized in this world; it certainly does not make eligible marriages—for that you need a dowry.

Recent criticism has concentrated on the economics of *Jane Eyre*, pointing out that Bertha is as much a victim of the mercenary marriage trade-off as is her husband. Nancy Pell says that Bertha was 'traded by her father . . . along with her dowry, to cover the Mason family's taints of insanity and Creole blood with the honor and protection of the Rochester name'.[17] Pell's assumption that 'Creole' means 'negro' or 'half-caste' and that this ancestry is to be considered a handicap, like insanity, is racist, but her idea that Bertha's revenge is that of the woman who has been traded fifteen years before is interesting. Certainly Bertha has plenty to be angry about, but Jane's narrative, Charlotte's vision, would seem to preclude all but conventional sympathy; the novel shows no empathy with the 'clothed hyena', and we have to wrench the narrative to find it. The problem with arguing about 'unconscious' meanings, or 'metonymic discourses', is that there can be no proof, only suggestion as to what images represent what fictional 'realities'. For Pell, Bertha is the psychological symbol, not of Charlotte Brontë's repressed hostility against the male universe, but of Edward Rochester's repressed awareness of his true social situation.[18] She is also, we may be in danger of forgetting, the literal lunatic wife the law at that time made no provision for him to get free of; divorce was not available. Symbolic readings of the death of Bertha often leave this dimension out. Karen B. Mann writes that both John Reed and Richard Mason represent 'a class gone sour'. 'Reed is bloated by the indulgent materialism of the bourgeoisie, while Mason is the weak and degenerate issue of the colonial system.'[19]

> It is . . . possible that Bertha's rage, expressed in fits of temper and in defiant acts of sexual indulgence—is the outward expression of malevolence bred by a system which denies her a separate will and imprisons her in a marriage which is primarily a monetary bargain. Much of her evil may, then, be unconscious retaliation.[20]

Perhaps; the question is, how much did Charlotte's conscious (or unconscious) mind know about Bertha's unconscious? While the twentieth-century reader sees acts of sexual indulgence as 'defiant', we have to remember that until recently in Western culture chastity was an absolute value, as it related to women, and its absence considered a proof, not of liberation, but of depravity. It is also hinted that Bertha's unchastity preceded the marriage bargain. Peter Grudin points out that

> Although some latitude and potential for salvation is offered to the sexually licentious man, Charlotte Brontë's independence of thought and incipient feminism do not extend such charity to the woman who transgresses society's code for feminine modesty and restraint. Sexual license in a woman is unforgivable, irreversible, and literally unspeakable.[21]

Mann sees the destruction of Thornfield as the destruction of
Rochester's property by 'an expression of Jane herself':
'Rochester is chastened economically and socially, not simply
physically.' For Mann, Bertha's rage is less 'unbridled sexual
passion' than due to 'a caste system which gives Rochester
power because he is male and wealthy'. Charlotte's is an
'extra-fictional plea for the economic and social independence
of women . . . through the figure of Bertha Mason, an integral
part of the progress Jane makes in coming to recognize herself
and her essential needs'.[22] Extra-fictional is right; Jane's story
cannot enact the emancipation of women: Bertha, who must
be destroyed, has to plead darkly for it. Interestingly, Bertha's
madness has made her dumb; she has no intelligible speech. If
such a degraded being, confined to a windowless cell, is
Charlotte's dumb spokeswoman for liberty, then *Jane Eyre* is a
dark fable indeed. It can be, though it rarely is, read as a
tragedy with the final catastrophe moderated through love,
but Rochester's redemption is at the price of his ruin. That
Bertha is a powerful symbol of the unacceptable face of
femininity (destructive rage, insatiable sexuality) is obvious.
Jane and Bertha are sisters under the skin: Bertha's attack on
her brother and Jane's attack on her cousin/foster brother,
John Reed, have their similarities. Both have their roots in
frustration and anger. While there is an economic dimension
to *Jane Eyre*, and a crucial one, it impinges more directly on the
figure of Jane than on that of Bertha. Bertha is the instrument
of Jane's repressed fury, destroying Thornfield and hitting
Rochester, that lordly male, over the head. But Jane's conscious mind must master her anger; Bertha's orgy of destruction is followed by the death of the angry woman, leaving
room for the loving, nurturing one.

Only recently has it been generally recognized that Rochester
is punished as much for his sultan-like propensities as for his
sexual sins. As Margaret Moan Rowe puts it,

> Rochester craftily seeks to subjugate Jane by elevating her . . .
> her idolatry . . . is short-lived as she refuses to be angel or object
> in Rochester's new world. Increasingly in the days before the
> wedding, Jane comes to understand that Rochester's idea of
> equality is very different from her own, and she struggles
> against his definition as she presses for her own. . . .[23]

After the reconciliation, 'Gone are the explicitly unequal components in the earlier imagery: father–child, master–bird, sultan–seraglio.'[24] Rowe concludes that

> Critics who focus on equality . . . as the central issue at the novel's close underestimate Brontë's radical vision of the ideal relationship between man and woman, a relationship which has at its centre the idea of mutuality and has as its goal 'perfect concord'.[25]

Maybe, but is there full equality, let alone concord above and beyond it, between a fit woman and a blind cripple? As Burkhart puts it,

> The almost ferocious ethic of Jane, her sense of duty, her Christian self-respect, are entirely victorious—Rochester now talks about God a good deal. She has brought him firmly into line, morally as well as sexually'.[26]

As Tromly writes, Jane 'talks glibly on behalf of her husband; her repeated assertions that they are one have the effect of making Rochester disappear'.[27] Ruth Bernard Yeazell puts forward a symbolic interpretation of the novel's resolution:

> Bertha's death and Rochester's maiming are not simply convenient twists of plot—they . . . become metaphors for the transformation within Jane. The madness which she fought has at last been destroyed; the passion whose consuming force she resisted has finally been controlled . . . the central focus for these events is not the violence done to Bertha or Rochester, but the symbolic change in Jane herself.[28]

This is what we hoped to find, traditionally. But is not this rather too comfortable? There is a temptation, when we come across an unpleasant or awkward piece of plotting, to elide it into the symbolic as a means of neutralizing it. The violence done to Bertha and to Rochester, the beloved husband, is, on the literal level, hideously bloody; both are smashed, like eggs.
As Maurianne Adams writes:

> If the 'romance' of *Jane Eyre* is a Cinderella story, although with a chastened and repentant Prince, the 'anti-romance' of *Jane Eyre* raises a psychological dilemma basic to the Victorian family and the institution of marriage seen from the underside of class and gender.[29]

Showalter says that

> Rochester's blindness ... [Robert] Moore's sickness ... are
> symbolic immersions of the hero in feminine experience. Men,
> these novels are saying, must learn how it feels to be helpless and
> to be forced unwillingly into dependency. Only then can they
> understand that women need love but hate to be weak. If he is to
> be redeemed and to rediscover his humanity, the 'woman's man'
> must find out how it feels to be a woman.[30]

Gilbert and Gubar see 'an element of truth' in Richard Chase's
theory of 'symbolic castration', which demonstrates that the
'tempo and energy of the universe can be quelled' by a 'patient,
practical woman',[31] but Gilbert and Gubar believe that
Rochester's punishment occurs so that Jane can 'strengthen
herself, ... make herself an equal of the world Rochester
represents'.[32] Carolyn Heilbrun writes that 'Rochester undergoes, not sexual mutilation as the Freudians claim, but the
inevitable sufferings necessary when those in power are forced
to release some of their power to those who previously had
none'.[33] Helene Moglen believes that Jane's development can

> be maintained only at the cost of Rochester's romantic self-
> image. Rochester's mutilation is, in terms of this nascent feminist
> myth, the necessary counterpart of Jane's independence: the
> terrible condition of a relationship of equality.[34]

Terrible indeed. Annette Schreiber thinks,

> perhaps his maiming symbolizes his inadequacy to save Jane
> from her own ... insignificance and helplessness. Perhaps only
> the heavenly father can achieve that mission ... the words that
> close the novel, ... end the quest.[35]

Schreiber believes the 'father-husband-saviour-lover cannot
rescue the deeply lonely, emotionally wounded heroine'. The
heroine is not badly wounded; she has learned to accept
compromise, and a mutilated happiness on earth, under God.
But Charlotte was wounded. The identification of Rochester as
father-husband-saviour-lover is too obvious, in my view, to
need arguing. Maurianne Adams writes, 'Jane's nurturing
custodianship of the blinded and maimed Rochester is again
parental rather than sexual.'[36] Charlotte here gave a tip to
Dickens, who as everybody knows had an unhappy relationship

163

with his father, and makes so many of his protagonists (Wemmick, Jenny Wren) stand in quasi-parental relationship to their progenitors. Adams wonders whether Rochester's maiming is 'the harsh biblical punishment for adultery . . . or whether its very harshness draws our attention to Jane's extreme, perhaps excessive, need to be needed. . . .'[37] Indeed it does. Charlotte's last-known letter to Heger, 18 November 1845, says:

> *Mon père me permet maintenant de lui lire et d'écrire pour lui, il me témoigne aussi plus de confiance qu'il ne m'en a jamais témoignée, ce qui est une grande consolation.* (My father allows me now to read to him and write for him; he shows me, too, more confidence than he has ever shown before, and that is a great consolation.)

Earl A. Knies notes that although critics have usually accepted Mrs. Gaskell's statement that *Jane Eyre* was begun in Manchester in August 1846, while Mr. Brontë's cataracts were being removed, the manuscript bears two dates, 16 March 1847, at the beginning, and 19 August 1847, at the end. The second date is the completion date. The question is whether Charlotte started the novel on 16 March 1847, or in August 1846. He argues that the novel's 'unity of tone' suggests that *Jane Eyre* was started later than we thought.[38] Whether or not Charlotte actually started writing at her father's bedside, the experience was profound and its relevance to *Jane Eyre* obvious. Moglen writes of Charlotte's 'resentment of the parent who has never loved her enough: the mother who died; the father who withdrew'.[39] For Moglen, *Jane Eyre* is

> a perfect fusion of experience and invention. The trauma of Cowan Bridge . . . the dreary years spent as a governess, the thwarted passion for M. Heger . . . the ambivalence of Charlotte's relationship with Branwell and with her father, her sense of isolation and alienation, the intensity of her imaginative functioning and yearning sexuality; a religious aspiration that transcended traditional belief.[40]

This I accept. To say that Charlotte wrote out of the pressure of her own emotional conflict is not inimical to respect for her art; to see that Jane's story solves, in wish-fulfilment, Charlotte's problems is not to identify author and heroine. But the shape of the heroine was dictated by Charlotte's needs. Rosamond Langbridge, in 1929, noted that what first drew Charlotte to M. Heger was the reminiscent tyranny, religiosity and temper which brought back Mr. Brontë to her homesick soul; while she was strongly attracted by the virility and vanity, the irascibility, it seems to us, and the sarcasm which suggested Branwell. . . .[41]

Moglen cites a revealing letter, also printed by Gérin,[42] from Heger to another former pupil. It is sentimental and flirtatious, alarmingly like a love-letter. Talking of 'communication' between himself and the girl, Meta Mossman, he writes (22 November 1887):

> Letters and the post are not, luckily, the only means of communication, or the best, between people who are really fond of one another: I am not referring to the telephone, which allows one to speak, to have conversations, from a distance. I have something better than that. I have only to think of you to see you. I often give myself the pleasure when my duties are over, when the light fades. I postpone lighting the gas lamp in my library, I sit down, smoking my cigar, and with a hearty will I evoke your image— and you come (without wishing to, I daresay), but I see you, I talk with you—you, with that little air, affectionate undoubtedly, but independent and resolute, firmly determined not to allow any opinion without being previously convinced, demanding to be convinced before allowing yourself to submit—in fact, just as I knew you, my dear M—— and as I have esteemed and loved you.

If Heger wrote or talked like this to his female pupils, then he seems to have been dangerously near the limits of professionalism. The language is romantic; there is a note of wooing, with the flattering suggestion that the recipient is an independent person, whose judgement must be convinced before she will 'submit'. This is the language of courtship. On the evidence of this letter, Heger's relations with his pupils, though no doubt scrupulously correct on the physical level, involved emotional seduction and the arousal of responses which could find no satisfaction. The 1847 portrait of the family by Ange François shows a man who looks not only highly intelligent, but darkly handsome. Frederika Macdonald tells us the real M. Heger was

> *not* tender-hearted; nor very tender in manner; nor even very pleasant and considerate; nor even kind, outside of his professorial character . . . his sympathy for his pupils, *as his pupils*, led him to work on their sympathies, as a way of inducing a

frame of mind in them and an emotional state of feeling, rendering them susceptible to literary impressions, and putting them in key with himself, in this very fine enthusiasm of his, not only for enjoying literature himself, but for throwing open to others, and to young votaries especially, the worship of beautiful literature. . . . But the very exclusive literary temperament of M. Heger left him rather cold-blooded than particularly warm-hearted, where his pupils' feelings interfered. . . .[43]

Can we be sure it was only the beauties of literature he wanted the girls to worship? The letter cited is not even to a pupil, but to a *former* pupil. Heger is continuing the game of emotional domination, advance and withdrawal, after the professional link has been snapped. Charlotte was perhaps too plain to get this sort of treatment; her letters to him do not suggest that he wrote such emotionally charged letters to her. But had his conversations with her, in French or in English, hovered on the edge of the lover-like caress, as this letter does? Heger wrote to Mr. Brontë, when the girls first returned from Brussels, that he felt for them an affection *'presque paternelle'*.[44] Paternal affection was what Charlotte was short of; she spent her life trying to be good to Papa, so that he would be grateful and love her (though at the end she stood up to him, forcing him to accept in his own house the husband who would help Charlotte take care of the old man: tangled loyalties indeed). When Branwell died, Charlotte wrote to W. S. Williams (2 October 1848):

My poor father naturally thought more of his *only* son than of his daughters, and, much and long as he had suffered on his account, he cried out for his loss like David for that of Absalom—my son! my son!—and refused at first to be comforted. And then when I ought to have been able to collect my strength and be at hand to support him, I fell ill. . . .

The wastrel son was worth more than five daughters, two dead: of those remaining, two, or perhaps all three, of them were women of genius, one of whom had just electrified England with her first novel. Charlotte may have found Papa's preference 'natural'; but she fell ill and we are not surprised. David Smith takes it for granted that *Jane Eyre* is an extended fantasy of father–daughter incest, and writes that in the Red Room Jane 'not only feared but committed, in fantasy, incest with Mr. Reed. . . . We will be more tolerant of [Jane's] flight from

166

Rochester, perhaps, if we are aware of the extent to which she dreaded the consummation of her sexual desires.'[45] Smith points out that against the bad father-figure of Brocklehurst stands the good father-figure, Mr. Lloyd the apothecary. Smith links Brocklehurst and St. John as superego figures, both associated with death. Smith takes up the notion of castration, though he accepts that, 'Permanently blind in one eye, temporarily in the other, and maimed by the loss of one limb, Rochester has suffered a symbolic *partial* castration.'[46] What, one wonders, would symbolic full castration involve? Smith continues,

> the father has lost some (but not all) of the sexual power which made him a fearful figure as well as a beloved one . . . and Jane can fulfil the de-sexualised daughter rôle of *service* to the helpless father. . . . Jane's superego actually joins forces with her passion. Blaming herself for his predicament, she concludes she can expiate only by lifelong servitude to her old master. The psychic conflict has been resolved, daughter and father, sans mother and segregated . . . live happily ever after.[47]

This is all very neat, but Jane does not blame herself for Rochester's predicament; it is all Bertha's fault. Jane never doubts that she did right in refusing to be Rochester's mistress. The slipperiness of the concept 'superego' is evident from the different interpretations put on it by different readers. They do not seem sure whether the superego is a 'good' principle holding the triadic personality together, or a 'bad' one, a force of repression. That this ambivalence is built into Western culture, especially since the advent of Romanticism, is a source of the disturbing strength of *Jane Eyre*. Which do we want to win? The forces of passion or the framework of Christian domesticity?

Diane Sadoff's analysis is heavily Lacanian. She invokes Freud's identification in 'The Uncanny' of the 'substitutive relation between the eye and the male organ'.[48] Since other commentators equate the penis with the hand, thereby concluding that when Jane becomes Rochester's 'right hand' she becomes a substitute penis, Charlotte seems to have missed no opportunities. Charlotte would not have needed to read Freud or his followers; she had the myths of Samson and of Oedipus to work on, and her father's literal blindness was suggestive for her. In *King Lear* the loss of Gloucester's eyes is his punishment for adultery: 'the dark and vicious place where thee he got cost him his eyes', says Edgar (*Lear*, Act V, sc. iii). The good Edgar is the instrument of vengeance on the wicked Edmund. Shakespeare's two brothers, the good son and the bad, exemplify, as do Lear's daughters, similarly divided, filial ambivalence. And *Lear* at its most poignant is the story of a wronged daughter tenderly reunited with the father who had rejected her. Sadoff reminds us that in *Villette* the relations between Polly Home and her father are implicitly seductive.[49] She points out that in *Shirley* Caroline's mad father raves and the daughter falls ill, 'both metaphors for desire in Brontë's narratives'.[50] For Sadoff 'What critics call "masochism" in Brontë's novels, then, we may interpret as stories about the female fantasy in a patriarchal and phallocentric culture, "I am being beaten by my father".'[51] Sadoff's analysis of the relations between Charlotte's characters and father-figures is persuasive:

> The structures I have traced of presence and absence, of sup-plementation, and of female desire, punishment and self-punish-ment as narratively linked to the father appear not only in Brontë's novels, but in her biography as well. The central figure in Brontë's imaginative confrontation with her own experience is not Branwell, as Winifred Gérin and Helene Moglen argue, but her father. . . . Since Elizabeth Gaskell mythologized him as a tyrant, on the word of a dismissed servant, the figure of Patrick Brontë has been vilified and—the current trend—domesticated. All we know about the father, however, we know from Brontë's imaginings: his paradoxical absence and hovering presence some-where in the godlike upper stories of the parsonage.[52]

Sadoff here makes a common mistake: many people imagine, erroneously, that there are attics at the parsonage, in reality a tiny house. Mr. Brontë's study was downstairs, across the hall from the family living room. It must have been a refuge from that cramped living room, overflowing with small children. That Papa withdrew when left with the demands of his brood (described optimistically to Mary Burder as a 'small, but sweet, little family') is understandable: his attempts to remarry were unsuccessful. He seems to have had an ulcer. Papa needed peace and quiet.

It is not too far-fetched to see the fusion in Charlotte's mind of Papa and of Heger, both stern and exigent, offering only crumbs of affection that had to be earned by strenuous good behaviour, transformed into tender lovers. Beating Rochester over the head (with falling *masonry?*), she makes Heger's imaginary wife the agent of his maiming, thus relieving her narrator/author persona, leaving her innocent; he melts into her dream of Papa, blinded and helpless, dependent on her, the puniest, weakest, and (as she felt herself to be) the least promising of his children. Papa, thundering from the pulpit in his Ulster accent (which Mrs. Gaskell thought of as Scotch) must have seemed to the small Charlotte like the voice of God. The children of clergymen notoriously have problems of identity and moral crises. *Jane Eyre* is on one level an Oedipal fantasy in which the daughter becomes the wife; in the original story, we remember, Antigone is both daughter and sister to the blind Oedipus. Jane is also something of a Delilah, in that finding Rochester shaggy and overgrown she sets about cutting his hair. But in choosing as her hero not a clergyman, no Brocklehurst or St. John figure, but a secular sinner, Charlotte was making her bid for emancipation from the dominance of Papa; and by turning Branwell's ravings into Bertha's, and giving Bertha an orgy of destruction, Charlotte satisfied, in imagination, her longing to escape from the patriarchal family into adult marriage with another widower, who would love and cherish her and be grateful. But the male had to be punished for arousing her passionate devotion and then ignoring her. Castration is a side-issue, particularly when different commentators equate either the eye or the hand with the penis: how many penises has Rochester to lose? To see Jane as becoming a substitute penis for her blinded hero (who later gives her a son) is to enter an Alice-in-Wonderland world of illusion where everything stands for something else but nobody knows what it is. The mutilation of Edward Rochester, distressing for readers, was a profoundly necessary resolution for Charlotte, as an assault on patriarchy and a complaint about the forced passivity, sexual and economic, of women. David Cowart writes,

> Critics uncomfortable with the psychological implications of his wounding have attempted to interpret it as condign punishment for his attempted bigamy (rather than as a displacement of the punishment deserved by the incestuously ambitious Jane).[53]

There is considerable truth in this. Paula Sullivan writes: '*Jane Eyre* is a woman's hostile fantasy about a man.'[54] Sadoff feels it is time for feminist critics to stop apologizing for Charlotte's 'narrative punishment of Rochester: his punishment indeed represents a "symbolic castration", one that does not signify "equality" but rather a fear of sexual difference and masculine power.'[55] The Marxist Feminist Literature Collective see it this way:

> In the vocabulary of Lacanian psychoanalysis, his maiming by the author is not so much a punitive castration, but represents his successful passage through the castration complex. Like all human subjects he must enter the symbolic order through an enforced acceptance of the loss of an early incestuous love-object, a process he initially tries to circumvent by bigamy. His decision to make Jane his bigamous wife attempts to implicate the arch-patriarch, God himself ("I know my maker sanctions what I do".) The supernatural lightning which this presumption provokes is less a re-establishing of bourgeois morality than an expression of disapproval by the transcendental phallic signifier of Rochester's Oedipal rivalry. It is God at the end of the novel who refuses to sanction Jane's marriage to St. John Rivers when invoked in its support, and who sends Rochester's supernatural cry to call Jane to him; and it is God's judgement which Rochester, in his maimed condition, finally accepts with filial meekness. By accepting the Law, he accepts his place in the signifying chain and enters the Symbolic order, as bearer rather than maker of the Law.[56]

The authors point out that the marriage legitimates sexuality, without attempting to rupture 'the dominant kinship structures'. While Charlotte would have been startled at the notion of God as 'transcendental phallic signifier', she might have accepted some of this analysis. What bothers me is the identification of Bertha as the 'early incestuous love-object'. This seems to mean that Rochester sees Bertha as a mother-figure, thus arousing God's jealousy. But Bertha was never much of a love-object; Rochester weakly agreed to marry her for her money because she was good-looking: it was a youthful mistake, made under family pressure. He is rather old to be working through castration complexes and the loss of early love-objects at the time of his first marriage.

The Maiming of Edward Rochester

In a private letter, the critic Nora Crook writes:

> One of the cruellest jokes that Charlotte plays on Mr. Rochester
> is that he gets exactly what all ardent men are supposed, in
> popular romantic fiction, to want: that one's love should always
> appear to be an angel. Jane graduates from being a *fairy* to a
> cloudy figure in blue as his eyesight gets better. She does allow
> him to have the dignity of being a Vulcan—so he has some
> Satanic majesty. He is the lame smith, godlike but imperfect—
> this Venus will never deceive him with Mars. . . . I think
> Charlotte engineers things so that you are so relieved to find that
> he is not dead . . . that you are prepared to put up with blindness
> and a stump as trifling imperfections. It is dead right for Jane's
> character that she never really asks herself whether she might not
> have preferred Mr. Rochester undamaged. But of course she
> would have—she set off for Thornfield before she heard of the
> fire, and her discovery of the 'blackened ruin' is one of the great
> 'too late!' moments in literature. So (and here's one of your
> instances of what's not said)—she accepts this maimed sacrifice
> of a husband because *she doesn't deserve better*. She didn't write
> herself a winning script when she was young, to use Eric Berne's
> terminology, and can only feel happy about marrying Mr. R.
> when he is no longer a desirable match as far as the world is
> concerned. She has early learned that getting one's heart's desire
> means getting what one doesn't want as well. She wants to go to
> school and thinks it will be a release, whereas (although she gets
> a good education) it turns out to be another kind of prison. So
> part of the message of the book is Axel Heyst's 'woe to the man
> who when young has not learned to put his trust in life!'* Jane's
> education has made her suspicious of good fortune, and she can
> really only trust her bad luck—or rather she can only relax in
> situations where she knows that she is not *too* fortunate.

Jane's happiness is not the fairy-tale kind. Religion has the
last word. St. John's closing words may mean that he has failed
in grace, and is egotistically torturing himself, as John Halperin
thinks,[57] in which case it is he, not Jane, who is the masochist;
or he may be a reminder that life on earth is spent in the shadow
of eternity. Perhaps we may read Charlotte's unexpected
obeisance to St. John, whose proposals are rejected because she
finds his brand of religion hateful, as an apology to Papa for

---

* Mrs. Crook paraphrases the hero of Joseph Conrad's novel, *Victory*.

wishing to leave him and his religious authority, to find a secular mate of her own. Eventually she managed to find a husband, but he was not the one she wanted: and he was a clergyman. In real life she brought her husband to the paternal hearth. Jane Eyre, on the run from Rochester, is reduced to eating pigs' food; the orphan is symbolically the prodigal daughter, who will return.

NOTES

1. Donald Stone, *The Romantic Impulse in Victorian Fiction*, p. 113.
2. Ibid., p. 120.
3. Annette Tromly, *The Cover of the Mask*, p. 60.
4. Ibid., p. 59.
5. Ibid., p. 61.
6. Lawrence Jay Dessner, *The Homely Web of Truth*, pp. 67–8.
7. Ibid., pp. 72–3.
8. Ibid., p. 74.
9. Quoted by Sidney Bidell, letter to Ellen Nussey, 15 February 1885.
10. Elizabeth Hardwick, *Seduction and Betrayal*, p. 29.
11. Adrienne Rich, '*Jane Eyre*: The Temptations of a Motherless Woman', in *Lies, Secrets and Silence*, p. 96.
12. Ibid., p. 92.
13. Raymond Williams, 'Forms of English Fiction in 1848', in *1848: The Sociology of Literature*, ed. Francis Barker *et al.*, p. 279.
14. The Marxist Feminist Literature Collective, 'Women's Writing: *Jane Eyre, Shirley, Villette, Aurora Leigh*', in *1848: The Sociology of Literature*, ed. Francis Barker *et al.*, p. 191.
15. Elizabeth Hardwick, *Seduction and Betrayal*, p. 13.
16. Lord David Cecil, *Early Victorian Novelists*, p. 87.
17. Nancy Pell, 'Resistance, Rebellion and Marriage: The Economics of *Jane Eyre*', *N.C.F.*, 31 (1977), 410.
18. Ibid., 411.
19. Karen B. Mann, 'Bertha Mason and Jane Eyre: The True Mrs. Rochester', *Ball State University Forum*, 19 (1978), 32.
20. Ibid., 33.
21. Peter Grudin, 'Jane Eyre and the Other Mrs. Rochester: Excess and Restraint in *Jane Eyre*', *Novel*, 10 (1977), 157.
22. Karen B. Mann, 'Bertha Mason and Jane Eyre', 34.
23. Margaret Moan Rowe, 'Beyond Equality: Ideas and Images in *Jane Eyre*', *Ball State University Forum*, 21:4 (Autumn 1980), 7.
24. Ibid., 8.
25. Ibid., 9.
26. Charles Burkhart, *Charlotte Brontë: A Psychosexual Study of her Novels*, p. 75.

27. Annette Tromly, *The Cover of the Mask*, p. 59.
28. Ruth Bernard Yeazell, 'More True than Real: Jane Eyre's Mysterious Summons', *N.C.F.*, 29 (1974), 142.
29. Maurianne Adams, 'Family Disintegration and Creative Reintegration: The Case of Charlotte Brontë and *Jane Eyre*', in *The Victorian Family: Stress and Structure*, ed. Anthony Wohl, p. 160.
30. Elaine Showalter, *A Literature of their Own*, p. 152.
31. Richard Chase, 'The Brontës: A Centennial Observance', in *Twentieth Century Views*, ed. Ian Gregor, p. 25.
32. Sandra Gilbert and Susan Gubar, *The Madwoman in the Attic*, p. 368.
33. Carolyn Heilbrun, *Towards Androgyny*, p. 59.
34. Helene Moglen, *Charlotte Brontë: The Self Conceived*, p. 142.
35. Annette Schreiber, 'The Myth in Charlotte Brontë', *Literature and Psychology*, 18:1 (1968), 67.
36. Maurianne Adams, '*Jane Eyre*: Woman's Estate', in *The Authority of Experience*, ed. Diamond and Edwards, p. 153.
37. Ibid., p. 158.
38. Earl A. Knies, *The Art of Charlotte Brontë*, pp. 215–16.
39. Helene Moglen, *Charlotte Brontë: The Self Conceived*, p. 109.
40. Ibid., p. 107.
41. Rosamond Langbridge, *Charlotte Brontë: A Psychological Study*, p. 83.
42. Winifred Gérin, *Charlotte Brontë*, pp. 262–63.
43. Frederika Macdonald, *The Secret of Charlotte Brontë*, p. 133.
44. Letter dated, according to Shorter's *Life and Letters*, 'Samedi, 5 Obre'. Gérin gives the date as 6 November 1842.
45. David Smith, 'Incest Patterns in Two Victorian Novels', *Literature and Psychology*, 15 (Summer 1965), 137.
46. Ibid., 143.
47. Ibid., 144.
48. Diane Sadoff, *Monsters of Affection*, p. 123.
49. Ibid., p. 130.
50. Ibid., p. 133.
51. Ibid., p. 134.
52. Ibid., p. 139.
53. David Cowart, 'Oedipal Dynamics in *Jane Eyre*', *Literature and Psychology*, 31 (1981), 37.
54. Paula Sullivan, 'Rochester Reconsidered: *Jane Eyre* in the Light of the Samson Story', *B.S.T.*, 16 (1973), 192.
55. Diane Sadoff, *Monsters of Affection*, p. 184n.
56. The Marxist Feminist Literature Collective, 'Women's Writing: *Jane Eyre, Shirley, Villette, Aurora Leigh*', in *1848: The Sociology of Literature*, ed. Francis Barker *et al.*, p. 193.
57. John Halperin, *Egoism and Self-Discovery*, p. 61.

13

Shirley: A Feminist Document?

> The character who most perfectly embodies Charlotte Brontë's romanticism and who occupies the central point about which the three concentric rings of characters seem to be arranged is, oddly enough, Shirley's dog Tartar.—Jacob Korg

Jane Eyre is in part about Charlotte's bitterness that her father could give her no dowry. *Shirley* is on the same theme: Shirley, the heiress, can woo her man, who is grateful, and hand over her money to him. This seems to be a symbolic gesture, as until the Married Women's Property Act 1870, a woman's property automatically became her husband's unless a separate settlement was made upon her. (Annette Schreiber sees Shirley's munificence as a form of 'castration'[1]: surely a pleasanter one than Rochester's mutilation?) Caroline's misery comes from poverty: Robert can only afford to marry her after he has firstly failed in his bid to marry Shirley and her wealth, and secondly benefited from the repeal of the Orders in Council which has helped the economy pick up. Jane, having acquired her fairy gold, proceeds to share it out. Charlotte has a recurrent fantasy of lavishing money on kinsfolk and lovers. Her novels are as much about the lack of money as the lack of love. *Shirley* could be sub-titled, 'Muck and brass'. Shirley was not a girl's name until Charlotte made it so; to get the full flavour of Captain Keeldar, we must imagine a girl with a name like Howard or Gary.

Margaret Smith writes of *Shirley*,

> Because it contains many small revisions, it reveals clearly Charlotte Brontë's *conscious* art. One feature that recurs here and in

174

Villette is a concern for rhythm and pattern: Charlotte repeatedly adds words to complete the balance of a sentence: 'sparkling clear' becomes 'sparkling bright in clear air', so that it matches the following phrase, 'shimmering dim through mist'; the 'lustre and softness of prayer' becomes 'the softness of love and the lustre of prayer'.[2]

Shirley also demonstrates Charlotte's wit and her analytical intelligence. Tastes differ about Charlotte's humour, and to some the account of the little boy who is hoping to get left-over cake and cries when he does not might be considered facetious and laboured; it delights me. We remember it is the three curates who have gobbled up the cake:

> Its elegy was chanted in the kitchen by Abraham, Mrs. Gale's son and heir, a youth of six summers; he had reckoned on the reversion thereof, and when his mother brought down the empty platter, he lifted up his voice and wept sore. (Ch. 1)

The quasi-biblical diction reminds us that the greedy clergymen have thoughtlessly deprived a child. We think of millstones and offended little ones. A howl of disappointment is elegantly transformed by irony into an elegiac chant for the cake that is no more. It has been said that Charlotte could not draw male characters; indeed, she said so herself (letter to James Taylor, 1 March 1849):

> Thank you for your remarks on *Shirley*. Some of your strictures tally with some by Mr. Williams. You both complain of the want of distinctness and impressiveness in my heroes. Probably you are right. In delineating male character I labour under disadvantages; intuition and theory will not always adequately supply the place of observation and experience. When I write about women I am sure of my ground—in the other case I am not so sure.

The complaints by Taylor and Williams surprise and puzzle me. The English novel contains few men to compare with the radical Mr. Yorke and the Tory Mr. Helstone, fully conceived and understood. Yet *Shirley* is considered an artistic failure and a shortfall in radical feminism.

It was produced in terrible conditions. Charlotte wrote to W. S. Williams on 3 July 1849:

> Lonely as I am, how should I be if Providence had never given me courage to adopt a career—perseverance to plead through two

long, weary years with publishers till they admitted me? How should I be with youth past, sisters lost, a resident in a moorland parish where there is not a single educated family? . . . As it is, something like a hope and a motive sustains me still. I wish all your daughters—I wish every woman in England, had also a hope and a motive. Alas, there are many old maids who have neither.

Martha Vicinus quotes a key passage from *Shirley*:

'Caroline,' demanded Miss Keeldar abruptly, 'don't you wish you had a profession—a trade?'

'I wish it fifty times a day. As it is, I often wonder what I came into the world for. I long to have something absorbing and compulsory to fill my head and hands, and to occupy my thoughts.'

'Can labour alone make a human being happy?'

'No, but it can give varieties of pain, and prevent us from breaking our hearts with a single tyrant master-torture. Besides, successful labour has its recompense; a vacant, weary, lonely, hopeless life has none.' (Ch. 12)

Vicinus continues:

When Mrs. Jameson, an early feminist, showed this passage to two men, one said the girl should emigrate, the other that she should marry. . . . The most popular alternative to vacuity for the middle classes was charity. Trained to be loving and emotional, without sexuality, young ladies threw themselves into church work, or . . . the serving of the family . . . religious fervor was often an unconscious form of sexual sublimation, whereby the most enthusiastic religious women found a suitable outlet for their passions.[3]

Charlotte was sceptical about religion as sublimation and her energetic satire on the 'Jew-basket' shows us what she thought of charitable needlework. When Mary Taylor read *Shirley*, she wrote from New Zealand, April 1850, 'You are a coward and a traitor.' Mary objected that only 'the few born to wealth' could escape working, and that a woman who worked was 'by that alone' better than one who did not. While this was true, it was no answer to the problem of girls like Caroline, whose social position made useful work and the power of earning impossible, so they were condemned to genteel poverty. Caroline's wish to work is negated by her uncle.

Janet Spens believed that 'Caroline was originally intended to die of a broken heart, but the death of Anne made this too sad an ending for Charlotte, who would not have wanted people to think that Anne's death was due to any such cause.'[4] Caroline has also been thought to be a combination of Ellen Nussey and Charlotte herself. For a review of opinions, see Herbert E. Wroot, *Sources of the Brontë Novels: Persons and Places.*[5] J. M. S. Tompkins writes, memorably, 'Two thirds of the way through *Shirley* Caroline Helstone's eyes change from brown to blue.'[6] Tompkins believes that Charlotte's original model was brown-eyed Ellen Nussey, but after Anne died, Charlotte turned to blue-eyed Anne as original. Tompkins argues that Caroline may have been intended to live single. Her recovery is due to her mother's love rather than Robert's return to her, and Louis only turns up halfway through the novel so that both girls can have husbands. Earl A. Knies, in 'Art, Death and the Composition of *Shirley*', questions Mrs. Gaskell's dating, on which Spens and Tompkins base their cases. Mrs. Gaskell wrote that Charlotte had nearly finished the second volume when Branwell died, and that the first chapter Charlotte wrote after Emily and Anne were dead was Chapter 24, 'The Valley of the Shadow of Death'. Knies notes that Louis Moore is mentioned as early as Chapter 5, although he does not appear until later. The end of the first volume is dated in manuscript September 1848, the month of Branwell's death, and was sent to W. S. Williams in February 1849, before Anne died. Knies argues that Louis cannot be an afterthought.[7] Margaret Smith agrees that the second and third volumes were completed after Branwell's death.[8] Knies concludes that 'Charlotte's failure in *Shirley* must, in the final analysis, be assessed in artistic, not personal, terms.'[9]

If there is a failure in *Shirley*, it seems to be in the ending, where Charlotte, besotted with the idea of Belgian school-teachers, awards one to Shirley as her prize. Shirley, we feel, deserves better. Though what ought Charlotte to have given her? Charlotte's control disappears when it comes to the marriages, with Martin's meddling and the lame contrivance of Louis's diary. Charlotte did not know how to end her novel, because the problems she wrote about were insoluble.

Jacob Korg notes in 'The Problem of Unity in *Shirley*' that the novel seems static because the facts are established from the start. 'The most exciting actions, like the battle at the mill, or

Shirley's clash with her uncle, do not develop the plot but simply reveal character and attitudes.'[10] Korg concludes that *Shirley*, patched together from diverse materials, is a philosophical novel: 'its philosophy often seems to encumber it seriously, but it does serve to pull the novel's parts together into a single fabric.'[11]

Arnold Shapiro defends the novel in 'Public Themes and Private Lives: Social Criticism in *Shirley*'. He argues persuasively that the novel is about selfishness, national, commercial and personal. All the men agree with Peter Malone about marrying for 'advantageous connexion',[12] and Shapiro is one of the few critics to recognize that Robert Moore is far from being idealized. 'Moore is that phenomenon so common to Victorian literature—the divided man. . . . There is, as he realizes, a sharp cleavage between "cousin Robert" and "Mr. Moore".'[13]

Carol Ohmann, in 'Charlotte Brontë: The Limits of her Feminism', summarizes critical response:

> At once G. H. Lewes, in the *Edinburgh Review*, called it 'a portfolio of sketches.' Lewes' judgment that the novel is conspicuously lacking in unity, has decidedly prevailed among the critics of *Shirley*. Janet Spens, for example, Lord David Cecil, Fannie Ratchford, Robert Heilman, Asa Briggs, J. M. S. Tompkins have all reiterated it. More recently, two younger critics, Jacob Korg and Arnold Shapiro, have argued strenuously on the other side, claiming, although from different interpretations of the novel's meaning, that *Shirley* is unified and its unity is thematic.[14]

Ohmann writes: 'In *Shirley*, Charlotte Brontë is consistently concerned with the right use and the misuse of power . . . the ambience of *Shirley* is cultural, social, economic, political, all four.'[15] Ohmann points out that 'While Caroline's experience testifies to the emptiness, the poverty, the indignity of the spinster's lot, two further characters in the novel bear witness to the keener griefs that come from marriage.'[16] Ohmann points out that 'Shirley's fate is not all that different from Caroline's, though Caroline thinks it is. . . .'[17] Ohmann continues:

> that Shirley claims exemption from under-estimation and from inaction by playing a rôle, by putting on a masculine identity is, finally, an insistent reminder of her constraints. Shirley claims

freedom only by an act of alienation from her genuine self and from her sex.[18]

Ohmann concludes that though Shirley herself suggests a new mythology, a new scripture and a new literature, in her myth of Eve the mother of Titans (Ch. 18), women experience what they experience as a class, even if they have money.

> They stand outside the corridors and bedrooms of power, outside the testaments of religion, culture, history. They need history rewritten and a new mythology. They are in want of a sweeping re-construction of social, economic, and political relationships.[19]

To offer a more radical solution, Charlotte would have had to be liberated 'from virtually an entire heritage'.[20]

Margaret A. Blom, in 'Charlotte Brontë, Feminist Manquée', discusses the 'half-doll, half-angel' (Ch. 20) view of women and concludes,

> . . . Brontë's own subjection to the cultural restrictions she argues against is demonstrated by her belief that, despite their capacity and need for independence, women wish to be dominated. This idea is stated explicitly by her most attractive, most fortunately endowed woman, Shirley Keeldar, who, though she consistently asserts her love of independence, ultimately remarks that when she chooses a husband, she will 'prefer a *master*. One in whose presence I shall feel obliged and disposed to be good. . . . A man whose approbation can reward—whose displeasure punish me. A man I shall feel it impossible not to love, and very possible to fear'.
> The desire to be both independent and mastered creates an inevitable and irresolvable conflict which runs through all of Charlotte Brontë's work . . . only when Louis Moore, whom she has long loved, at last discards the rôle of tutor for that of master, and forces her to acknowledge that he is determined to become her 'keeper' can she respond to him sexually. . . . Shirley accedes to the loss of self-hood imposed by marriage only because her own sexual desire is finally stronger than her desire for independence, but she puts off the wedding as long as possible, even after accepting Louis, who himself describes the agony her conflicting drives cause her: 'Pantheress!—beautiful forest-born!—wily, tameless, peerless nature! She gnaws her chain; I see the white teeth working at the steel!'[21]

What is Charlotte's attitude to this painful (even embarrassing) passage? What ought ours to be?

Roslyn Belkin, in 'Rejects of the Marketplace: Old Maids in Charlotte Brontë's *Shirley*', argues that *Shirley* is 'the least understood of Charlotte's novels'.[22] Belkin quotes the novel: 'Old maids like the houseless and unemployed poor should not ask for a place and an occupation in the world; the demand disturbs the happy and rich'.[23] (Ch. 22).

Belkin's original reading makes sense of much that readers have found puzzling in *Shirley*. It is no use looking to Charlotte for radical political opinions: she told Miss Wooler on 13 April 1853, that a correspondent 'thinks me a much hotter advocate for *change*, and what is called "political progress" than I am. . .'. None of the Victorian novelists who dealt with industrial life were radicals; they all showed generous indignation, pleaded for sympathy with the sufferings of the poor, and advocated compromise solutions, Christian or conservative. We see this from the novels of Disraeli, Dickens and Mrs. Gaskell. Aged 30, Charlotte wrote to Miss Wooler, 30 January 1846 (letter 2, Fitzwilliam Museum, Cambridge):

> . . .—it seems that even 'a lone woman' can be happy, as well as cherished wives and proud mothers—I am glad of that—I speculate much on the existence of unmarried and never-to-be married women nowadays and I have already got to the point of considering that there is no more respectable character on this earth than an unmarried woman who makes her own way through life quietly perseveringly—without support of husband or brother and who having attained the age of forty-five or upwards—retains in her possession of a well-regulated mind—a disposition to enjoy simple pleasures—fortitude to support inevitable pains, sympathy with the sufferings of others and willingness to relieve want as far as her means extend. . . .

(Shorter, incidentally, prints 'husband or mother'.) Belkin writes,

> As the narrative unfolds, the reader is led to examine the moral implications of the use and misuse of power by the more fortunate members of Briarfield society over its powerless and weak. What emerges is a remarkable portrayal of the effects of persecution not only on the victims, but on the culprits as well. *Shirley* also provides one of the few accurate portrayals either in nineteenth

180

or twentieth century fiction of the indignities which society inflicts on elderly spinsters, and, as well, gives the lie direct to the fallacy, still perpetuated in modern literature, that the chief problems of single, older women are sexual rather than social and economic.[24]

Belkin points out Robert Moore's contempt for Miss Ainley and Miss Mann, and reminds us that to punish Miss Ainley for helping the workers who were wounded when they attacked Robert's mill, he 'utters, what seems to him, the most cutting remark he can make about an elderly spinster, "Miss Ainley, that *very* plain old maid, sent in a stock of lint and linen to help the wounded." '[25]

Belkin recognizes that Robert is a 'flawed hero', a point clearly enough made by Caroline's comparison of him with Coriolanus. Belkin observes: 'Nineteenth-century literary convention demanded that a flawed hero undergo a moral conversion in order to be worthy of marriage to the heroine', so Moore repents. Belkin points out that only Mr. Hall (beloved by Briarfield's older women and its poor) and Louis Moore, 'a tutor and therefore, himself, a member of an oppressed group, are not self-serving'.[26]

> In treating women and the unemployed poor like business commodities instead of sentient human beings, 'the manufacturers', as Brontë calls them, lose something of their own humanity. . . .[27] Unlike the unemployed who can draw attention to their plight through oral protest or, when necessary, violent disturbances, Briarfield's single women are condemned to silence by their powerlessness. Rejects of the fiercely competitive marital market, they can rebel only in covert ways. Penniless and poorly educated . . . Caroline suffers stoically and in secret. . . .[28]

Belkin quotes:

> A lover masculine so disappointed can speak and urge explanation; a lover feminine can say nothing; . . . Take the matter as you find it: ask no questions; utter no remonstrances; it is your best wisdom. You expected bread and got a stone; break your teeth on it, and don't shriek because the nerves are martyrized: do not doubt that your mental stomach—if you have such a thing—is strong as an ostrich's—the stone will digest. You held out your hand for an egg, and fate put into it a scorpion. Show no consternation; close your fingers firmly upon the gift; let it sting

through your palm. Never mind, in time, after your arm and hand have swelled and quivered long with torture, the squeezed scorpion will die and you will have learned the great lesson how to endure without a sob. (Ch. 7)

It is worth noting that Charlotte twice uses the word 'torture' to describe Caroline's silent, passive suffering, total frustration and boredom. *Shirley* raises uncomfortable questions: is Shirley's conflict about being dominated by Louis culturally conditioned, dictated by a psychological peculiarity of Charlotte's, or a biological given? Do increased job opportunities really offer any alternative comfort to the girl whose lover rejects her? Has society really changed the situation of women so that they 'can speak and urge explanation' when disappointed?

Caroline visits the two old maids, who fill her with respect. They are morally better, less selfish, than the males who deride them. Shirley herself, unlike them, is good-looking and has the power of riches. Charlotte told Mrs. Gaskell that 'many traits in Shirley's character were taken from Emily.'[29] Mrs. Gaskell found it puzzling that the gay and charming Shirley could be a portrait of the morose and reserved Emily, stripped, naturally, of her genius and the 'harshness of her peculiar character'. Shirley, the lady of the manor, resembles Emily in little more than in the possession of a fierce dog and the unfeminine habit of whistling (a whistling woman and a crowing hen, is neither fit for God nor men, as the old English proverb has it, probably because witches were believed to be able to whistle up ill winds). Shirley, unlike Emily, affords and enjoys wearing beautiful clothes, rich silk dresses.

Belkin does not believe the character of Shirley is based on Emily Brontë; rather she is 'a construct of her author's imagination', Charlotte's answer to the question, 'How would a single woman, with (in Brontë's view) impeccable values, act if she had power equivalent to that of the privileged males in her society?'[30] Shirley, unlike the powerful males, is not so greedy that she ignores suffering. She is determined to defend her property, but believes it her moral responsibility to help the unemployed poor (the standard humane Victorian compromise). It is only with a trusted female friend that Shirley can express her feminism. And Shirley ends up like other women, subordinate to her husband.

182

Susan Gubar, in 'The Genesis of Hunger, According to *Shirley*', writes that Shirley is Caroline's double, a projection of all her repressed desires; what Shirley does, for example throwing the hated curate out of her house, is what Caroline would like to do. Shirley gives Robert a loan. And Shirley provides Caroline with her long-lost mother. 'Shirley seems slightly unreal to most readers, and this very unreality serves to remind us that she is part of a fantastic wish-fulfilment, an affirmation of what ought to be possible for women.'[31]

Criticism has been silent on one of Charlotte's artistic triumphs in *Shirley*, the portrait of Hortense Moore. In it Charlotte's astringent wit shows how a woman of sufficient, but limited, intelligence can become a petty tyrant, the victim of her own rigidity; Hortense's chief interests in life are censoriously abusing the British, among whom she lives, and endlessly rearranging, or as Charlotte so expressively puts it, 'rummaging', her drawers. Her energy is displaced, like that of so many women, into a futile obsession with order, endless tidying up to no real purpose. Hortense acts towards her cousin and pupil, Caroline, like a repressive mother, though Hortense's quirks have a lot to do with not being married. Caroline's real mother, Mrs. Pryor, has had a nightmare marriage, leading only to separation. So damaged has Mrs. Pryor been that her trust in life and nature is broken. Mrs. Yorke is married, and the mother of a large family, but she is neither happy, nor fulfilled, nor beloved by her children. Rose (modelled on Mary Taylor, who recognized and acknowledged her own family portrait) rebels. Mary Cave has died of her husband's neglect. *Shirley* is a clear-sighted analysis of the place of women in commercial society. It is not about Chartism, because Chartism was current, and would have been too near the bone. The novel is only superficially about industrial relations; it is about un- employed working men and unemployed middle-class women driven to desperation by physical and spiritual hunger. The extended metaphors of bread and stone, egg and scorpion, are about how to cope when starving. Charlotte was no facile optimist. When Caroline goes to see kind Miss Ainley,

> she bent her own mind before Miss Ainley's in reverence. What
> was her love of nature, what was her sense of beauty, what were

her more varied and fervent emotions, what was her deeper power of thought, what her wider capacity to comprehend, compared to the practical excellence of this good woman? Momently they seemed only beautiful forms of selfish delight; mentally she trod them under foot. (Ch. 10)

Intelligent people, confronted with simple goodness, frequently decide, 'momently', that it is more important to be good than to be clever. Caroline forces herself to do good works for the benefit of the poor under Miss Ainley's direction, and perseveres in keeping busy so that 'fevered thoughts' can no more poison her. But it does not work; the best is that

> gleams of satisfaction chequered her gray life here and there. . . . I must speak truth; these efforts brought her neither health of body nor continued peace of mind . . . her memory kept harping on the name of Robert Moore . . . the mind's soil and its treasures were freezing gradually to barren stagnation. (Ch. 10)

Caroline struggles to tire herself out with long walks in all weathers, but still cannot sleep. Obsessed with Robert, she writes letters to him, which she does not send. Charlotte here flings down a challenge to the Victorian pieties about the single woman's ability to find satisfaction in being useful. Yet what sets Caroline on the road to recovery when she falls ill is not sexual love, but the recovery of her mother. It is poignant to read Charlotte's imaginary portrayal of a loving mother: someone who tenderly urges you to wear your shawl, for fear you catch cold. In *Shirley*, Charlotte acknowledges that women need men; but in the bonds of friendship between Shirley and Caroline, between Mrs. Pryor and her surrogate daughter, the motherless Shirley to whom she is governess, and her true daughter, Caroline, Charlotte acknowledges the strength of female bonding, of sisterhood. *Shirley*, with its two heroines, one active, the other passive, is a memorial tribute to Emily and Anne, and to the loving bonds which women can forge among themselves in a hard, selfish world, dominated by males and by money.

Shirley is classed as an 'industrial novel'. Patricia Beer writes that Charlotte 'not only shows the changes brought about by the growth and spread of the industrial revolution, but tends to approve of them',[32] accepting Robert Moore's visions of a bright

future, when 'the green natural terrace shall be a paved street
. . . the rough pebbled track shall be an even, firm, broad,
black, sooty road, bedded with the cinders from my mill'
(Ch. 37). Beer thinks the narrator's voice describing the 'Hollow,
which tradition says was once green, and lone, and wild', with
its 'manufacturer's daydreams' of a 'mighty mill, and a chimney,
ambitious as the tower of Babel', is the quietly elegiac voice of
acceptance. However, the tower of Babel brought dissension
and disaster; its result was social strife, like that of industrial
society. To assume that Caroline 'knows that progress must
come before prettiness' is to assume complacency on Charlotte's
part where I read a wry ambivalence. George Gissing, who
wrote, 'in no modern writer have I such intense personal
interest as in Charlotte Brontë,'[33] exhibited hostility to the
commercial spirit and industrial development in his novel
Demos (1886), which echoes this passage. Charlotte perceived
the environmental cost of industrialization: in Yorkshire the
encroachment on once green and pleasant land is still the most
striking feature of the landscape. Her regrets about this inter-
penetration, now a commonplace, then a new issue, she
bequeathed to D. H. Lawrence. Charles Burkhart has accused
Charlotte of bad writing, condemning her 'violence',[34] when she
tells us, in *The Professor*, 'The mill was before us, vomiting soot
from its long chimney, and quivering through its thick brick
walls with the commotion of its iron bowels' (Ch. 2). The
metamorphosis whereby the mill becomes a sort of foul dragon,
a powerful mechanical beast, seems to me brilliant, like
Dickens's melancholy mad elephants in Coketown. Both Dickens
and Charlotte respond to both the ugliness and the magnificence
of the industrial landscape, reflecting Carlyle's ambivalent
account of Manchester in *Past and Present*. Charlotte's was one of
the earliest industrial novels. Together with Emily, she invented
the Yorkshire novel. *Shirley* may be read as a defence of poetry
and the romantic imagination, threatened by people like the
industrialist Hiram Yorke, who despite his intelligence has no
time for them, by a clergy who are spiritually moribund, and by
a money-mad society which excludes educated women from the
means to acquire money except by the marriages which are
impossible unless they have money already.

Charlotte Brontë: Truculent Spirit

NOTES

1. Annette Schreiber, 'The Myth in Charlotte Brontë', *Literature and Psychology*, 18:1 (1968), 50.
2. Margaret Smith, 'The Manuscripts of Charlotte Brontë's Novels', *B.S.T.*, 18 (1983), 200.
3. Martha Vicinus, *Suffer and Be Still*, Introduction, p. xi.
4. Janet Spens, 'Charlotte Brontë', in *Essays and Studies by Members of the English Association*, 14 (1929), 63–4.
5. Herbert E. Wroot, Supplementary Part 4, *B.S.T.*, 8 (1935), 99–101.
6. J. M. S. Tompkins, 'Caroline Helstone's Eyes', *B.S.T.*, 14 (1961), 18.
7. Earl A. Knies, 'Art, Death and the Composition of *Shirley*', *Victorian Newsletter*, 28 (Fall 1965), 22.
8. Margaret Smith, 'The Manuscripts of Charlotte Brontë's Novels', *B.S.T.*, 18 (1983), 197.
9. Earl A. Knies, 'Art, Death and the Composition of *Shirley*', 24. Against Knies' arguments that Charlotte wrote little between Branwell's death and Anne's and that only the first volume can have been completed, we must set Charlotte's own letter of 30 October 1852, to George Smith, with the manuscript of the first two volumes of *Villette*: 'I can hardly tell you how much I hunger to have some opinion besides my own, and how I have sometimes desponded and almost despaired because there was no one to whom to read a line—or of whom to ask a counsel. "Jane Eyre" was not written under such circumstances, nor were two-thirds of "Shirley".'
10. Jacob Korg, 'The Problem of Unity in *Shirley*', *N.C.F.*, 12 (September 1957), 135.
11. Ibid., 136.
12. Arnold Shapiro, 'Public Themes and Private Lives: Social Criticism in *Shirley*', *Papers on Language and Literature*, 4 (Winter 1968), 75.
13. Ibid., 78.
14. Carol Ohmann, 'Charlotte Brontë: The Limits of her Feminism', *Female Studies*, 6 (1972), 156.
15. Ibid., 157.
16. Ibid., 158.
17. Ibid.
18. Ibid., 160.
19. Ibid.
20. Ibid., 161.
21. Margaret A. Blom, 'Charlotte Brontë, Feminist *Manquée*', *Bucknell Review*, 21 (Spring 1973), 100–1.
22. Roslyn Belkin, 'Rejects of the Marketplace: Old Maids in Charlotte Brontë's *Shirley*', *International Journal of Women's Studies*, 4:1 (1981), 50.
23. Cited Belkin, 51.
24. Belkin, 52.
25. Ibid., 54.
26. Ibid., 55.
27. Ibid., 56.

28. Ibid., 57.
29. Mrs. Gaskell, *Life*, Ch. 18.
30. Belkin, 60.
31. Susan Gubar, 'The Genesis of Hunger, According to *Shirley*', *Feminist Studies*, 3 (1976), 11. Gubar points out that 'the man who offers stones instead of sustenance in return for the woman's love will receive as his punishment the rocks and stones cast by the other victims of his competitive egotism, the workers' (Gubar, 9). Shirley herself imagines her views on the woman question might earn her a 'cairn of avenging stones'.
32. Patricia Beer, *Reader, I Married Him*, p. 84.
33. See J. M. W. Bemelmans, 'A Permanent Interest of a Minor Kind: Charlotte Brontë and George Gissing's *The Unclassed*', *B.S.T.*, 18 (1985), 383.
34. Charles Burkhart, *Charlotte Brontë: A Psychosexual Study of her Novels*, p. 53.

14

Villette

. . . the most interesting novel about being a schoolteacher before
D. H. Lawrence.—Laurence Lerner

While the reading public has always enjoyed *Jane Eyre* most
among Charlotte's novels, critics have often considered *Villette*
caviare to the general. Janet Spens thought it

> her greatest book because in it the essence of her passionate,
> gloomy race finds expression. Lucy Snowe's temperament is her
> fate, and is linked with the stormy skies and seas which are the
> constant background of her story and at last the terrific agent of
> her doom. The author wrote to her publishers who had apparently
> pled for happiness for Lucy: 'Lucy must not marry Dr. John; he
> is far too youthful, handsome, bright-spirited, and sweet-tempered;
> he is a "curled darling" of Nature and of Fortune . . . he must be
> made very happy indeed. If Lucy marries anybody, it must be
> the Professor—a man in whom there is much to forgive, much to
> "put up with". But I am not leniently disposed towards Miss
> Frost: from the beginning I never meant to appoint her lines in
> pleasant places'—a fact which ought to have been obvious to all.
> Mr. Brontë too pled for a happy ending. 'But the idea of M. Paul
> Emmanuel's death at sea was stamped on her imagination until
> it assumed the distinct force of reality.'[1]

Jane Eyre, despite its description of suffering and its terrible
ending, leaves its heroine triumphant. *Villette* is often found
depressing. We do not believe in Jane's 'plainness'; we see Lucy
as pale, meagre and unattractive. We do not identify with her,
as we do with Jane (and to a certain extent with Caroline); we
do not even like her. Lucy has attracted much attention as an
'unreliable narrator'. The problem is the ironic distance between
her and Charlotte; we know she shares some of Charlotte's

188

opinions and experiences, yet Charlotte did not like her either. Lucy lies to herself, denying that she has 'an overheated and discursive imagination' (Ch. 2) and to us; she has recognized Dr. John, the object of Madame Beck's pursuit, all along as the handsome, careless Graham, but she has concealed her knowledge from us. She denies, in her narrative, any warm feelings for him, but fetishises his letters, a grovelling monomaniac. Lucy's unsuccessful struggle is to repress emotion and the imagination, as her unattractive exterior and her social situation demand; *Villette* is a painfully ironic account of the price of frustration, socially imposed and unsuccessfully internalized. The novel has been seen as disjointed. Like *Jane Eyre*, it has the unity of a fable about the growth of a psyche, but the reconciliation is harder, and *Villette* is even more possessed by death than was *Jane Eyre*, with its thoughts of the Styx as 'down the sable flood we glided' (Ch. 5), its howling banshee winds and storms. Is poor Marie Broc, the 'cretin' Lucy is forced to care for, an image of what Lucy might become, as many critics assure us? Or is it a nervous tic induced by the Other of French criticism to see all peripheral characters as 'doubles' of the heroine and to become solemnly excited over mirrors and the images they reflect? Is the nun a piece of melodramatic nonsense or a symbol of repression and enclosure finally exposed as another lie? Why does Lucy seem to enjoy being bullied and insulted by M. Paul? Do we really believe in a man whose saintly 'revenge' on the relatives of his dead love, kept from him because of his poverty, is to keep them in comfort when they fall on hard times? These coals of fire have the effect of impoverishing him and making marriage doubly impossible, because of the tie of sentiment and the drain on his resources. M. Paul's mixture of irascibility and tenderness may (just about) convince, but the socio-economic plight into which his religious allegiance has allegedly led him does not. He is willing to o'erleap these barriers for the love of Lucy, but is thwarted by Fate. Helene Moglen argues that this is because 'Brontë's fantasy relationship with Heger would not then have been laid to rest',[2] but while this is true, there are other complicated reasons for Lucy's solitary state. As Robert Colby points out, the ending of *Villette* echoes and reverses that of *Paul et Virginie* by one of the authors Heger introduced Charlotte to, Bernadin de Saint-Pierre, in which Paul survives, but his beloved, Virginie, is drowned. The ship Paul sails away on is the *Paul et Virginie*.[3] Could Catholic Paul and Protestant Lucy ever have been happy together? Is the Charlotte who brilliantly satirized Hortense Moore for her pugnacious national prejudices in an alien context exposing Lucy's little Englandism to our mockery, or is her resistance to Catholic culture intended to be understood as a manifestation of her integrity? *Villette* evinces a stronger and more sincere commitment to Protestant Christianity than any of Charlotte's previous works. Yet we know too that the freak of the confessional represented Charlotte's own experience.

Her progress as a novelist seems to have been from a first attempt to convert raw experience into fiction by the transparent device of changing the sex of the narrator (*The Professor*), to an egotistical novel written from inspiration, to the novel of 'research' and social exploration (*Shirley*), to a final facing of her worst fears and the aspects of herself she most disliked. A similar progression can be traced in other novelists and could explain why, whereas Charlotte punishes Rochester in *Jane Eyre*, she punishes her narrator, Lucy, for everything she most disliked in herself: as Lucy exorcizes the nun, the goblin, the spectre, and shakes her loose, so Charlotte in the persona of Lucy distances her own isolation and 'morbid' weakness.

She alienates us at the start. Our sympathies are with the heroic child Paulina, struggling with abandonment and desolation, and Lucy's dismissal of her as 'a little busybody' (Ch. 1) detaches us from Lucy and alerts our suspicions. It shows her as jealous, mean-spirited and cold-hearted. Yet we like the adult Paulina, so submissive to her possessive father, less than Lucy does. Has Lucy learned to be generous? At this point, it seems we are invited to admire Paulina and reject Ginevra, but Paulina's intellectual refinement is never established, although her Victorian scruples are, and Ginevra has all the life. What are we to make of Lucy's admitted attraction to the featherheaded and selfish Ginevra, and the strange episode of the mock courtship, with Lucy wearing a man's collar and jacket over her own long skirts? Lucy here has been precipitated by Paul into acting, into feeling and publicly displaying sexual emotion, simultaneously make-believe and real, in that Lucy, a woman, is unwillingly attracted by another woman, Ginevra, and is playing at wooing Ginevra away from the man Ginevra despises and Lucy would like to have, Dr. John, who is in the audience. Lucy is exalted by this emotional tangle and her violent reaction to the demand that she play a man's rôle is to make herself ridiculous by retaining her skirt, reminder to herself and the world that she too is a female. She is both excited and afraid to demonstrate courtship behaviour towards an unworthy object whom Lucy partly envies and would like to identify with, because she, Ginevra, is attractive and beloved, though undeserving. Lucy is initially reluctant, but finally stimulated to such excitement that she feels forced to renounce all emotional indulgence for the future. She fears the emotions and the arts which imitate, feed on and fan them. Stage acting can be inflammatory: Vashti's 'immoral' acting is followed by a fire in the theatre. (Here Charlotte's imagination failed her: whereas she knew that the sleeping Rochester would have been 'stupefied by the smoke' she does not bother to imagine the panic-stricken trampling of a crowded theatre on fire.) Is it relevant that Charlotte's reaction to the acting of Rachel in London was similar to that of Lucy in Brussels?[4] How much is to be laid at the door of Evangelical hostility to the theatre? Charlotte's reactions to theatrical performance, as recorded in her letters to Miss Wooler, were shrewd and original, and it is clear that, unlike strict Evangelicals, she had no objection to the theatre as such.

It is Paul who first liberates Lucy into emotion, by locking her in an attic with the rats, cockroaches, black-beetles and the 'spectre', a punitive experience Lucy finds strangely enlivening. This seems to be because she is not used to being noticed; she seems to prefer being attacked by Paul to being ignored. Eventually Paul's surreptitious acts of kindness and generosity, despite verbal abuse, liberate her into feeling and a faith in human love, after the pair of them have defied the triple-headed Catholic junta of Père Silas, Madame Beck and Madame Walravens. The nun has been critized as melodramatic, and Robert Colby has valuably pointed out the background of *Villette* in genres such as the Gothic novel and the governess novel, in particular Julia Kavanagh's *Natalie*.[5] The nun, who in true Radcliffean fashion turns out to have a rational explanation, is handled with sober realism compared with Madame

Walravens, the hunchback barbarian queen, three feet high, in
her brocade and jewels which Paul (crazily) insists she keep.
She lives in an enchanted castle with portraits on walls which
mysteriously unroll to reveal steps down which the sorceress
comes tapping with her stick. While the cool, calculating
Zoraide Reuter and Madame Beck have been universally
recognized as hostile portraits of Madame Heger, so are the
grotesques, Bertha Mason and Madame Walravens. Madame
Walravens represents the economic and sentimental barrier
between Paul and Lucy. As the grandmother of Paul's dead
love, now reduced to living on Paul's charity, Madame
Walravens is degraded into a hideous object, a parasite, totally
undeserving. She is not self-sustaining, as is that wily widow,
Madame Beck, enemy of Madame Walravens in that Madame
Beck wishes to entrap Paul into marriage and diminish Madame
Walravens's pickings. Madame Beck has the talent and energy
to earn a good living. Madame Beck 'ought to have swayed a
nation', 'should have been the leader of a turbulent legislative
assembly . . .'; her procedures 'comprised the duties of a first
minister and a superintendent of police' (Ch. 8). Charlotte
envied Madame Heger and Madame Beck their administrative
efficiency, their successful careers as pedagogues, administrators
and business women. In the city of London, the heart of the
business world, where money is made, Lucy has felt 'deeply
excited' (Ch. 6). Charlotte was forced into unwilling respect for
Madame Heger and Madame Beck. On the projections of
Madame Heger as the 'clothed hyena' of *Jane Eyre* and as the
poison dwarf of *Villette*, battening on the generosity of M. Paul,
Charlotte let rip her murderous jealousy. Charlotte's work
shows a pattern of bad mother-figures and good mother-figures:
Mrs. Reed, Miss Temple; Mrs. Yorke, Mrs. Pryor. The step-
mother figures thwart and trample. The good mother-figures
nourish and cherish. Lucy's god-mother, Mrs. Bretton, is an
ambiguous figure, whose possessive pride in, and flirtation with,
her son, Graham/Dr. John, is more threat than nurture to
Lucy. Mrs. Bretton's relationship with her son parallels that
between Mr. Home/Count Bassompierre and his daughter
Polly/Paulina. Mrs. Bretton is both mother-figure and rival to
Lucy for her son's affections. Madame Walravens, on the other
hand, is the focus of all Charlotte's stored-up hatred, which

could never be openly expressed, for that 'rosy sugar-plum', Madame Heger. The real Heger was a married Catholic: in Charlotte's fable, another wish-fulfilment, again muted, Paul is single because loyal to a memory, a phantom, a nun. Charlotte denies the fruitful sexuality of the Heger union in making Paul the victim of sentimental attachment and consequent insane self-sacrifice, which she characteristically blames on religious pressure. His attachment to the wraith of his dead fiancée can be dissolved (though with Madame Walravens draining his resources, how could he afford to furnish Lucy's scholastic Wendy-house?). Charlotte displaces the real man's unavailability from his marriage to his religion, hence the Catholic conspiracy against Lucy. The outburst against Madame Beck, who fails to separate Lucy and Paul before his departure, is also a wish-fulfilment for Charlotte, with something of *l'esprit de l'escalier* in it: ' "Keep your hand off me, and my life, and my troubles. Oh, Madame! in *your* hand there is both chill and poison. You envenom and you paralyze." ' Madame's reply is,

> '. . . You must not marry Paul. He cannot marry.'
> 'Dog in the manger!' I said; for I knew she secretly wanted him, and had always wanted him . . . she did not love, but she wanted to marry, that she might bind him to her interests . . . she was *my* rival, heart and soul, though secretly, under the smoothest bearing, and utterly unknown to all save her and myself. (Ch. 38)

It is possible to feel considerable sympathy for Madame Heger, watching the plain, clever, intense young *Anglaise* falling in love with Monsieur, and behaving correctly to protect her marriage, only to find herself recognizably vilified in print. It is unsurprising that she refused to see Mrs. Gaskell.

Villette ponders the problem of those who deserve love and get it, like Paulina; those who do not deserve love, but get it, like Ginevra; those who neither deserve love nor get it, like Madame Beck and Zélie; and Lucy, who is not sure she deserves love, but gets it just the same. But like Miss Marchmont's, her happiness is brief, snatched away by premature death of the loved one. Lucy's emotional capacity, which she has done her best to bury with Graham/Dr. John's letters, bursts out in 'the strange necromantic joys of fancy', like the bright hair she vividly imagines growing out of coffin-chinks. Contact with Paul has freed Lucy's frozen emotions, just as contact with Heger freed Charlotte's confidence as a writer. Paul gives Lucy one brief kiss and disappears; but whereas Heger gave Charlotte a diploma, Paul gives Lucy her own school, thus giving her independence and putting her on an equal social footing with Madame Beck. Once again, it is fairy gold that emancipates Lucy; even the power to earn a decent living, free of prying and oppression, comes to her not as something she has saved for out of her own earnings, but as a magical gift, snatched from the witch-mother, the evil queen. (Did Paul cut Madame Walravens's allowance? Did she have to sell some of those jewels adorning her knobbed old fingers?)

While, as we have seen, Moglen and Eagleton see Charlotte as a masochist, wishing to be dominated, Schreiber sees her novels as castrating their heroes. My own feeling is that Charlotte does not believe in happy endings. She did not care for single life and the struggle to earn a living, but her view of marriage was clear-eyed (some would say jaundiced). Many women in her situation would have settled for being Mrs. James Taylor. It was only with reluctance that Charlotte married at all. Kate Millett's was one of the earliest feminist readings of *Villette*. With hindsight, we wonder how it was possible to read Charlotte Brontë any other way. Millett points out that Lucy, though a gentlewoman, is a servant by occupation; the low-status, low-pay occupations open to women

> involve 'living in' and a twenty-four hour surveillance tantamount to imprisonment. The only circumstances under which Lucy is permitted an occupation are such that they make financial independence and personal fulfillment impossible. . . . One of the most interesting cases of inferiority feelings in literature, Lucy despises her exterior self, and can build an inner being only through self-hatred. Yet living in a culture which takes masochism to be a normal phenomenon in females, and even conditions them to enjoy it, Lucy faces and conquers the attractions Paul's sadism might have held. . . . Brontë pretends to compromise; convention is appeased by the pasteboard wedding of Paulina Mary and Prince John; cheated in Lucy's escape.

> Escape is all over the book; *Villette* reads like one long meditation on a prison break. Lucy will not marry Paul even

after the tyrant has softened. He has been her jailer all through the novel, but the sly and crafty captive in Lucy is bent on evading him anyway. . . . She plays pupil to a man who hates and fears intelligent women and boasts of having caused the only woman whose learning ever challenged his own to lose her job . . . in his simplicity he has been hoodwinked into giving her the keys. The moment they are in her hand, and she has beguiled him into lending her money, renting her a school of her own, and facilitated her daring in slipping from the claws of Madame Beck—she's gone. The keeper turned kind must be eluded anyway; Paul turned lover is drowned.

Lucy is free. Free is alone; given a choice between 'love' in its most agreeable contemporary manifestation, and freedom, Lucy chose to retain the individualist humanity she had shored up, even at the expense of sexuality. The sentimental reader is also free to call Lucy 'warped', but Charlotte Brontë is hard-minded enough to know that there was no man in Lucy's society with whom she could have lived and still been free. On those occasions when Brontë did marry off her heroines, the happy end is so fraudulent, the marriages so hollow, they read like satire, or cynical tracts against love itself. . . . As there is no remedy to sexual politics in marriage, Lucy very logically doesn't marry. But it is also impossible for a Victorian novel to recommend a woman not to marry. So Paul suffers a quiet sea burial.[6]

The Marxist Feminist Literature Collective agree:

By admitting to the incompatibility of Romanticism and Victorian 'romance', creative potency and marriage as defined by Victorian ideology, Lucy at last becomes a truly reliable narrator. . . . Lucy's two letters express a duality articulated elsewhere in the novel, in the visionary passage in which Reason plays the part of wicked and 'envenomed' step-mother, while Imagination is celebrated as the succouring, nourishing, consoling 'daughter of heaven'. It is within this primal relationship that the novelist herself is constituted as woman and writer— nurtured on Romanticism, fostered by an uncongenial Reason.[7]

This fine reading of *Villette* points out that Lucy finds herself liberated by acting.

Vashti too is an iconoclast and breacher of sexual convention, an importantly female version of the central Romantic protagonist, the satanic rebel and fallen angel whose exclusion and damnation is a function of divine tyranny. . . . *Villette* can only be silent

195

about the true nature and origin of Lucy's oppression—that is, the enshrining of marriage and the home in Victorian ideology and its consequences for women. But the ideological not-said is eloquently inscribed in the margin of the text—in the 'discursive' activity of Lucy's (over) heated imagination. Here we witness also, in contrast to Lucy's fascination, Graham Bretton's sexual judgement on 'a woman, not an artist: it was a branding judgement'. Branded as a fallen woman, a rebel against conventional morality, Vashti is at once excluded from the home and thereby permitted to retain her potency—a daemonic symbol of sexual energy and revolt, created by a woman (actress/author) in contrast to the static, male-fabricated icons of women exhibited in an earlier chapter; Cleopatra or the Jeune Fille/Mariée/Jeune Mère/Veuve (women as sexual object or bearer of ideology).[8]

As Gilbert and Gubar say, in their excellent analysis of *Villette*, Charlotte 'explores why and how the aesthetic conventions of patriarchal culture are as imprisoning for women as sexist economic, social and political institutions'.[9]

Paul as a lover fills the female reader with deep anxiety, culminating at the picture exhibition (Ch. 19). Here we empathize with Lucy's independence of judgement and her refusal to be bullied. The scene is crucial, for here she is being told what to think, what to feel, and ordered to restrict the use of her own eyes *because* she is a single woman. One would like to know more about the picture of the fat, underdressed lady Lucy identifies as Cleopatra. People have assumed, because of another reference, in Chapter 23, to Rubens's fat women, that the picture must be by Rubens, but no picture by Rubens fits the description. Gustave Charlier has found a catalogue for the Brussels salon in 1942, which identifies a picture by De Biefve, called *Une Almée*, of 'an indolent and abundant beauty stretched out in a flaccid, so-called Oriental style on the cushions of a sofa', which scandalized Brussels society in 1842. He describes a lithograph of this picture, but unfortunately does not reproduce it.[10] He also identifies a set of pictures by Madame Fanny Geefs labelled *La Vie d'une Femme*, the very pictures Paul recommends to Lucy and which she rightly scorns. Contemporaries found them insipid: Victor Joly wrote that all the heads 'bear the cachet of that romantic sentimentality which is the deplorable fruit of contemporary literature.'[11]

The whole of Chapter 19 is delightfully spirited and witty;
Lucy applies her Ruskinian demand for 'truth' in painting to
'complacent fat women' who struck her

> as by no means the goddesses they appeared to consider them-
> selves . . . and yet there were fragments of truth here and there
> which satisfied the conscience, and gleams of light which cheered
> the vision. Nature's power here broke through in a mountain
> snow-storm. . . . An expression in this portrait proved clear
> insight into character. . . .

Lucy sits down in front of

> the huge, dark-complexioned gipsy-queen; of whom, indeed, I
> soon tired, and betook myself for refreshment to the contempla-
> tion of some exquisite little pictures of still life: wild flowers,
> wild-fruit, mossy wood-nests, casketing eggs that looked like
> pearls seen through clear green sea-water; all hung modestly
> beneath that coarse and preposterous canvas.

Paul Emmanuel marches in, scolds Lucy for looking at an
immodest picture, and recommends to her attention the four
'*Anges*',

> grim and grey as burglars, and cold and vapid as ghosts. What
> women to live with! insincere, ill-humoured, bloodless, brainless
> nonentities! As bad in their way as the indolent gipsy-giantess,
> the Cleopatra, in hers.

Paul absurdly tells Lucy that married women may look on
the scantily-draped fat woman, but no 'demoiselle' should
glance at her.

> I assured him plainly I could not agree in this doctrine, and did
> not see the sense of it; whereupon, with his usual absolutism, he
> merely requested my silence, and also, in the same breath,
> denounced my mingled coldness and ignorance. A more despotic
> little man than M. Paul never filled a professor's chair. I noticed,
> by the way, that he looked at the picture himself quite at his ease,
> and for a very long while: he did not, however, neglect to glance
> from time to time my way, in order, I suppose, to make sure that
> I was obeying orders, and not breaking bounds.

Here Charlotte takes a sly swipe at the double standard of
morality: men, it seems, are permitted to look at indecent
pictures of women, whereas decent women are not. This is in

197

itself absurd, as pictures of female nakedness are presumably more inflaming to the male than to the female. Charlotte, writing about Paul's attempts to control Lucy's morals and behaviour, is in full control of her narrative. We know that Paul has no 'right' to tyrannize over Lucy; she is a colleague, not a daughter, and not yet a pupil, in no way inferior to him except in her sex. His presumption of authority, based only on this gender distinction, is illegitimate. Jane Eyre's view of Rochester was romantic, idolatrous, though mockery and teasing kept breaking through. Here Lucy shows us Paul Emmanuel as absurd; such despotic fussing would drive any woman mad. Generous he may be, but he is presented with a great deal of comic irony, an irony which amuses readers so that until recently few have recognized that the 'adorable' M. Paul is quite intolerable, to Lucy as well as to us. Only an emotionally starved girl, despising herself and her attractions, would put up with him for five minutes. But Lucy is such a girl: plain, lonely, foreign and vulnerable, so that even the Scarlet Woman of Rome appears temporarily seductive. *Villette* seems to be saying that no woman in her right mind would fall in love with a Paul Emmanuel; Lucy's wretchedness and isolation are her only excuse for such an error of judgement. Dr. John is coarse in fibre, lacking the finer feelings. Paul is supersensitive, and as neurotic as Lucy. As misfits, they make a pair, but they are not well-matched. How could Lucy's cool irony and analytical intelligence 'put up with', in Charlotte's own words, such a little monster? As she wrote to George Smith early in 1853, 'Drowning and matrimony are the fearful alternatives'. In *Villette* Charlotte was paying off several old scores; as well as blackening Madame Heger, she made M. Heger into a figure of ridicule. Charlotte wrote to Ellen from Brussels in 1842:

> He is a professor of rhetoric, a man of power as to mind, but very choleric and irritable in temperament; a little black being, with a face that varies in expression. Sometimes he borrows the lineaments of an insane tom-cat, sometimes those of a delirious hyena; occasionally, but very seldom, he discards these perilous attractions and assumes an air not above 100 degrees removed from mild and gentleman-like. He is very angry with me just at present, because I have written a translation which he chose to

198

stigmatize as *peu correcte*. . . . When he is very ferocious with me I cry; that sets all things straight.

Clearly at the time, Charlotte enjoyed being bullied and responding with the woman's defensive weapon of tears; it was, after all, attention which implied that the man cared what she achieved. Yet ten years afterwards, Charlotte seems to be recollecting in tranquillity, and wondering what an 'insane tom-cat', a 'delirious hyena' would really have been like as an avowed lover? She exposes the faults of Paul, whom she says she loves, as nakedly as those of Madame, whom she says she hates. Admittedly, Paul's are the faults of warmth, whereas Madame's are those of coldness. But we are made uneasy by the relentless mockery of the 'loved one' in *Villette*.

Charlotte, as is well known, changed Lucy's surname from Snowe to Frost and back again to Snowe (letter to W. S. Williams, 6 November 1852). Charlotte adds:

> You say that she may be thought morbid and weak, unless the history of her life be more fully given. I consider that she *is* both morbid and weak at times; her character sets up no pretensions to unmixed strength, and anybody living her life would necessarily become morbid. It was no impetus of healthy feeling which urged her to the confessional, for instance; it was the semi-delirium of solitary grief and sickness. . . .

Charlotte had lived Lucy's life and had 'become morbid'. But in *Villette* she was able to transcend her wretchedness by writing a radically experimental novel. As Annette Tromly quotes:

> . . . I got books, read up the facts, laboriously constructed a skeleton out of the dry bones of the real, and then clothed them, and tried to breathe into them life, and in this last aim I had pleasure. (Ch. 25)

Tromly continues:

> For Lucy the written word not only promises to complete the self; it also promises to resurrect the self. Faced with the dry bones of her experience, she writes, rather than lives, her life. Her autobiography mediates between herself and the world; it enables her to forge a reconstructed image.

(This can be said of all autobiographies, diaries, writing generally.) Tromly continues:

199

Yet if writing brings comfort, it also—like the more physical enclosures in the novel—involves confinement. With Lucy Snowe as narrator, Charlotte Brontë posits the darkest view of art that she has yet suggested. For not only does Lucy, like Jane and Crimsworth, use her autobiography as a means of deceiving herself, but she also, as we have noted, uses it quite deliberately to deceive others. As Lucy encloses herself in her autobiography, then, Charlotte Brontë is again raising the spectre of art's ethical ambiguity.[12]

Tromly sees Paul Emmanuel as having 'the loftiest perspective' in the novel; he is also 'the consummate artist'.

> Unlike Lucy and the others, Paul does not abuse the arts; his total engagement with life makes the false comforts which others seek from art unnecessary. Lucy directs the drama of her life with devious control, but of Paul we are told, 'There was no sham and no cheat and no hollow unreal in him'. Paul tells stories, though he is not a man to write books: he tells Lucy 'My book is this garden; its contents are human nature . . .' He has a 'careless, unconscious prodigality, such mental wealth as books seldom boast; his mind was indeed my library, and whenever it was opened to me, I entered bliss.'

As Tromly points out, sending letters which are 'real food that nourished, living water that refreshed',

> Paul, until his death, makes the substitutions of art unnecessary for Lucy; his letters contain his 'living presence'. Once this living presence is removed, however, there is no longer anything to pull Lucy out of herself.[13]

But, as Tromly tells us,

> Staged, contrived, self-protective, dishonest, distorted—the creation of Lucy's dark muse is an ironic monument indeed to a dead love. . . . She pretends to hold out hope for a happy ending, yet at the reader who would wish for such an ending, she lashes out suddenly with a tone of bitter scorn. In Paul Emmanuel's death at sea, his bereaved fiancée smugly recognizes the final stroke of a hostile Fate—part of her preordained personal mythology.[14]

The relation between Lucy and her imagination is, I believe, even more complicated than Tromly recognizes. In Chapter 30, M. Paul again dictates action to Lucy and again she resists; he asks her to lead a class in improvising a composition in French, without grammar or lexicon (we know that Heger forbade these tools to Charlotte and Emily). Lucy tells us:

> I knew what the result of such an experiment would be. I, to whom nature had denied the impromptu faculty; who, in public, was by nature a cypher; whose time of mental activity, even when alone, was not under the meridian sun; who needed the fresh silence of morning, or the recluse peace of evening, to win from the Creative Impulse one evidence of his presence, one proof of his force; I, with whom that Impulse was the most intractable, the most capricious, the most maddening of masters (him before me always excepted)—a deity, which sometimes, under circumstances apparently propitious, would not speak when questioned, would not hear when appealed to, would not, when sought, be found; but would stand, all cold, all indurated, all granite, a dark Baal with carven lips and blank eye-balls, and breast like the stone face of a tomb; and again, suddenly, at some turn, some sound, some long-trembling sob of the wind, at some rushing past of an unseen stream of electricity, the irrational demon would wake unsolicited, would stir strangely alive, would rush from its pedestal like a perturbed Dagon, calling to its votary for a sacrifice whatever the hour—to its victim for some blood or some breath, whatever the circumstance or scene, rousing its priest, treacherously promising vaticination, perhaps filling its temple with a strange hum of oracles, but sure to give half the significance to fateful winds, and grudging to the desperate listener even a miserable remnant—yielding it sordidly, as though each word had been a drop of the deathless ichor of its own dark veins. And this tyrant I was to compel into bondage, and make it improvise a theme, on a school estrade, between a Mathilde and a Coralie, under the eye of a Madame Beck, for the pleasure and to the inspiration of a bourgeois of Labassecour!

For a girl who denies having an 'overheated and discursive imagination', this is a remarkable outburst. What has Lucy to do with the Creative Impulse? This characteristically magnificent passage shows Charlotte in full control of her Creative Impulse, although the subject is its absence. The Creative Impulse, like the passions, is 'heathen'; for Lucy, it is like the false gods of the Old Testament, to which Lucy is an unwilling sacrifice. Incidentally, Charlotte uses the word 'sordidly' with precision, as she frequently does the Latinate word 'fruition' (which properly means not 'fructition' but 'enjoyment'). M. Paul is asking Lucy to expose her creative self, the quick of her nature which she studiously holds in check, to the dull gaze of the school inspectors, as he has forced her to perform a disturbingly ambiguous rôle in the play. Paul acts as a stimulus to Lucy's emotions, here identified with the 'creative impulse' which can only be Charlotte's, not Lucy's. Heger channelled Charlotte's creativity and here she records the mingled pain and pleasure of the experience. The choice of imagery shows that she identified her stern teacher with a grim and remote idol, with sacrifice—compare *Jane Eyre*, Ch. 27, and the poems. In 'He saw my heart's woe' the unmoved lover is described as an idol cut in rock, a 'Baal'. What seems to be another version of this poem, with its various drafts, is in the Berg Collection, New York public library.[15] One stanza reads:

> Cold as a statue's grew his eye,
> Hard as a rock his brow,
> Cold hard to me—but tenderly
> He kissed my rival now.

In the second version of this same poem, we read of a painful parting and tears because 'my ship was soon to sail.' Thus we see that in Charlotte's mind the sea is an emblem of parting and images of the 'Creative Impulse' enmesh with images of her tyrant master. Her dreams were tormented with images of those she loved (her sisters Maria and Elizabeth, Monsieur) being cold to and angry with her. Yet in her imaginative re-creations, as Helen Burns, as Paul Emmanuel, although they sternly correct her, they offer nourishment and love. Lucy's reluctance to make an exhibition of herself in public represents Charlotte's own shyness and diffidence; in the images of power, rejection and obdurate idols, her feelings about her imagination fuse with those she felt for Heger.

Four rejected fragments, early drafts of *Villette*, in the Brontë Parsonage Museum, Haworth, are reprinted in the Clarendon *Villette*. The first fragment is narrated by an 'Elizabeth Home', who describes herself, after some reflection, as unimaginative, but with a 'gift of inventing tales and games', but then says these were adaptations of what she had read: 'I was a very literal person.' The second fragment is narrated by Polly and consists of her early memories and attachment to her father. It is the third fragment which has the bite: an older girl (unnamed) cruelly teases small Rosa about her loyalty to 'an old wooden doll', which the older girl threatens to 'split into chips for firewood'. This older girl shows a cruelty to small Rosa that is rejected in *Villette* as too harsh for Lucy or for Graham, whose cruelty to little Polly comes from the careless arrogance of the teenage male towards an adoring little girl. Polly and Graham, like so many Victorian couples, start with what is basically a brother–sister relation. The violence in *Villette* is not acted out by Lucy towards Polly; it is turned upon herself, in self-torture, expressed in images of Jael, Sisera, tentpegs, nails, symbolic crucifixions. In *Villette* Charlotte gave us the first nervous break-down novel, and its disruptions enact those of a mind at the end of its tether, losing coherence and control. Yet the drug administered by Madame to soothe Lucy stimulates her to visionary power, so that she sees everybody assembled in the park at midnight like a clairvoyant; her bonnet pulled forward to conceal her face, she gains, by watching, nearly all the information she needs. The sight of the second Justine Marie reveals to Lucy the true state of her own feelings: '. . . something tore me so cruelly under my shawl, something so dug into my side, a vulture so strong in beak and talon, I must be alone to grapple with it' (Ch. 39). And when Lucy goes home and finds the nun's clothing in her bed, the mystery is dispelled, and Lucy is no longer the prey of hallucination. Her emotions have survived their premature burial and the ghostly visitant is shown to be not the ghost of a girl walled up alive for unchastity, but a flesh-and-blood male, intent on seduction, who has defeated Madame's surveillance and penetrated, via the *allée défendue*, the virginal convent-like fastnesses of a girls' boarding school.

Russell Goldfarb argues that *Villette* is about a 'sexually frigid young woman who learns to come to terms with her abnormal sexuality . . . at the end of *Villette* Lucy is happy, healthy, and emotionally secure'.[16] But Goldfarb interprets the passage about a 'dell, deep-hollowed . . . its herbage pale and humid' (Ch. 23) as 'vaginal imagery',[17] evidence of an imaginary sexual intercourse experienced while reading Dr. John's letters in the garret, and a psychoanalytic catharsis. Goldfarb believes that 'With the jar containing the letters thrust deeply within the secret hole, Lucy re-enacts her sexual experience with Dr. John before she inters it for good . . . she will have no future desire for sexual experience.'[18] Certainly, in Chapter 35, Paul calls Lucy his *'Petite soeur'* and, as Goldfarb points out, Paul has buried his sexual potential with Justine Marie. Paul and Lucy are thus 'two of a kind'.[19] Goldfarb praises Charlotte for anticipating Freud, a comment which should set off warning bells. It might make more sense to see the burial traditionally, as the end of a hopeless love and the beginning of a fruitful one.

Feminist critics have generally felt that Charlotte was herself trapped in the culture she anatomized; as Margaret Blom puts it, 'for her there was no way to adjust the inevitably ambivalent desires or to alleviate the consequent rage and pain.'[20] Judith Newton argues, in a fine analysis,[21] that Charlotte could not emancipate herself from the dominant ideology. Of course she could not; novels articulate the ongoing struggle of the self with whatever ideology is current.

Villette ends, 'Farewell.' Charlotte is closing a chapter in her life; while it is a cliché of modernist criticism to say that the heroine of a first-person novel, despite its fractured utterances, eventually finds coherence in the act of writing, etc. (obviously so, or there would be no novel), in the case of *Villette* this seems true of Charlotte as well as of Lucy. The image of the unplumbed, salt, estranging sea as symbol of separation haunts Charlotte's writing: for example, in the poem quoted in Chapter 7, in the references to Mrs. O'Gall of Bitternut Lodge, Ireland. Heger/Paul Emmanuel had been laid to rest and Charlotte/Lucy accepts spinsterhood. But the 'little man' has left Charlotte/Lucy with a priceless gift: that of a career. Emmanuel gives Lucy her school, the school that Charlotte thought she wanted, but never achieved. For Charlotte, even a school would have been a less desirable goal than her true vocation, that of novelist. Heger provided Charlotte with experience she was able to use as fictional material, and an education which provided her with discipline, models and standards. He brought her no happiness, but such fulfilment as she found came from contact with him. *Villette* is a requiem for a one-sided love, symbolized by the burying of letters and the drowning of Paul. It is also an exorcism: the ghostly figure of the nun, like Charlotte's own fears that her imagination might be a form of neurosis, has been reduced to an image not of death, but of sex as enjoyed by other people. Like Roman Catholicism, of which it is metonymic emblem, the ghostly figure of the nun represents for Lucy sacrifice in the form of Justine-Marie. But she is not called upon to sacrifice her religion (her cultural identity), even by her Catholic lover; she is not called upon to stay unloved for ever. Both these bogies disappear with the disappearance of the *revenant* nun and the emergent love of Paul Emmanuel. Lucy is finally free, by the establishment of her own career and the knowledge she is loved, of masochism. Now she has letters which are 'living water, that refreshed', she is rid of the 'incubus' (an ambiguous term, meaning both nightmare and a demon-seducer who appears in erotic dreams). Lucy has 'three happy years'. Charlotte was not so fortunate. Jane Eyre represented, despite the feint of making her 'plain', a romanticized self, although Jane's happiness can only come at the cost of punishment and suffering; Lucy has all Charlotte's real miseries. Symbolically, the relationship with Paul Emmanuel brings her wholeness, independence and self-respect. In *Villette*, Charlotte faced her intolerable griefs, and found a fictional compromise with the problem that had haunted her since the days of the Roe Head journal and the snub administered by Southey: how to reconcile emotional frustration and self-control with the exercise and release of her unique creative imagination, in the belief (Ch. 31) that 'this life is not all; neither the beginning nor the end. I believe while I tremble; I trust while I weep.'

NOTES

1. Janet Spens, 'Charlotte Brontë', *Essays and Studies*, 14 (1929), 65.
2. Helene Moglen, *The Self Conceived*, p. 227.
3. Robert Colby, *Fiction with a Purpose*, p. 207.
4. David Isenberg, 'Charlotte Brontë and the theatre', *B.S.T.*, 15 (1968), 237–41. See also Alan Dent, 'Rachel in London', *Manchester Guardian*, 9 May 1941.
5. Colby, p. 196.
6. Kate Millett, *Sexual Politics*, pp. 145–47. For dissenting views, see Patricia Meyer Spacks, *The Female Imagination*; Carolyn V. Platt, 'How Feminist is *Villette?*', *Women and Literature*, 3 (1975), 16–27; Margaret Lenta, 'The Tone of Protest: An Interpretation of Charlotte Brontë's *Villette*', *English*

Charlotte Brontë: Truculent Spirit

Studies, 64 (October 1983), 423 and 428, and Toril Moi, *Sexual/Textual Politics: Feminist Literary Theory* (London: Methuen, 1985), p. 28.
7. The Marxist Feminist Literature Collective, in *The Sociology of Literature 1848*, ed. Francis Barker *et al.*, p. 200.
8. Ibid., 198–99.
9. Sandra M. Gilbert and Susan Gubar, *The Madwoman in the Attic*, p. 419.
10. Gustave Charlier, transl. Phyllis Bentley, *B.S.T.*, 12 (1955), 388.
11. Cited Charlier, 387.
12. Annette Tromly, *The Cover of the Mask*, p. 86.
13. Ibid., p. 87.
14. Ibid., p. 88.
15. See Tom Winnifrith, *Brontë Facts and Brontë Problems*, Ch. 1.
16. Russell Goldfarb, *Sexual Repression and Victorian Literature*, p. 139.
17. Ibid., p. 152.
18. Ibid., p. 153.
19. Ibid., p. 156.
20. Margaret A. Blom, 'Charlotte Brontë, Feminist *Manquée*', *Bucknell Review*, 21 (Spring 1973), 102.
21. Judith Newton, *Women, Power and Subversion*, Ch. 3.

Selective Bibliography

ADAMS, MAURIANNE, '*Jane Eyre*: Woman's Estate', in *The Authority of Experience: Essays in Feminist Art*, ed. Arlyn Diamond and L. R. Edwards (Amherst, Mass.: Massachusetts University Press, 1977)
——, 'Family Disintegration and Creative Reintegration: The Case of Charlotte Brontë and *Jane Eyre*', in *The Victorian Family: Stress and Structure*, ed. Anthony Wohl (London: Croom Helm, 1978)
ALEXANDER, CHRISTINE, *The Early Writings of Charlotte Brontë* (Oxford: Blackwell, 1983)
——, 'Some New Findings in Brontë Bibliography', *N.Q.*, n.s. 30, No. 3 (Vol. 228 continuous series) (June 1983), 233–37
ALLEN, WALTER, *The English Novel* (London: Phoenix House, 1954; repr. Pelican, 1960)
ALLOTT, MIRIAM (ed.), *Charlotte Brontë: 'Jane Eyre' and 'Villette'—A Casebook* (London: Macmillan, 1973)
——, *The Brontës: The Critical Heritage* (London and Boston: Routledge and Kegan Paul, 1974)
ALTER, ROBERT, *Partial Magic: The Novel as Self-Conscious Genre* (Berkeley, Los Angeles, and London: University of California Press, 1975)
ANDERSON, RUTH L., 'As Heart Can Think', *Shakespeare Association Bulletin*, 12 (1973), 246–51
ANDREWS, W. L., 'The *Times* Review that Made Charlotte Brontë Cry', *B.S.T.*, 11 (1950), 359–69
AUERBACH, NINA, 'Charlotte Brontë: The Two Countries', *University of Toronto Quarterly*, 42:2 (Summer 1973), 328–42
BACON, ALAN, 'Jane Eyre's Paintings and Milton's "Paradise Lost"', *N.Q.*, 31:1, 229 continuous series (March 1984), 64–5
BAILLIE, J. B., 'Religion and the Brontës', *B.S.T.*, 7 (1927), 59–69
BAKER, ERNEST, 'The Brontës, Charlotte', in *The History of the English Novel* (London: H. F. and G. Wetherby, Ltd., 1937)
BARKER, FRANCIS (ed.), *The Sociology of Literature 1848*: Proceedings of the Essex Conference on the Sociology of Literature, July 1977 (Colchester: University of Essex, 1978)
BARKER, JULIET R. V., 'Charlotte Brontë's Photograph', *B.S.T.* 19 (1986), 27–8
——, 'Subdued Expectations: Charlotte Brontë's Marriage Settlement', *B.S.T.*, 19 (1986), 33–9
BATES, MADISON C., 'Charlotte Brontë and the Kay-Shuttleworths, with a New Brontë Letter', *Harvard Library Bulletin*, 9 (1955), 376–91

BAYNE, PETER, *Two Great Englishwomen* (London, 1881)

BEATY, JEROME, '*Jane Eyre* and Genre', *Genre*, 10 (Winter 1977), 619-54

BECKWITH, FRANK, 'Letters of the Rev. Patrick Brontë to *The Leeds Intelligencer*', *B.S.T.*, 13 (1960), 433–36

BEER, PATRICIA, *Reader, I Married Him* (London: Macmillan, 1974)

———, 'Charlotte Brontë and Currer Bell', *B.S.T.*, 18 (1981), 1–14

BELKIN, ROSLYN, 'Rejects of the Marketplace: Old Maids in Charlotte Brontë's *Shirley*', *International Journal of Women's Studies*, 4:1 (1981), 50–66

BEMELMANS, JOS, 'Some Neglected Responses to Charlotte Brontë's Novels', *B.S.T.* 18 (1982), 120–27

———, 'A Permanent Interest of a Minor Kind: Charlotte Brontë and George Gissing's *The Unclassed*', *B.S.T.*, 18 (1985), 383

BENSON, E. F., *Charlotte Brontë* (London: Longmans, 1932)

BENTLEY, PHYLLIS, *The Brontës and their World* (London: Thames and Hudson, 1969)

———, 'Love and the Brontës', *Contemporary Review*, 217 (November 1970), 225–30

BENVENUTO, RICHARD, 'The Child of Nature and the Child of Grace and the Unresolved Conflict of *Jane Eyre*', *English Literary History*, 39 (December 1972), 620–38

BERMAN, RONALD, 'Charlotte Brontë's Natural History', *B.S.T.*, 18 (1984), 271–78

BJORK, HARRIET, *The Language of Truth: Charlotte Brontë and the Woman Question* (Lund Studies in English, 1974)

BLACKALL, JEAN FRANZ, 'Point of View in *Villette*', *Journal of Narrative Technique*, 6 (1976), 14–28

———, 'A Suggestive Book for Charlotte Brontë?', *Journal of English and Germanic Philology*, 76 (1977), 363–83

BLACKBURN, RUTH HARRIET (ed.), *The Brontë Sisters: Selected Source Materials for College Research Papers* (New York: State University of New York at Stony Brook, 1964)

BLAMIRES, HARRY, *A Short History of English Literature* (London: Methuen, 1974)

BLEDSOE, ROBERT, 'Snow Beneath Snow: A Reconsideration of the Virgin of *Villette*', *Women and Literature*, n.s. 1 (1980), 214–22

BLOM, MARGARET A., 'Charlotte Brontë: Feminist *Manquée*, *Bucknell Review*, 21 (Spring 1973), 87–102

———, '*Jane Eyre*: Mind as Law Unto Itself', *Criticism*, 15 (1973), 350–64

———, *Charlotte Brontë* (New York: Twayne, 1977)

BODENHEIMER, ROSEMARIE, 'Jane Eyre in Search of her Story', *Papers in Language and Literature*, 16 (1980), 387–402

BOSTRIDGE, MARK, 'Charlotte Brontë and George Richmond: Idealisation in the Sitter', *B.S.T.*, 17 (1976), 58

BRADBY, GODFREY FOX, *The Brontës and Other Essays* (London: Oxford University Press, 1932)

Selective Bibliography

BRAMMER, MARGARET (*afterwards Smith*), 'The Manuscript of *The Professor*', *Review of English Studies*, 11 (May 1960), 157–70

BRANTLINGER, PATRICK, 'The Case Against Trade Unions in Early Victorian Fiction', *Victorian Studies*, 13 (September 1969), 37–52

BRIGGS, ASA, 'Private and Social Themes in *Shirley*', *B.S.T.*, 13 (1958), 203–19

BRONTË, CHARLOTTE, 'Albion and Marina', *B.S.T.*, 6 (1920), 5

——, *Five Novelettes* (London: Folio Press, 1971)

——, 'The Story of Willie Ellin', *B.S.T.*, 9 (1936), 3–22

——, 'Two Unpublished Manuscripts Foreshadowing *Villette*', *B.S.T.*, 7 (1931), 277ff.

——, 'Napoleon and the Spectre: A Ghost Story' (London: privately printed by Clement Shorter, 1919)

——, *Something About Arthur*, ed. Christine Alexander (Austin, Texas: Humanities Research Centre, the University of Texas at Austin, 1981)

——, *Emma, a Fragment* (repr. with *The Professor*, Everyman edition)

——, *The Moores*, pr. with *Jane Eyre*, introductn. by W. Robertson Nicoll (London: Hodder and Stoughton, 1902)

BRONTË, PATRICK, *Collected Works* (Bingley, 1898)

BUCKLEY, JEROME, *The Victorian Temper* (Cambridge, Mass.: Harvard University Press, 1951)

BURKHART, CHARLES, 'Another Key word for *Jane Eyre*', *N.C.F.*, 16 (September 1961), 177–79

——, 'The Moon in *Villette*', *Explicator*, 21 (September 1962)

——, 'The nuns of *Villette*', *Victorian Newsletter*, 44 (Fall 1973), 8–13

——, *Charlotte Brontë: A Psychosexual Study of her Novels* (London: Gollancz, 1973)

BURNS, WAYNE, 'The Critical Relevance of Freudianism', *Western Review*, 20 (1956), 301–14

BUSHNELL, NELSON S., 'Artistic Economy in *Jane Eyre*: A Contrast with *The Old Manor House*', *English Language Notes*, 5 (March 1968), 197–202

CARLISLE, JANICE, 'A Prelude to *Villette*: Charlotte Brontë's Reading 1850–52', *Bulletin of Research in the Humanities*, 82 (1979), 403–23

CARUS-WILSON, WILLIAM WILSON, *The Children's Friend* (1833)

——, *Child's First Tales: Chiefly in Words of One Syllable—For the Use of Infant Schools and Little Children in General* (Kirkby Lonsdale and London, 1836)

CAZAMIAN, LOUIS, *The Social Novel in England 1830–1850* (originally *Le Roman Social en Angleterre*, Paris: 1904, transl. Martin Fido; London: Routledge and Kegan Paul, 1973)

CECIL, LORD DAVID, *Early Victorian Novelists* (London: 1934, Penguin reprint, 1948)

CHAPONE, MRS. HESTER, *Letters on the Improvement of the Mind*, bound with Dr. Gregory's *A Father's Legacy to His Daughters* and *Reflections on the Seven Days of the Week* by Catharine Talbot, with the Lives of the Authors (Edinburgh: John Anderson and Thomas Tegg, 1824)

CHARLIER, GUSTAVE, 'Brussels Life in *Villette*: A Visit to the Salon in 1842', *B.S.T.*, 12 (1955), 386–90

CHASE, KAREN, *Eros and Psyche: The Representation of Personality in Charlotte Brontë, Charles Dickens and George Eliot* (New York: Methuen, 1984)

CHASE, RICHARD, 'The Brontës: A Centennial Observance', *Kenyon Review*, 9 (Autumn 1947), 478–506

CHITHAM, EDWARD, and WINNIFRITH, TOM, *Brontë Facts and Brontë Problems* (London: Macmillan, 1983)

CHRIST, CAROL, 'Imaginative Constraint, Feminine Duty and the Form of Charlotte Brontë's Fiction', *Women's Studies*, 6 (1979), 287–96

CHRISTIAN, A (*Pseud.*), *The Veil Uplifted and Mesmerism Traced to its Source, being an Exposure of the Leading Error of Phrenology; of the Object of Mesmerism to Confirm that Error; and an Examination of the Pretensions of Electro-Psychology* (London: Benjamin L. Green, 1852)

CHRISTIAN, MILDRED, 'The Brontës', in *Victorian Fiction: A Guide to Research*, ed. Lionel Stevenson (Cambridge, Mass.: Harvard University Press, 1964), pp. 214–44

———, 'The Brontës', *Victorian Newsletter*, 13 (Spring 1968), 19

COLBY, ROBERT A., '*Villette* and the Life of the Mind', *P.M.L.A.*, 75 (September 1960), 410–19

———, *Fiction with a Purpose; Major and Minor Nineteenth-Century Novels* (Bloomington, Indiana, and London: Indiana University Press, 1967)

COOTER, ROGER, *The Cultural Meaning of Popular Science: Phrenology and the Organisation of Consent in Nineteenth-Century Britain* (Cambridge: Cambridge University Press, 1984)

CORNISH, DOROTHY, 'The Brontës' Study of French', *B.S.T.*, 11 (1947), 97–100

COVENEY, PETER, *The Image of Childhood* (orig. publ. by Rockliff as *Poor Monkey*, 1957; Harmondsworth: Peregrine revised, 1967)

COWART, DAVID, 'Oedipal Dynamics in *Jane Eyre*', *Literature and Psychology*, 31 (1981), 33–8

COX, STEPHEN D., *The Stranger Within Thee: Concepts of the Self in Late Eighteenth-Century Literature* (Pittsburgh, 1980)

CRAIG, G. ARMOUR, 'The Unpoetic Compromise: On the Relation Between Private Vision and Social Order in Nineteenth-century English Fiction', *English Institute Essays*, 1955 (New York: Columbia University Press, 1956)

CRAIK, W. A., *The Brontë Novels* (London: Methuen, 1968)

———, 'The Brontës', in the *Sphere History of Literature in the English Language*, ed. Arthur Pollard, Vol. 6, pp. 140–68

CROSBY, CHRISTINA, 'Charlotte Brontë's Haunted Text', *Studies in English Literature 1500–1900*, 24 (Autumn 1984), 701–15

CRUMP, R. W., *Charlotte and Emily Brontë, A Reference Guide 1846–1915* (Boston, Mass., 1982)

CUNNINGHAM, VALENTINE, *Everywhere Spoken Against: Dissent in the Victorian Novel* (Oxford: Clarendon Press, 1975)

CURTIS, DAME MYRA, 'Cowan Bridge School: an old prospectus examined'. *B.S.T.*, 12 (1953), 187–92

DAVIES, STEVIE, 'Recent Studies of the Brontës', *Critical Quarterly*, 27 (Autumn 1985), 35–40

DAY, MARTIN S., 'Central Concepts of *Jane Eyre*', *Personalist*, 41 (October 1960), 495–505

DELAFIELD, E. M., *The Brontës: Their Lives Recorded by their Contemporaries* (London: Hogarth Press, 1935)

DESSNER, LAWRENCE J., 'Charlotte Brontë's *Le Nid*, an Unpublished Manuscript', *B.S.T.*, 16 (1973), 213

———, *The Homely Web of Truth* (The Hague and Paris: Mouton, 1975)

DIMNET, ERNEST, *The Brontë Sisters*, trans. Louise Morgan Sill (London: Cape, 1927)

DINGLEY, R. J., 'Rochester as Slave: An Allusion in *Jane Eyre*', *N.Q.*, 31:1, 229 continuous series (March 1984), 66

DODDS, M. HOPE, 'The Howitts' Review of *Jane Eyre*, 1847', *B.S.T.*, 13 (1960), 438–39

DOODY, MARGARET ANNE, 'Fiction, Ruins and Troubled Waters: Female Dreams in Fiction and the Development of the Gothic Novel', *Genre*, 10 (1977), 529–72

DRABBLE, MARGARET, 'The Writer as Recluse', *B.S.T.*, 16 (1974), 259–69

———, Introduction to *Villette* (London: Dent, 1983)

DREW, PHILIP, 'Charlotte Brontë as a Critic of *Wuthering Heights*', *N.C.F.*, 18 (March 1964), 365–81

DRY, FLORENCE SWINTON, *The Sources of 'Jane Eyre'* (Cambridge: Heffer, 1940)

DU MAURIER, DAPHNE, *The Infernal World of Branwell Brontë* (London: Gollancz, 1960)

DUNBAR, GEORGIA S., 'Proper Names in *Villette*', *N.C.F.*, 15 (June 1960), 77–80

DUNBAR, JANET, *The Early Victorian Woman: Some Aspects of her Life* (London: Harrap, 1953)

DUTHIE, ENID L., 'Charlotte Brontë and Constantin Heger', *Contemporary Review*, 187 (March 1955), 169–73

———, 'Charlotte Brontë's Translation: The First Canto of Voltaire's *Henriade*', *B.S.T.*, 13 (1959), 347–51

———, *The Foreign Vision of Charlotte Brontë* (London: Macmillan, 1975)

———, *The Brontës and Nature* (London: Macmillan, 1986)

EAGLETON, T., 'Class, Power and Charlotte Brontë', *Critical Quarterly*, 14 (Autumn 1972), 223–35

———, *Myths of Power: A Marxist Study of the Brontës* (London: Macmillan, 1975)

EASSON, ANGUS, 'Two Suppressed Opinions in Mrs. Gaskell's *Life of Charlotte Brontë*', *B.S.T.*, 16 (1974), 281–83

———, 'Domestic Romanticism: Elizabeth Gaskell and *The Life of*

Charlotte Brontë', *Durham University Journal*, 73, n.s. 42:2 (June 1981), 169–76

ERICKSEN, DONALD H., 'Imagery as structure in *Jane Eyre*', *Victorian Newsletter*, 30 (Fall 1966), 18–22

EWBANK, INGA-STINA, *Their Proper Sphere: A Study of the Brontë Sisters as Early Victorian Female Novelists* (London: Arnold, 1966)

FABER, RICHARD, *Proper Stations: Class in Victorian Fiction* (London: Faber, 1971)

FALCONER, J. A., '*The Professor* and *Villette*: A Study of Development': *English Studies*, 9 (April 1927), 33–7

FIELDING, K. J., 'The Brontës and the *North American Review*: A Critic's Strange Guesses', *B.S.T.*, 13 (1956), 14–18

FITZGERALD, J. A., 'Death of an Elderly Primigravida in Early Pregnancy: Charlotte Brontë', *New York State Journal of Medicine*, 79 (1979), 796–99

FOISTER, SUSAN R., 'The Brontë Portraits', *B.S.T.*, 18 (1985), 339

FOSTER, SHIRLEY, 'A Suggestive Book: A Source for *Villette*', *Etudes Anglaises*, 35 (1982), 177–84

FREEMAN, JANET H., 'Speech and Silence in *Jane Eyre*', *Studies in English Literature*, 24 (Autumn 1984), 683–700

FULTON, E. MARGARET, '*Jane Eyre*: The Development of a Female Consciousness', *English Studies in Canada*, 5 (Winter 1979), 432–47

GALLAGHER, H. W., 'Charlotte Brontë: A Surgeon's Assessment', *B.S.T.*, 18 (1985), 363–70

GALLOP, MARJORIE, 'Charlotte's Husband', *B.S.T.*, 12 (1964), 297–99

GARY, FRANKLIN, 'Charlotte Brontë and George Henry Lewes', *P.M.L.A.*, 51 (June 1936), 518–42

GATES, BARBARA, ' "Visionary Woe" and its Revision: Another Look at Jane Eyre's Pictures', *Ariel*, 7:4 (1976), 36–49

GÉRIN, WINIFRED, 'Byron's influence on the Brontës', *Keats–Shelley Memorial Bulletin*, 17 (1966), 1–19

———, *Charlotte Brontë: The Evolution of Genius* (London: Oxford University Press, 1967)

———, *Elizabeth Gaskell* (London: Oxford University Press, 1976)

GEZARI, JANET K., 'Marriage or Career: Goals for Women in Charlotte Brontë's Novels', *Bucknell Review*, 24:1 (1978), 83–94

GILBERT, SANDRA M., and GUBAR, SUSAN, *The Madwoman in the Attic: The Woman Writer and the Nineteenth-Century Literary Imagination* (New Haven and London: Yale University Press, 1979)

GIRDLER, LEW, 'Charlotte Brontë's *Shirley* and Scott's *The Black Dwarf*', *Modern Language Notes*, 51 (March 1956), 187

GOLDFARB, RUSSELL, *Sexual Repression and Victorian Literature* (Pennsylvania: Bucknell University Press, 1970)

GRAYSON, LAURA, '*Shirley*: Charlotte Brontë's Own Evidence', *B.S.T.*, 14 (1963), 31

GREEN, JOHN ALBERT, *Catalogue of the Gleave–Brontë Collection at the Moss Side Free Library* (Moss Side, 1907)

Selective Bibliography

GRIBBLE, JENNIFER, 'Jane Eyre's Imagination', *N.C.F.*, 23 (1968), 279–93

GRIFFIN, GAIL, 'The Humanisation of Edward Rochester', *Women and Literature*, n.s. 2 (1981), 118–29

GRUDIN, PETER, 'Jane and the Other Mrs. Rochester: Excess and Restraint in *Jane Eyre*', *Novel*, 10 (1977), 145–57

GUBAR, SUSAN, 'The Genesis of Hunger, According to *Shirley*', *Feminist Studies*, 3 (1976), 5–21

HADOW, SIR W. H., 'Education, as Treated by the Brontës', *B.S.T.*, 6 (1925), 261–75

HALPERIN, JOHN, *Egoism and Self-Discovery in the Victorian Novel: Studies in the Ordeal of Knowledge in the Nineteenth Century* (New York: Burt Franklin, 1974), pp. 33–79

HANNAH, BARBARA, *Striving Towards Wholeness* (New York: G. P. Putnam's Sons, 1971)

HANSON, LAWRENCE and E. M., *The Four Brontës* (London: Oxford University Press, 1949)

HARDWICK, ELIZABETH, *Seduction and Betrayal* (London: Weidenfeld, 1974)

HARDY, BARBARA, *The Appropriate Form: An Essay on the Novel* (London: Athlone Press, 1964)

———, *Forms of Feeling in Victorian Fiction* (London: Peter Owen, 1985)

HARKNESS, BRUCE, review of the Clarendon *Jane Eyre*, *N.C.F.*, 25 (December 1970), 355–69

HARRISON, GRACE ELIZABETH, *Haworth Parsonage: A Study of Wesley and the Brontës* (London: Epworth Press, 1937)

———, *The Clue to the Brontës* (London: Methuen, 1948)

HART, ANNE, 'Studies, Time, the Author as Wife', *B.S.T.*, 16 (1975), 376–81

HAWTHORN, JEREMY, *Narrative: From Malory to Motion Pictures* (London: Arnold, 1980)

HEATON, HERBERT, 'The Economic Background of *Shirley*', *B.S.T.*, 8 (1932), 3–19

HEILBRUN, CAROLYN G., *Towards Androgyny: Aspects of Male and Female in Literature* (London: Gollancz, 1973)

HEILMAN, ROBERT B., 'Charlotte Brontë's "New" Gothic', in *From Jane Austen to Joseph Conrad*, ed. Robert C. Rathburn and Martin Steinmann, Jr. (Minneapolis: University of Minnesota Press, 1958), pp. 118–32

———, 'Charlotte Brontë, Reason and the Moon', *N.C.F.*, 14 (March 1960), 283–302

———, 'Tuliphood, Streaks and Other Strange Bedfellows: Style in *Villette*', *Studies in the Novel*, 14 (1982), 223–47

HENELLY, MARK M., 'Jane Eyre's Reading Lesson', *English Literary History*, 51 (Winter 1984), 693–718

HINKLEY, LAURA L., *The Brontës, Charlotte and Emily* (London: Hammond, Hammond and Co., Ltd., 1947)

HOAR, NANCY COWLEY, 'And my Ending is Despair; *Villette*, Charlotte Brontë's Valediction', *B.S.T.*, 16 (1974), 185–91

HOEVELER, DIANE LONG, 'The Obscured Eye: Visual Imagery as Theme and Structure in *Villette*', *Ball State University Forum*, 19 (1978), 23–30

HOFSTADTER, DOUGLAS, and DENNETT, DANIEL C., *The Mind's I* (Brighton: Harvester, 1981)

HOLGATE, IVY, 'The Structure of *Shirley*', *B.S.T.*, 14 (1962), 27–35

HOLROYD, ABRAHAM, *Currer Bell and her Sisters*, repr. from the *Bradford Advertiser* (Keighley series of *Poems, Tales and Sketches*, No. 4, 1855)

HOPEWELL, DONALD, 'Cowan Bridge', *B.S.T.*, 6 (1921), 43–9

HOPKINS, ANNETTE BROWN, *Elizabeth Gaskell: Her Life and Work* (London: John Lehmann, 1952)

———, *The Father of the Brontës* (Baltimore: Johns Hopkins University Press, 1958)

HORNE, MARGOT, 'From the Window-seat to the Red Room: Innocence to Experience in *Jane Eyre*', *Dutch Quarterly Review*, 10 (1980), 199–213

HOUGHTON, WALTER E., *The Victorian Frame of Mind* (New Haven: Yale University Press, 1957)

HUGHES, R. E., '*Jane Eyre:* The Unbaptised Dionysos', *N.C.F.*, 18 (1964), 347–64

HUGUENIN, CHARLES A., 'Bronteana at Princeton University: The Parrish Collection', *B.S.T.*, 12 (1955), 391–400

HUTTON, JOANNA, 'Items from the Museum Cuttings Book', *B.S.T.*, 14 (1963) 26–30

ISENBERG, DAVID R., 'Charlotte Brontë and the Theatre', *B.S.T.*, 15 (1968), 237–41

JACK, IAN, 'Physiognomy, Phrenology and Characterisation in the Novels of Charlotte Brontë', *B.S.T.*, 15 (1970), 377–91

———, 'Novels and those Necessary Evils: Annotating the Brontës', *Essays in Criticism*, 32:4 (October 1982), 321–37

JACOBUS, MARY, '*Villette*'s Buried Letter', *Essays in Criticism*, 28 (July 1978), 228–44

JAMES, DAVID, 'Charades at Thornfield Hall and at Gaunt House', *B.S.T.*, 17 (1976), 35–41

JEFFARES, A. NORMAN, '*Shirley*: A Yorkshire Novel', *B.S.T.*, 15 (1969) 281–93

JOHNSON, E. D. H., ' "Daring the dread glance": Charlotte Brontë's Treatment of the Supernatural in *Villette*', *N.C.F.*, 20 (March 1966), 325–36

JONES, MARNIE, 'George Smith's Influence on *The Life of Charlotte Brontë*', *B.S.T.*, 18 (1984), 279–85

KARL, FREDERICK, 'The Brontës: The Outsider as Protagonist', in *An Age of Fiction: The Nineteenth-Century British Novel* (New York: Farrar, Straus and Giroux, 1964), pp. 77–103

KEARNS, MICHAEL SHANNON, 'Anatomy of the Mind: Mid-nineteenth Century Psychology and Nathaniel Hawthorne, Charlotte Brontë,

Charles Dickens and Herman Melville', unpubl. dissertation, University of California, Davis (DA 41:2613A)

KEEFE, ROBERT, *Charlotte Brontë's World of Death* (Austin, Texas: University of Texas Press, 1979)

KELLY, J. D., 'Jane Eyre's Paintings and Bewick's *History of British Birds*', *N.Q.*, 29, 226 cont. series (June 1981), 230–32

KING, JEANNETTE, *Jane Eyre* (Milton Keynes: Open University Press, 1986)

KINKEAD-WEEKES, MARK, 'The Place of Love in *Jane Eyre* and *Wuthering Heights*', in *The Brontës: A Collection of Critical Essays*, ed. Ian Gregor (Englewood Cliffs, New Jersey: Prentice Hall International, 1970)

KNIES, EARL A., 'Art, Death and the Composition of *Shirley*', *Victorian Newsletter*, 28 (Fall 1965), 22–4

——, 'The "I" of *Jane Eyre*', *College English*, 27 (1966), 546–56

——, *The Art of Charlotte Brontë* (Athens, Ohio: Ohio University Press, 1969)

KORG, JACOB, 'The Problem of Unity in *Shirley*', *N.C.F.*, 12 (September 1957), 125–36

KRAMER, DALE, 'Thematic Structure in *Jane Eyre*', *Papers on Language and Literature*, 4 (Summer 1968), 288–98

KROEBER, KARL, *Styles in Fictional Structure: the Art of Jane Austen, Charlotte Brontë, George Eliot* (Princeton, New Jersey: Princeton University Press, 1971; London: Oxford University Press, 1971)

LANE, MARGARET, *The Brontë Story* (London, Heinemann, 1953; Fontana reprint, 1969)

——, 'The Drug-like Brontë Dream', *B.S.T.*, 12 (1952), 79–87

LANGBRIDGE, ROSAMOND GRANT, *Charlotte Brontë: A Psychological Study* (Garden City, New York: Doubleday, 1929)

LANGFORD, THOMAS, 'The Three Pictures in *Jane Eyre*', *Victorian Newsletter*, 31 (Spring 1967), 47–8

——, 'Prophetic Imagination and the Unity of *Jane Eyre*', *Studies in the Novel*, 6 (1974), 228–35

LEDERER, CLARA, 'Little God-sister', *N.C.F.*, 2 (December 1946), 169–75

LEE, HERMIONE, 'Emblems and Enigmas in *Jane Eyre*', *English*, 30 (1981), 233–55

LENTA, MARGARET, 'The Tone of Protest: An Interpretation of Charlotte Brontë's *Villette*', *English Studies*, 64 (October 1983), 422–33

LINDER, C. A., 'The Ideal Marriage as Depicted in the Novels of Jane Austen and Charlotte Brontë', *Standpunte*, 24 (1971), 20–30

——, *Romantic Imagery in the Novels of Charlotte Brontë* (London: Macmillan, 1978)

LODGE, DAVID, 'Fire and Eyre: Charlotte Brontë's War of Earthly Elements', in *The Language of Fiction* (London: Routledge and Kegan Paul, 1966), pp. 114–43

——, *Working with Structuralism* (London: Routledge, 1981)

MACDONALD, FREDERIKA, *The Secret of Charlotte Brontë* (London: T. C. & E. Jack, 1914)

McGUINNESS, ARTHUR, *Henry Home, Lord Kames* (New York: Twayne, 1970)

McKENZIE, ALAN T., 'The Countenance you Show me: Reading the Passions in the Eighteenth Century', *Georgia Review*, 32:3 (1978), 758–73

McLAUGHLIN, M. B., 'Past and Future Mindscapes: Pictures in *Jane Eyre*', *Victorian Newsletter*, 41 (1972), 22–4

MacLEAN, KENNETH, 'Imagination and Sympathy; Sterne and Adam Smith', *Journal of the History of Ideas*, 10:3 (1949), 399–410

MANN, KAREN B., 'Bertha Mason and Jane Eyre: The true Mrs. Rochester', *Ball State University Forum*, 19 (1978), 31–4

MARGOLIOTH, DANIEL, 'Passion and Duty: A study of Charlotte Brontë's *Jane Eyre*', *Hebrew University Studies in Literature* (1979), 182–213

MARSHALL, WILLIAM H., 'The Self, the World and the Structure of *Jane Eyre*', *Révue des Langues Vivantes*, 27 (1961), 416–25

MARTIN, N. D. S., 'Two Unpublished Letters of Charlotte Brontë', *Bodleian Library Record*, 5 (October 1855), 222–23

MARTIN, ROBERT BERNARD, 'Charlotte Brontë and Harriet Martineau', *N.C.F.*, 7 (December 1952), 198–201

———, *The Accents of Persuasion* (London: Faber and Faber, 1966)

MARTIN, ROBERT K., '*Jane Eyre* and the World of Faery', *Mosaic*, 10 (Summer 1977), 85–95

MASON, LEO, 'Charlotte Brontë and Charles Dickens', *Dickensian* (Summer 1947), 118–24

MAYNARD, JOHN, *Charlotte Brontë and Sexuality* (Cambridge: Cambridge University Press, 1984)

MILLER, NANCY, 'Emphasis Added: Plots and Plausibilities in Women's Fiction', *P.M.L.A.*, 96:1 (January 1981), 36–48

MILLETT, KATE, *Sexual Politics* (London: Hart-Davis, 1971)

MILLGATE, JANE, 'Narrative Distance in *Jane Eyre*: The Relevance of the Pictures', *Modern Language Review*, 63 (April 1968), 315–19

———, 'Jane Eyre's Progress', *English Studies*, 50 (1969), xxi–xxix

MIRSKY, PRINCE, 'Through Foreign Eyes', *B.S.T.*, 6 (1923), 147 ff.

MOERS, ELLEN, 'Performing Heroinism', in *The Worlds of Victorian Fiction*, ed. Jerome H. Buckley (Cambridge, Mass., and London: Harvard University Press, 1975)

MOGLEN, HELENE, *Charlotte Brontë: The Self Conceived* (New York: Norton, 1976)

MOI, TORIL, *Sexual Textual Politics: Feminist Literary Theory* (London: Methuen, 1985)

MOMBERGER, PHILIP, 'Self and World in the Works of Charlotte Brontë', *Journal of English Literary History*, 32 (1965), 349–69

MOSER, LAWRENCE E., 'From Portrait to Person: A Note on the Surrealistic in *Jane Eyre*', *N.C.F.*, 20 (December 1965), 275–81

MUSSELWHITE, DAVID, 'The Novel as Narcotic', in *The Sociology of*

Selective Bibliography

Literature: 1848, ed. Francis Barker *et al.* (Colchester: University of Essex, 1978)

NESTOR, PAULINE, *Female Friendships and Communities* (London: Oxford University Press, 1985)

NEWTON, J. N. L., *Women, Power and Subversion: Social Strategies in British Fiction 1778–1860* (London: Methuen, 1985)

NICOLL, W. ROBERTSON, 'The Brontë Sisters', *B.S.T.*, 1 (1898), 2–23

——, 'Charlotte Brontë and Ann Mozley', *B.S.T.*, 5 (1919), 255–64

NIXON, INGEBORG, 'The Brontë Portraits: Some Old Problems and a New Discovery', *B.S.T.*, 13 (1958), 232–38

OFFOR, RICHARD, 'The Brontës: Their Relation to the History and Politics of their Time', *B.S.T.*, 10 (1943), 150–60

OHMANN, CAROL, 'Charlotte Brontë: The Limits of her Feminism', *Female Studies*, 6 (1972), 152–63

OLDFIELD, JENNIFER, 'The Homely Web of Truth: Dress as the Mirror of Personality in *Jane Eyre* and *Villette*', *B.S.T.*, 16 (1973), 177–84

PARKER, ROZSIKA, *The Subversive Stitch* (Women's Press, 1984)

PASCAL, ROY, 'The Autobiographical Novel', *Essays in Criticism*, 9 (1959), 134–50

PASSELL, ANNE, 'The Three Voices in Charlotte Brontë's *Shirley*', *B.S.T.*, 15 (1969), 323–26

——, *Charlotte and Emily Brontë: An Annotated Bibliography* (New York: Garland, 1979)

PATTERSON, SALLY, 'An Examination of the Rôle of Women in Society as Portrayed by Charlotte Brontë in *Jane Eyre* and *Villette* and Anne Brontë in *Agnes Grey* and *The Tenant of Wildfell Hall*', *B.S.T.*, 19 (1986), 55–9

PELL, NANCY, 'Resistance, Rebellion and Marriage: The Economics of *Jane Eyre*', *N.C.F.*, 31 (1977), 397–420

PETERS, MARGOT, *Charlotte Brontë: Style in the Novel* (Madison, Wisc.: University of Wisconsin, 1973)

——, *Unquiet Soul: A Biography of Charlotte Brontë* (New York: Doubleday; London: Hodder and Stoughton, 1975)

PETERSON, W. S., 'Henry James on *Jane Eyre*', *Times Literary Supplement* (30 July 1971), 919–20

PHYSICIAN, A (*Pseud.*), *Short Sketch of Animal Magnetism* (London: J. Hatchard & Son, 1838)

PICKERING, SAMUEL, 'Using and Controlling the Imagination in *Jane Eyre*', *Illinois Quarterly*, 42:1 (1979), 16–28

POLLARD, ARTHUR, 'The Brontës and their Father's Faith', *Essays and Studies*, n.s. 37 (1984), 46–61 (repr. from *Australasian Victorian Studies Association Conference Papers*, 1977)

——, 'Admiration and Exasperation: Charlotte Brontë's Relationship with William Makepeace Thackeray', *B.S.T.*, 17 (1978), 171–81

PRATT, BRANWEN BAILEY, 'Charlotte Brontë's "There was once a little girl": The Creative Process', *American Imago*, 39:1 (Spring 1982), 31–9

PRESCOTT, JOSEPH, '*Jane Eyre*: A romantic Exemplum with a Difference', in *Twelve Original Essays on Great English Novels*, ed. Charles Shapiro (Detroit: Wayne State University Press, 1960), pp. 87–102

PRESTON, ALBERT H., 'John Greenwood and the Brontës', *B.S.T.*, 12 (1951), 34–8

PUTZELL, SARA MOORE, 'Rights, Reason and Redemption: Charlotte Brontë's Neo-Platonism', *Victorian Newsletter*, 55 (Spring 1979), 5–7

QUALLS, BARRY, *The Secular Pilgrims of Victorian Fiction: The Novel as Book of Life* (Cambridge: Cambridge University Press, 1981)

QUARM, JOAN, 'Purified by Woe: On Faith and Suffering', *B.S.T.*, 19 (1986), 17–26

RAPAPORT, HERMAN, '*Jane Eyre* and the "*Mot Tabou*"', *Modern Language Notes*, 94 (1979), 1093–104

RHODES, MARGARET G., 'Where are the Letters?', *B.S.T.*, 15 (1968), 250

RHODES, PHILIP, 'A Medical Appraisal of the Brontës', *B.S.T.*, 16 (1972), 101–9

RICH, ADRIENNE, '*Jane Eyre*: The Temptations of a Motherless Woman', in *On Lies, Secrets and Silence* (New York: Norton, 1979), pp. 88–106

RIGNEY, BARBARA HILL, *Madness and Sexual Politics in the Feminist Novel* (Madison, Wisc.: Wisconsin University Press, 1978)

ROBERTS, DOREEN, '*Jane Eyre* and the Warped System of Things', in *Reading the Victorian Novel: Detail into Form*, ed. Ian Gregor (London: Vision; New York: Barnes and Noble, 1980), pp. 131–49

RODOLFF, REBECCA, 'Providential Encounters in Charlotte Brontë's Fiction', *Studies in the Novel*, 12 (1980), 316–26

ROGAL, SAMUEL, 'The Methodist Connection in Charlotte Brontë's *Shirley*', *Victorian Institute Journal*, 10 (1981–82), 1–13

ROWE, MARGARET MOAN, 'Beyond Equality: Ideas and Images in *Jane Eyre*', *Ball State University Forum*, 21:4 (1980), 5–9

SADOFF, DIANNE F., *Monsters of Affection: Dickens, Eliot and Brontë on Fatherhood* (Baltimore: Johns Hopkins University Press, 1982)

SAINTSBURY, GEORGE, 'The Position of the Brontës as Origins in the History of the English Novel', *B.S.T.*, 2 (April 1899), 18-30

SCARGILL, M. H., ' "All passion spent": A Revaluation of *Jane Eyre*', *University of Toronto Quarterly*, 19 (January 1950), 120–25

SCHMIDT, EMILY T., 'From Highland to Lowland: Charlotte Brontë's Editorial Changes in Emily's Poems', *B.S.T.*, 15 (1986), 221–27

SCHORER, MARK, *The World We Imagine: Selected Essays* (New York: Farrar, Straus and Giroux, 1986)

SCHREIBER, ANNETTE, 'The Myth in Charlotte Brontë', *Literature and Psychology*, 18:1 (1968), 48–67

SCRUTON, WILLIAM, *Thornton and the Brontës* (Bradford: John Dale, 1898)

SELINCOURT, ERNEST DE, 'The Genius of the Brontës', *B.S.T.*, 2 (1906), 234–55

Selective Bibliography

SENSEMAN, WILFRED M., 'Charlotte Brontë's Use of Physiognomy and Phrenology', *B.S.T.*, 12 (1954), 286–89 (extracts from *Papers of the Michigan Academy of Science, Art and Letters*, 38 (1952), 475–86)

SHANNON, EDGAR F., JR., 'The Present Tense in *Jane Eyre*', *N.C.F.*, 10 (September 1955), 141–45

SHAPIRO, ARNOLD, 'Public Themes and Private Lives: Social Criticism in *Shirley*', *Papers on Language and Literature*, 4 (Winter 1968), 74–84

———, 'In Defense of *Jane Eyre*', *Studies in English Literature 1500–1900*, 8 (1968), 681–98

SHARMA, P. P., 'Charlotte Brontë: Champion of Woman's Economic Independence', *B.S.T.*, 14 (1965), 38–40

SHIPTON, HELEN, '*Jane Eyre* and an Older Novel', *Monthly Packet* (November 1896), 556–61

SHORTER, CLEMENT, 'New Light on the Brontës', *B.S.T.*, 1 (1898), 10–19

SHOWALTER, ELAINE, *A Literature of their Own: British Women Novelists from Brontë to Lessing* (Princeton: Princeton University Press, 1977)

SHUTTLEWORTH, SALLY, 'The Surveillance of the Sleepless Eye: The Constitution of Neurosis in *Villette*' (forthcoming)

SIEBENSCHUH, WILLIAM R., 'The Image of the Child and the Plot of *Jane Eyre*', *Studies in the Novel*, 8 (Fall 1976), 304–17

SLATTERY, E. M., 'The Brontës: Refined Gothic', *University of South Africa English Studies*, 12:3 (1974), 24–7

SMITH, DAVID, 'Incest Patterns in Two Victorian Novels: Part I, "Her master's voice: *Jane Eyre* and the Incest Taboo"', *Literature and Psychology*, 15 (Summer, 1965), 135–44

SMITH, GEORGE, 'Charlotte Brontë', *Cornhill Magazine*, 9 (December 1900), 778–95

SMITH, MARGARET, 'The Manuscripts of Charlotte Brontë's Novels', *B.S.T.*, 18 (1983), 189–205

SNOWDEN, J. KEIGHLEY, 'The Brontës as Artists and as Prophets', *B.S.T.*, 4 (1909), 78–92

SOLOMON, ERIC, '*Jane Eyre*: Fire and Water', *College English*, 25 (December 1963), 215–17

SPACKS, PATRICIA MEYER, *The Female Imagination* (New York: Knopf, 1975)

SPENS, JANET, 'Charlotte Brontë', *Essays and Studies by Members of the English Association*, 14 (1929), 54–70

STANG, RICHARD, *The Theory of the Novel in England* (London: Routledge and Kegan Paul, 1959)

STEDMAN, JANE W., 'Charlotte Brontë and Bewick's *British Birds*', *B.S.T.*, 15 (1966), 36–40

STEINER, GEORGE, *On Difficulty* (Oxford: Oxford University Press, 1972)

STEPHEN, LESLIE, Introduction to the *Works of Samuel Richardson* (London: Henry Sotheran & Co., 1883)

STEVENS, JOAN, 'A Sermon in Every Vignette', *Turnbull Library Record*, 1, n.s. No. 3 (March 1968), 12–24

Charlotte Brontë: Truculent Spirit

STEVENS, JOAN, 'Woozles in Brontë-land', *Studies in Bibliography*, 24 (1971), 99–108

——, 'A Brontë Letter Corrected', *B.S.T.*, 16 (1971), 46

STONE, DONALD D., *The Romantic Impulse in Victorian Fiction* (Cambridge, Mass.: Harvard University Press, 1980)

STONEMAN, P. M., 'The Brontës and Death: Alternatives to Revolution', in *The Sociology of Literature: 1848* (Colchester: University of Essex, 1978)

STUART, J. ERSKINE, 'Brontë Nomenclature', *B.S.T.*, 1:3 (1895), 14–18

SULLIVAN, PAULA, 'Rochester Reconsidered: *Jane Eyre* in the Light of the Samson Story', *B.S.T.*, 16 (1973), 192–98

——, 'Fairy-tale Elements in *Jane Eyre*', *Journal of Popular Culture*, 12 (1978), 60–74

SWINBURNE, A. C., *A Note on Charlotte Brontë* (London: Chatto and Windus, 1877)

TANNER, TONY, Introduction to *Villette* (Harmondsworth: Penguin Classic, 1979)

TASCH, PETER A., 'Jane Eyre's "three-tailed bashaw"', *N.Q.*, n.s. 29 (June 1982), 232

TIFFANY, LEWIS K., 'Charlotte and Anne's Literary Reputation', *B.S.T.*, 16 (1974), 284–87

TILLOTSON, KATHLEEN, *Novels of the Eighteen-Forties* (London: Oxford University Press, 1954)

TODD, J., 'Charlotte Brontë's Mercurialism', *British Medical Journal*, (1967, i.), 799

TOMPKINS, J. M. S., 'Jane Eyre's Iron Shroud', *Modern Language Review*, 22 (1927), 195–97

——, 'Caroline Helstone's Eyes', *B.S.T.*, 14 (1961), 18–28

TRAVERSI, DEREK, 'The Brontë Sisters and *Wuthering Heights*', in *Pelican Guide to English Literature*, 6 (Harmondsworth, 1958)

TROMLY, ANNETTE, *The Cover of the Mask: The autobiographers in Charlotte Brontë's Fiction* (Victoria: English Literary Studies Monograph 26)

TWITCHELL, JAMES, 'Heathcliff as Monomaniac', *B.S.T.*, 16 (1975), 374

TYTLER, GRAHAM, *Physiognomy in the European Novel* (Princeton: Princeton University Press, 1982)

VICINUS, MARTHA (ed.), *Suffer and Be Still* (Bloomington: Indiana University Press; London: Methuen University paperback, 1980)

WAGNER, GEOFFREY, *Five for Freedom: A Study of Feminism in Fiction* (London: Allen and Unwin, 1972)

WARE, JOHN M., 'Bernardin de Saint-Pierre and Charlotte Brontë', *Modern Language Notes*, 40 (June 1925), 381–82

WATSON, MELVIN R., 'Form and Substance in the Brontë Novels', in *From Jane Austen to Joseph Conrad*, ed. Robert C. Rathburn and Martin Steinmann, Jr. (Minneapolis: University of Minnesota Press, 1958), pp. 106–17

WATTS, ISAAC, *The Doctrine of the Passions Explained and Improved, to Which are Subjoined, Moral and Divine Rules for the Regulation or Government of Them* (Coventry, 178–)

WEST, REBECCA, 'Charlotte Brontë', in *Great Victorians*, ed. H. J. and Hugh Massingham (London: Nicholson and Watson, 1932), pp. 49–61

WHEELER, MICHAEL D., 'Literary and Biblical Allusion in *The Professor*', *B.S.T.*, 17 (1976), 46–51

————, *The Art of Allusion in Victorian Fiction* (London: Macmillan, 1979)

WILLIAMS, RAYMOND, 'Forms of English Fiction in 1848', in *The Sociology of Literature: 1848*, ed. Francis Barker *et al.*, pp. 277–90

WILLS, JACK C., 'The Shrine of Truth: An Approach to the Work of Charlotte Brontë', *B.S.T.*, 15 (1970), 392–99

WILSON, F. A. C., 'The Primrose Wreath: The Heroes of the Brontë Novels', *N.C.F.*, 29 (1974), 40–57

WINNIFRITH, TOM, 'Charlotte Brontë and Calvinism', *N.Q.*, n.s. 17, 215 cont. series (January 1970), 17–18

————, 'Charlotte Brontë's Letters to Ellen Nussey', *Durham University Journal*, 63 (December 1970), 16–18

————, *The Brontës and their Background: Romance and Reality* (London: Macmillan, 1973)

———— [with Edward Chitham], *Brontë Facts and Brontë Problems* (London: Macmillan, 1983)

YABLON, G. ANTHONY, and TURNER, JOHN R., *A Brontë Bibliography* (London: Ian Hodgkins; Connecticut: Meckler, 1978)

YEAZELL, RUTH B., 'More True than Real: Jane Eyre's Mysterious Summons', *N.C.F.*, 29 (1974), 127–43

ZEMAN, ANTHEA, *Presumptuous Girls* (London: Weidenfeld and Nicolson, 1977)

Index

223

Index

Freud, Sigmund, 74, 98, 167, 204; Freudian readings, 22, 74, 94, 97, 99–103, 136–39, 163, 167

Gaskell, Elizabeth, 12, 14, 17–20, 21, 40, 49, 59, 65, 74, 76, 86, 89, 93, 98, 103, 125, 164, 168, 169, 180, 182
Gauthier, Théophile: *Emaux et Camées*, 24
Gosse, Edmund, 13
Greenwood, John, 28n., 145
Grimshaw, Rev. William, 65

Hartley, David, 57
Heger, Constantin, 23, 24, 26, 44, 97, 98, 164, 165–66, 169, 189, 198–99, 201, 202
Heger, Zoe Parent, 44, 145, 148, 192, 198
Holroyd, Abraham, 63

James, Henry, 14
Jung, Carl Gustav, 98; Jungian reading, 98

Kavanagh, Julia, 94, 191, 194
Kay-Shuttleworth, Sir James, 24, 95

Lamartine, Alphonse de, 23
Lawrence, D. H., 32, 151, 185, 188
Leeds Mercury, 30
Lewes, G. H., 12, 27n., 41, 42, 91, 94, 178

Martineau, Harriet, 46, 53n., 84, 94, 97
Martyn, Henry, 68
Marxism, 35
Marxist criticism, 98; Marxist readings, 137, 158, 170, 195–96
Methodism, 51, 58–77, 130
Methodist Magazine, 55
Methodist Monthly, 51
Milton, John, 25, 30, 116, 147, 149; *Paradise Lost*, 70, 150; *Samson Agonistes*, 70, 146–48

Nicholls, Rev. A. B., 16, 20, 40, 62, 77, 86, 97
Nietzsche, Friedrich: *The Birth of Tragedy*, 73
North American Review, 41
Nussey, Ellen, 12, 17, 18–20, 21, 24, 42, 49, 54, 56, 57, 61, 68, 71, 76, 85, 89, 91, 92, 95
Nussey, Henry, 68

Parsonage Museum, Haworth, 15, 18, 44, 56, 86, 152n., 168, 202
Pilgrim's Progress, The, 34
Plato, 47; *The Phaedrus*, 73; Platonic ladder, the, 74; Neo-Platonism, 74
Pratt, Samuel Jackson, *Sympathy*, 127–28

Quarles, Francis: *Emblems*, 34

Quarterly Review, 41, 99
Queen Victoria, 107–8

Rhys, Jean: *Wide Sargasso Sea*, 144
Richardson, Samuel, 30, 44
Rigby, Elizabeth, 40, 121
Rousseau, Jean-Jacques, 128
Rubens, Peter Paul, 196

Saint-Pierre, Bernardin de, 23, 117, 189
Sand, George, 76, 79n.
Scott, Sir Walter, 76, 79n., 113, 116
Selina, Countess of Huntingdon, 60
Seymour, Henry H., 63
Shakespeare, 13, 34, 149; *A Midsummer Night's Dream*, 116; *Antony and Cleopatra*, 114–15; *Hamlet*, 115–16; *Coriolanus*, 181; *King Lear*, 148, 168; *Macbeth*, 11, 14, 33, 70, 109; *The Winter's Tale*, 114
Shelley, Percy Bysshe, 125, 128, 134n.
Shepheard-Walwyn, Clement Carus-Wilson, 66
Shorter, Clement, 20, 85
Smith, Adam, 128
Smith, George, 18, 21, 75
Southey, Robert, 75, 95–6, 124
Stephen, Leslie, 13, 30–1
Sterne, Lawrence, 42, 44
Swinburne, Algernon Charles, 30

Taylor, James, 25, 42, 175, 194
Taylor, Mary, 12, 20, 59, 71, 83, 95, 97, 124, 125, 176, 183
Thackeray, William Makepeace, 13, 44, 91, 113; *Vanity Fair*, 33, 40, 99, 159
Tom Jones, 33
Turner, J. Horsfall, 20, 82n.
Turner, J. M. W., 39

Ward, Mrs. Humphry, 13, 23, 75
Watts, Isaac, 44–50
Weightman, Rev. William, 61, 62–3, 73
Wesley, John, 51, 55, 59, 60, 63, 64, 75
Whipple, Edwin Percy, 40
Whitefield, George, 55, 60, 64
Whitfield, George, 55
Williams, W. S., 12, 41, 42, 71, 76, 84, 94, 123, 143, 150, 166, 175, 199
Wise, T. J., 20
Wollstonecraft, Mary, 149
Wooler, Margaret, 16, 18–20, 39, 40, 54, 75, 84, 85, 88, 180
Woolf, Virginia, 108, 117, 117n., 144
Wordsworth, William, 114, 128

Yarnall, Ellis, 38